KNOW HIS
Spirit
BIBLE STUDY

KNOW HIS *Spirit* BIBLE STUDY

*An Inductive Bible Study
for Youth and Adults*

BY JENNIFER B. PRICE
FOREWORD BY
BISHOP ROBERT E. WOODARD, JR.

CITI OF
BOOKS

CITIOFBOOKS, INC.
3736 Eubank NE Suite A1
Albuquerque, NM 87111-3579
www.citiofbooks.com

Hotline:	1 (877) 389-2759
Fax:	1 (505) 930-7244

Ordering Information:

Quantity sales. Special discounts are available on quantity purchases by corporations, associations, and others. For details, contact the publisher at the address above.

Printed in the United States of America.

ISBN-13:	Softcover	979-8-89391-608-9
	eBook	979-8-89391-610-2
	Hardback	979-8-89391-609-6

Library of Congress Control Number: 2025905597

Know His Spirit Bible Study is a second edition version of the book "Now is the Time for God's Children to be Filled with His Holy Spirit" which the author Jennifer B. Price copyrighted through the Library of Congress in 1998 and self-published in 1999.

In 1997, the author was divinely inspired to produce a workbook about being filled with the Holy Spirit. She was moved to write a book that documented what she learned about the Holy Spirit from studying the Bible for herself, which was affirmed in her Christian life experiences.

The Holy Spirit led her to format the book in a way that even young people could understand the information. This led to the book's first edition design as a youth-friendly workbook. The content was organized so readers could learn in an inductive study style.

In 2025, the Lord opened the door for the author to publish a second edition version of the book through Citi of Books, Inc. For the second edition, the Holy Spirit led the author to add a new dimension to the content that would provide a greater benefit to adults who were new believers in Christ and to adults who were mature Christians. This included changing the title of the book to "Know His Spirit Bible Study."

The 2025 title of the book, **Know His Spirit Bible Study**, more accurately reflects the nature of the second edition updated content. This Bible study curriculum serves as a tour guide for anyone who wants to learn about the Holy Spirit and have His presence manifest in their life.

Learn more about the author, Jennifer B. Price,
and her other published written and music works,
on her ministry website:
knowbiblestudies.com

Acknowledgements

Family

I thank my husband, Robert,

and our four children—Chris, Joe, Candi and Alex—

for their patience and understanding during the writing

of this book. My achievements are yours, too!

Your loving wife and mother,

Jennifer

Special thanks to my mother Lillian and my sister Janis who have supported me in all my adventures. Thank you for your love and prayers.

Acknowledgements

Spirit-Filled Preachers and Teachers

The author thanks the many Spirit-filled Preachers and Teachers who have imparted, to the author, the truth of God's Word by declaring His precepts in their messages and by living godly lives. You have truly demonstrated by your example what it means to "work out your own salvation with fear and trembling." There are too many people to name, but God knows who you are, and I know He will reward each of you for a job well done. Yet, I do acknowledge that all you imparted to me was not in vain. I thank those who know me personally, such as my Pastors past and present, and those who do not, such as the authors of spiritual works whose writings have also been instrumental in my spiritual growth.

Holy Spirit Teacher

Dear Heavenly Father, I thank you from the depths of my heart, for sending your darling Son Jesus Christ to die on the cross for my sin, and to rise from the dead so that by my faith in the risen Jesus Christ, I am a child of the One True and Living God.

Thank you, God, for pouring out Your Holy Spirit on the earth to help all of us who believe on the Lord Jesus Christ, as the scripture has said, to be born of the Spirit, empowered by the Spirit, and taught by the Spirit.

I acknowledge that God the Holy Spirit is the GREATEST TEACHER OF ALL TIME! I pray that this work, divinely inspired by the Holy Spirit Teacher, is pleasing, Abba Father, in your sight. I pray, too, that I please you as your child and as your servant.

This is my prayer, with my earnest thanks, and my sincere love,
In Jesus Name, Amen.

Jennifer B. Price

Contents

PURPOSE AND WORKS OF THE SPIRIT

Contents

Contents

Contents

Tables

Foreword

&

Commendation

1998: The Foreword that follows was written by Bishop Robert E. Woodard, Jr., for the first edition publication of this book that Jennifer B. Price self-published in 1999 under the title, "**Now is the Time for God's Children to be Filled with His Holy Spirit,**" and renamed to **Know His Spirit Bible Study**.

2025: The Commendation that follows is provided by Eld. Craig I. Carter, who was one of the original exhorters for the first edition book and a mentee under Bishop Robert E. Woodard, Jr. At the time of this second edition **Know His Spirit Bible Study** publication, Eld. Carter is the Pastor of Williams Temple Church of God in Christ, which was previously pastored by Bishop Robert E. Woodard, Jr. Pastor Carter's Commendation is based on his review and approval of the updated content.

Foreword

I have read many books by very famous authors concerning the operation of the Holy Spirit, but I firmly believe that this book/workbook "Now is the Time for God's Children to Be Filled with His Holy Spirit," authored by Jennifer Price, is the best that I have ever read.

The Holy Spirit has placed a burden on her heart to teach children the operation and application of the Holy Spirit. In her zeal to target 10–13-year-olds, she displayed a writing style that is so profound, yet so simplistic that it will answer questions for a great number of adults also. Based on what the Holy Spirit has placed in this workbook through Jennifer Price, I believe that thousands will be filled with the Spirit. These numbers will include vast quantities of adults.

The timing of this workbook is phenomenal. Our children have watched as our national leaders have been dragged through one scandal after another throughout the years. They are asking questions we cannot always answer.

The hope of our future rests with our children.

The power to change the future depends on what we teach our children.

Our children are our hope for the nation and the church.

Every time a child is filled with the Holy Spirit it is a seed that will bring forth a harvest in the future. The only way we can ensure that our children become conquerors and victors is to help them be filled with The Spirit and know how to use spiritual weapons.

Satan's plan is always to kill the children. He tried to kill Joseph, Moses, John the Baptist, and Jesus.

Don't just read this book and put it down. Leave a deposit in the earth for the next generation by seeing to it that the information in this workbook is planted in every child you come in contact with.

Bishop Robert E. Woodard, Jr., 1998

Bishop Robert E. Woodard, Jr. was the beloved Bishop over the First Ecclesiastical Jurisdiction of Texas Southeast Churches of God in Christ (1996–2001) and Pastor of Williams Temple–Woodard Cathedral Church of God in Christ until he went to be with the Lord in 2001.

Commendation

My name is Craig I. Carter. I am the senior pastor at the Williams Temple Church of God in Christ located in Houston Texas.

I have been a part of the Church of God in Christ, International, Inc. Pentecostal-Holiness Christian denomination for over 60 years. The Church of God in Christ was birth out of the experience of the baptism of the Holy Ghost by its Founder Bishop Charles Harrison Mason in 1907.

Throughout my childhood and adult Christian life, I have witnessed the importance and the necessity of the baptism of the Holy Ghost.

I have read and appreciate the time, effort and research that has gone into this book **Know His Spirit Bible Study** by its author, Jennifer B. Price. I have known Jennifer for over 25 years, and I have witnessed firsthand her hard work and dedication, meticulous attention to detail, her love for God and His people, and her desire to see God's people receive the fullness of God's Power and blessings in their life.

This book is filled with a wealth of information and has a progressive, step-by-step format that will give the reader a thorough understanding of the Person of the Holy Ghost and how to receive Him. The material is easy to read and comprehend. I am confident, that after reading this book you will be mentally and spiritually positioned to experience what God promised throughout the scriptures, and that is the Baptism of The Holy Ghost.

The contents of this book will empower the believer to live a victorious life, and I also believe (because it is filled with the Word of God) that it can lead sinners to Christ.

Thank you, Sister Price, for the job well done.

Sincerely,

Pastor Craig I. Carter

---

*Pastor Craig I. Carter delivered this Commendation to Jennifer B. Price for her second edition book publication, **Know His Spirit Bible Study**, on March 28, 2025.*

Author Introduction

Know His Spirit Bible Study is designed to help you, the reader, go from studying about God's Holy Spirit to becoming filled with His Holy Spirit. It is an inductive study. This means that the content is formatted to guide you in immersing yourself in the Word of God so you can learn the truth about the person of the Holy Spirit for yourself.

The text serves as a tour guide on what the Bible says about the Holy Spirit's purpose and work to manifest God's presence on earth, with a focus on understanding His work within Christians. This includes helping you to see for yourself what the Bible says about being born of the Spirit, filled with the Spirit and allowing the fruit and gifts of the Spirit to empower you to be an effective witness on earth for Jesus Christ.

The teaching style in this study includes both the elements of the simple and the deep. The content has an appeal for youth and new believers in Christ, and for adults and mature Christians. For example, the study preparation section entitled "From Pneumatology to Dumanis Power!" and the last Chapter 8 entitled "This Spirit's for You: Adult Bible Study Handouts" will especially appeal to adults and mature Christians. Lessons 1 to 28 are the inductive study section. The early lessons begin simplistically to establish the most basic understanding of the Holy Spirit and then guide you in building a deeper knowledge as you progressively work through the lessons. This inductive study section is intended to appeal to both youth and adults.

At the end of **Know His Spirit Bible Study**, you will have gained enough information to know what it means to be filled with the Holy Spirit and how to receive Him in your life.

Helpful Study Resources:

- Bible - King James Version (KJV): This study was developed using the KJV so you will want that Bible readily available. You can also use your Bible version of choice as an additional study resource.

- Dictionary: To research words you are unfamiliar with in scriptures.

- Way to Record Your Answers: The Lessons have questions. Appendix A has the answers to the questions. However, you should write your own answers from the reading. The Holy Spirit Himself can help you understand answers to the questions that may be clearer than the answers you find in Appendix A.

- Prayer: Ask God to help you Know His Spirit, in Jesus Name, Amen!

How To Use this Bible Study

Know His Spirit Bible Study Lessons 1 through 28 are designed as an inductive study to allow adults and youth to study independently, after youth have obtained parent/guardian approval.

Helpful Study Resources:

- Bible: King James Version; Optional, another version of your choice
- A way to record answers to the questions in the lessons
- Dictionary to reference as needed
- Quiet place to study so you can focus and hear the Holy Spirit

General Organization of the Lessons:

- Introductory information about the Holy Spirit
- Lesson exercise
- Questions to answer
- Space provided to allow for recording answers in the book

Helpful Tips:

- **Tip 1:** Write your answers down. Doing this could strengthen your ability to remember what you have learned. Also, if you want to review this study later, you will have your answers available.

- **Tip 2:** The lessons are designed so that a teacher can instruct students in a class session, or a student can work alone. To facilitate this, the author has provided answers in Appendix A.

- **Tip 3:** Pray and ask God's Holy Spirit to guide you on an answer before looking in Appendix A.

- **Tip 4:** The Bible is the Living Word of God. God's Holy Spirit can help you understand an answer clearer than what is in Appendix A.

Jesus said,

"Ask, and it shall be given you; Seek, and you shall find; Knock, and it shall be opened unto you." (Luke 11:9)

"Blessed are they which do hunger and thirst after righteousness: for they shall be filled." (Matthew 5:6)

Preachers and Teachers present God's Word to you as plain as they can. However, it is God's Holy Spirit who will bring the final clarity of understanding deep within your heart!

*Pray for
Understanding Before
You Begin!*

Have Fun Learning!

From Pneumatology To Dunamis Power!

From studying about the Holy Spirit
to being filled with the Holy Spirit!

Know His Spirit Bible Study is designed to help you, the reader, go from studying about God's Holy Spirit to becoming filled with His Holy Spirit.

Simply put, as you read, do the Lesson exercises, and meditate on the study content, you will be equipped with enough information to transition from learning about the Holy Spirit to becoming filled with the Holy Spirit, with the understanding of WHY doing so will be a blessing in your life.

Bible Study Preparation
Section Outline:

Below is the outline of this Bible Study Preparation section content.

The content in this section has basic explanations on each topic.

For a deeper study, consider reviewing
the reference works in the Appendices.

Note: HS is short for Holy Spirit.

- **Definitions:**   **Pneumatology and Dunamis**
- **Bible Reveal:**   **Who the Holy Spirit Is**
- **HS in Old Testament:**   **How He Worked in People**
- **HS Prophecies:**   **His New Work in People is Coming**
- **HS in New Testament:**   **His New Work in People Arrives**
- **HS Today:**   **How He Works in People**
- **Required:**   **Decent and In Order**
- **Climax:**   **YOU GO!**
  from Pneumatology to Dunamis Power!

Definitions:

Pneumatology — "pneuma" is a Greek word that means "wind", "air", "spirit"; "ology" is a Greek word that means "the study of"[1]

"Pneumatology" refers to the study of God the Holy Spirit in the field of Systematic Theology. Systematic Theology is the study of what the entire Bible teaches on a topic or doctrine.[2] The below table includes a representative list of Systematic Theology study topics, with the study of Pneumatology highlighted. The Table is reprinted from the Apologetics section of "Know His Word Bible Study" by author Jennifer B. Price.[3]

Systematic Theology Doctrinal Topics

Topic "ology"	Topic "Doctrine" Description
Bibliology	The Doctrine of the Bible (Word of God)
Theology	The Doctrine of God (Trinity, God the Father)
Christology	The Doctrine of Christ (God the Son)
Pneumatology	**The Doctrine of the Holy Spirit (God the Holy Spirit)**
Angelology	The Doctrine of angels (angels and fallen spirits)
Anthropology	The Doctrine of man
Hamartiology	The Doctrine of sin
Soteriology	The Doctrine of salvation
Misthology	The Doctrine of rewards
Israelology	The Doctrine of Israel (nation of Israel in past, present)
Ecclesiology	The Doctrine of the Church
Israelology	The Doctrine of Israel (nation of Israel in future)
Eschatology	The Doctrine of last things

Dunamis — Dunamis is the Greek word translated into the English word "power" in Acts 1:8, "But ye shall receive **power**, after that the Holy Ghost is come upon you: and ye shall be witnesses unto me…" This same word is the root of the English words, "dynamite" and "dynamic."[1]

Know His Spirit Bible Study…
helps you learn enough information about the Holy Spirit so you can go **"from Pneumatology to Dunamis", meaning from just studying about the Holy Spirit to becoming filled with the Holy Spirit so His power can help you to be a dynamite, dynamic witness for Christ.**

Bible Reveal: Who the Holy Spirit Is

The Christian faith is a monotheistic faith. This means that we serve only ONE GOD. Our ONE GOD is made up of three divine persons. The Holy Spirit is the third divine person. Each person in the Godhead IS God. This is why God is sometimes referred to as God the Father, God the Son, and God the Holy Spirit. This "three-in-one" nature of God is also referred to as the Trinity or Triune God.

Scripture References: One God, Three-in-One

- "Hear, O Israel: The LORD our God is one LORD." (Deut. 6:4)
- "…Hear, O Israel; The LORD our God is one LORD" (Mark 12:29)
- "Let us make man in our image… So God created man in his own image" (Genesis 1:26, 27)
- "For there are three that bear record in heaven, the Father, the Word, and the Holy Ghost: and these three are one." (1 John 5:7)
- "but to us there is but one God, the Father, of whom are all things" (1 Corinthians 8:6a)
- "In the beginning was the Word, and the Word was with God, and the Word was God… and the Word was made flesh" (John 1:1, 14, 17)
- [Jesus said] "I and my Father are one." (John 10:30)
- "But Peter said, Ananias, why hath Satan filled thine heart to lie to the Holy Ghost… thou hast not lied unto men, but unto God." (Acts 5:3-4)

Scripture References: Triune God at work

- In Creation: God the Father, Spirit of God and Jesus worked in unity to create the heaven and earth. (Genesis 1:1-2, John 1:1-18)
- At Jesus' baptism: The Trinity was present at Jesus' baptism to affirm and empower Him in public ministry. (Luke 3:21-22)

Holy Spirit in the Old Testament: How He Worked in People

The Holy Spirit was said to be IN, INTO or WITHIN these O.T. men:

1.	Joseph	Genesis 41:38
2.	Moses	Isaiah 63:10-14
3.	Joshua	Numbers 27:18
4.	David	Psalm 51:10-11
5.	Ezekiel	Ezekiel 2:2, 3:24
6.	Daniel	Daniel 4:8, 18, 5:11-14; 6:3

Holy Spirit in the Old Testament: How He Worked in People continued

More Old Testament saints' experiences with the Holy Spirit:

-	Filled with the Spirit	Exodus 28:3; 31:3; Deuteronomy 34:9, Micah 3:8
-	Spirit Upon	Numbers 11:17-29; Judges 3:10; 6:34 Judges 11:29; 14:6, 19; 15:14
-	Spirit "moved" many	Judges 13:25; 2 Peter 1:21

He's Coming!

Holy Spirit Prophecies: His New Work in People is Coming

God sent prophecies about pouring out His Spirit on all flesh.

- Ezekiel 36:26-27 – Ezekiel foretold that God planned to put His Spirit in people and give them a new heart so they could keep His judgments and do them. (Galatians 3:13-29, Ephesians 2:17-22, Acts 2:38-39, Hebrews 9:13-22)

- Joel 2:28-29 – Joel foretold that God would pour out His Spirit upon all flesh so all could prophesy (Acts 2:1-22)

Old Testament Feasts of the Lord for Israel represented major New Testament spiritual events. One of those feasts represented the Holy Spirit's coming, which would occur 50 days after Jesus' resurrection. The Old Testament purpose of this feast was to worship God at the kickoff of the harvest season. The New Testament purpose was to initiate the worldwide harvest of souls. (Acts 1:8)

- Feast of Firstfruits represented Jesus' resurrection. (Leviticus 23:9-14, 1 Corinthians 15:20, 23)

- Feast of Weeks, which was also known as the Feast of Harvest, and as Pentecost, occurred 50 days after the Feast of Firstfruits. This feast represented the time when the Day of Pentecost would fully come in the New Testament, when God would pour out His Spirit upon all flesh. (Lev. 23:15-21, Exodus 23:16; Acts 1:3, 2:1)

John the Baptist understood from the Lord that the Messiah would baptize people with the Holy Spirit.

- Matthew 3:11-12, Mark 1:8, John 1:33

He's Arrived!

HS in New Testament: His New Work in People Arrives

Jesus promised the disciples that He would send them the Holy Spirit after His Ascension back to heaven.

"He that believeth on me,
as the scripture hath said,
out of his belly shall flow
rivers of living water.
(But this spake he of the Spirit,
which they that believe on him should receive:
for the Holy Ghost was not yet given;
because that Jesus was not yet glorified.)"
John 7:38-39

"Nevertheless I tell you the truth;
It is expedient for you that I go away:
for if I go not away, the Comforter will not come unto you;
but if I depart, I will send him unto you…

Howbeit, when he,
the Spirit of truth, is come,
he will guide you into all truth:
for he shall not speak of himself;
but whatsoever he shall hear, that shall he speak:
and he will shew you things to come.
He shall glorify me: for he shall receive of mine,
and shall shew it unto you."
John 16:7, 13-14

"And behold, I send the promise of my Father upon you:
but tarry ye in the city of Jerusalem,
until ye be endued with power from on high."
Luke 24:49 (Acts 1:5)

Jesus kept His Promise.

After His Ascension, He sent the Holy Spirit on the Day of Pentecost.

"And when the day of Pentecost was fully come,
they were all with one accord in one place…

…And they were all filled with the Holy Ghost, and
began to speak with other tongues, as the Spirit gave them utterance."
Acts 2:1, 4

HS Today: How He Works in People

[Jesus said]

**"Verily, verily, I say unto you, He that believeth on me,
the works that I do, shall he do also;
and greater works than these shall he do;
because I go unto my Father."**
John 14:12

[Apostle Peter said]

**"Repent, and be baptized every one of you
in the name of Jesus Christ for the remission of sins,
and ye shall receive the gift of the Holy Ghost.
For the promise is unto you,
and to your children,
and to all that are afar off,
even as many as the Lord our God shall call."**
Acts 2:38-39

[Apostle Paul said]

Have ye received the Holy Ghost since ye believed?
Acts 19:2

The Holy Spirit works today in people, who believe in Jesus Christ as the scriptures have said, just as He did in the New Testament. When the Day of Pentecost "was fully come," the outpouring of God's Holy Spirit upon all flesh initiated the worldwide harvest of souls.

When Jesus returned to heaven, He did not leave His disciples then, nor does He leave His disciples today, "comfortless." On the contrary, He has given us the Holy Spirit to bring God and Jesus to live inside us, to develop the fruit of God's character in us, and to gift us with portions of His dynamic power to equip us to bring in the harvest of souls. We can only do the greater works than Jesus did with the help of God's Holy Spirit. (Matthew 9:37-38, John 14:23, Galatians 5:22-23, 1 Corinthians Chapters 12–14, Romans 12:6-8)

The remainder of this study will help you to Know God's Holy Spirit so you can become filled with Him and enjoy all the benefits of living a victorious life in Christ with the Holy Spirit's help.

REQUIRED: DECENT AND IN ORDER

"And the spirits of the prophets
are subject to the prophets.

For God is not the author of confusion,
but of peace, as in all churches of the saints.

Let all things be done decently and in order."

1 Corinthians 14:32, 33, 40

**"Beloved, believe not every spirit,
but try the spirits whether they are of God:
because many false prophets are gone out into the world**."

1 John 4:1

Despise not prophesyings.
**Prove all things; hold fast that which is good.
Abstain from all appearance of evil.**
And the very God of peace sanctify you wholly;
and I pray God your whole spirit and soul and body
be preserved blameless unto the
coming of our Lord Jesus Christ.
1 Thessalonians 5:20–23

Warning:

There are false prophets, phony spirit gift experiences, and many risk factors in growing in the things of God, especially things related to spiritual gifts. Yet the Holy Spirit is well able to lead us into all truth and preserve our whole spirit and soul and body until Jesus returns for us.

God requires all things be done decent and in order. We just simply need to follow the order that God has identified. As you go through this study, you will also learn some of God's order for having His Spirit operate in your life, then the Holy Spirit will continue to teach you.

You Go! From Pneumatology to Dunamis Power!

Common enemies of the Church are ignorance, unbelief, and fear. There are consequences in yielding to these enemies (Hosea 4:6, Matthew 13:58, 1 John 4:18). Just remember 2 Timothy 1:7 & **YOU GO!**

After you complete this study, consider going through the entire Bible with **Know His Word Bible Study** curriculum also by Jennifer B. Price. You can access the curriculum at any major book outlet. You can also access the curriculum at the author's site: knowbiblestudies.com

Chapter 1:

?

WHO HE IS!

Chapter 1

Detailed Contents

Additional Study
- Chapter 8: Adult Bible Study Handouts
- Appendix C: Youth Lessons 1-28 Study Handouts
- Appendix H: KHS Video Lessons Synopsis

LESSON 1.

HOLY GHOST = HOLY SPIRIT = THE SPIRIT = THE SPIRIT OF GOD
(ALSO = COMFORTER = SPIRIT OF TRUTH = OTHER NAMES)

Just as "2 + 2 = 4, 2 x 2 = 4, 8 – 4 = 4, and 12 – 8 = 4" are different ways to talk about the number "4", the King James Version (KJV) of the Bible uses all the words in the Lesson title to refer to the third person of the Divine Trinity.

God is one God, who is made up of three (3) divine persons. This is why God is referred to as the Trinity or Triune God. The three divine persons are God the Father, God the Son (Jesus Christ), and God the Holy Spirit. Read 1 John 5:7 KJV which explains "these three are one."

God the Holy Spirit has been sent to believers by God the Father and God the Son to be our divine helper on earth. (John 14:16–17, 26; John 16:7, 13–15) Review the Study Prep section for background info.

Some versions of the Bible have changed all references to the 'Holy Ghost' to be 'Holy Spirit.' In this Bible Study, the King James Version of scriptures are used. For the commentary, the terms Holy Ghost and Holy Spirit/Spirit are used interchangeably.

Exercise:

From Acts 2:4 write down which words are used to talk about the Holy Spirit. Notice that He is talked about twice in this verse:

1) _____; **2)** _____

From Romans 8:14 write down which words are used to talk about the Holy Spirit. **3)** _____

From Ephesians 1:13 write down which words are used to talk about the Holy Spirit. **4)** _____

There are also other names used to refer to the Holy Spirit. Look up the examples in the passages below.

Read John 14:16 and 26. What is the Holy Ghost called? **5**_____

Can you guess by looking at the name why the Holy Ghost is called by this name? **6)** _____

Read John 14:17 and **John 16:13** for another name. **7)** _____

Can you guess why He is also called by this name? **8)** _____

Do not be confused by the different ways the scriptures talk about the Holy Spirit. You will learn more about these names for the Spirit in future lessons.

Three Types of Spirits...

There are really three (3) different types of spirits talked about in the Bible. They are the 1) Holy Spirit of God, 2) human spirit of man, and the 3) spirit of the world.

1 Corinthians 2:11–12 says,
For what man knoweth the things of a man, save the spirit of man which is in him? Even so the things of God knoweth no man, but the Spirit of God. Now we have received, not the spirit of the world, but the spirit which is of God; that we might know the things that are freely given to us of God.

This scripture tells us five important things about the 3 types of spirits:

1. The spirit of man, which is the human spirit, is the part of us that has feelings and knowledge learned from living on earth.
2. The Spirit of God understands how God thinks and feels.
3. The human spirit does not know the things of God.
4. We can receive the Spirit of God in a way that helps us to know the things of God.
5. The spirit of the world is not of God.

The spirit of the world comes from God's adversary the devil (satan) and his demons. These demonic spirits are described in different ways in the Bible. One description is found in Ephesians 2:2. This passage explains that the spirit of the world is the spirit that is working on the inside of the "children of disobedience."

When you read scriptures in the Bible that talk about a spirit, read carefully to understand which kind of spirit is being talked about.

...but One Holy Spirit

Read on to find out more about the Holy Spirit. As you learn who He is and how He operates, you will better understand whether what you read and hear is from the Spirit of God or the spirit of the world. When you are filled with the Spirit of God and know how to listen to Him, He will help you to know God's great plans for your life.

LESSON 2.   THE HOLY GHOST IS **NOT** REALLY A "GHOST"

The dictionary defines a ghost as the "soul of a dead person" that is believed to exist in an unseen world, but it appears to the living in a way to look like that dead person.

First and foremost, the Holy Ghost is the Spirit of the True and Living God, who is very much alive. For this reason alone, the Holy Ghost is not a ghost. In fact, the Bible describes the Holy Ghost as a living divine person with a mind. The Holy Ghost speaks to us in our human spirit, but He only talks to us about what Jesus (God the Son) and God the Father want us to know. Let us look in the Bible for proof that the Holy Ghost is a person who has a gender (meaning male or female), a will (meaning decision-maker), intelligence (meaning smart), and emotions (meaning to have feelings). He also communicates (hears and speaks). We can also know Him, but we do not see Him.

Exercise:

➢ **Gender**

From **1 Corinthians 12:11**, write down whether the Holy Ghost is a male (he) or a female (she). **1)** _____

➢ **Will**

From that same scripture, write down what the Holy Ghost does with the gifts of the Spirit. (**Also read 1 Corinthians 12:4, 7–11.**) **2)** _____

➢ **Intelligence**

If the Holy Ghost decides who will receive certain gifts, does that make Him unintelligent or intelligent? **3)** _____

➢ **Emotions**

Ephesians 4:30 says that we should not do what to the Holy Ghost? **4)** _____ Does this mean the Holy Ghost has feelings? **5)** _____

➢ **Communication**

From **Romans 8:27** we can learn two more things about the Holy Ghost. He has a **6)** _____ to think with and He **7)** _____ to God to intercede for us.

➢ **Knowable**

Read John 3:8. Write down what "thing" Jesus described in the earth that we cannot see, but we know it is real. **8)** _____ ; He explains that similarly the Spirit is not seen, but we can know He is real. **Read John 14:17**. How or where can we "know" the Holy Spirit? **9)** _____

The Holy Spirit speaks to us from within us.

Warning that the devil will also try to speak to us through his evil spirits. Let us take a little time to understand how we can know the difference between what the Holy Spirit will speak and what evil spirits will speak.

Read 1 John 4:1–3.

> [Note: For this passage, make sure you look at 1 John (First John) which is near the end of the Bible instead of John, which is the 4th book in the New Testament.]

Write down what the passage says about how to tell whether a person is speaking by the Spirit of God or by an evil spirit.

(Verse 2) The Spirit of God will confess **10)** _____

(Verse 3) The spirits that are not of God will not confess **11)** _____

(Verse 3) What is the spirit that is not from God called? **12)** _____

Read John 15:26.

Who will the Holy Spirit "testify" or speak about? **13)** _____

[Hint: Find out who "me" is by reading John 14:23.]

Read John 16:13–14.

14) Write down six things Jesus said the Holy Spirit will do.

a) _____ ; b) _____

c) _____ ; d) _____

e) _____ ; f) _____

... but follow only the Holy Spirit

LESSON 3.   A PROMISE AND A GIFT

After Judas Iscariot left the Last Supper to go betray Jesus to the Chief Priests and Pharisees, Jesus tried to prepare His disciples one final time for His soon coming death, burial and resurrection. Jesus also took this opportunity to tell them more about the Holy Ghost, which would replace Him in His role on the earth.

In John 16:7, Jesus explained that if He did not go away, the Comforter could not come. If He went away (meaning "went back to heaven"), then He would send the Holy Ghost to comfort them and help them live for God on earth.

Exercise:

Read John 16:7 and John 14:26.

What is another word used to refer to the Holy Ghost? **1)** _____

What would the Holy Ghost do after Jesus was physically gone from the earth? (John 14:26) **2)** _____

The prophet Joel foretold (meaning to predict) the coming of the Holy Spirit hundreds of years before Jesus walked on the earth.

Read Joel 2:28–29, then **Acts 1:4–5**, then **Acts 2:1–8, 12–18**.

From the title of this Lesson (Lesson 3), which of those two words describes what the coming of the Holy Ghost represented God keeping? (see Acts 1:4) **3)** _____

Now read Acts 2:38–39.

What is referred to as the "gift" and the "promise?" **4)** _____

Note:

Joel 2:28–29 and Acts 2:38–39 explain that children are to receive this "promise" and "gift" of the Holy Ghost just like adults of all ages.

Here are some questions for you to think about.

Feel free to write your thoughts below in the space provided.

When a friend keeps their promise to you, what do you usually do or how do you feel?

5) _____

_____

What do you usually do when you receive gifts such as Christmas gifts or birthday gifts?

6) _____

_____

How can the fact that the coming of the Holy Ghost in Acts was a promise kept by God to you, be compared to a promise a friend keeps to you?

7) _____

_____

How can the fact that the coming of the Holy Ghost is a gift from God to you, be compared to a gift you receive from a family member or friend?

8) _____

_____

LESSON 4. BEFORE YOU CAN BE FILLED WITH THE SPIRIT, YOU MUST BE BORN OF THE SPIRIT!

There are two personal experiences to have with the Holy Spirit.
You can be born of the Spirit, and then you can be filled with the Spirit.

PART 1. BORN OF THE SPIRIT

Jesus told Nicodemus in John Chapter 3 verse 3 that no one can be a part of the Kingdom of God unless they are born again. In Chapter 3 verses 4 through 8, Jesus explained to Nicodemus that to be born again a person must be born of the Spirit. Then Jesus made Himself even clearer when He explained in verses 16–18 that everyone who believes in Him (Jesus Christ) is saved = born again = born of the Spirit.

Romans 10:9–10 explains that the way to be saved is by believing on the risen Jesus Christ and by telling others that He is your Lord (meaning the Lord and Savior of your life).

John 1:12–13 further explains that believing on Jesus causes you to become born of God, which means you become a child of God.

Exercise:

The passages that follow give more insight into what it means to be born of the Spirit.

Look in 2 Corinthians 5:17 to find out what changes after you become born of the Spirit.

What becomes "new? **1)** _____

What makes him or her a new creature? **2)** _____

[Note: New creature means to be born again as a new spiritual creation or a new inner spiritual person.]

What happens to the old? **3)** _____

Read Romans 8:15–16 to discover your spiritual Father. **4)** _____

Read Colossians 1:12–14 to discover your spiritual kingdom.
5) _____

> [Note: Verse 12 tells who translates us. Verse 13 tells where He translates us. Verse 14 tells why He translates us.]

Read Ephesians 2:2–3 to find out who controlled our old self or inner spiritual person. **6)** _____

Look at Colossians 3: 9–10 to answer the next three questions.

Write down what was put on "new"? (v. 10); **7)** _____

How is the man (meaning person) made "new" or renewed? (v. 10);
8) _____

What happened to the old person? (v. 9); **9)** _____

Think About This

When a baby is born, they usually have parents/guardians, a home, and a name given to them by their parents. Then, their parents or guardians begin teaching them who they are and teaching them about life itself. The above scriptures show us how these same ideas apply to the person who is "saved" or "born again" or "born of the Spirit."

When we are born of the Spirit:

We become new spiritual people. (2 Corinthians 5:17)

Our new spiritual Father is God. (Romans 8:15–16)

Our new spiritual relationship position is child of God. (Romans 8:16)

Our new spiritual home is the Kingdom of God's dear son Jesus Christ. (Colossians 1:13)

Our new spiritual parent-teacher is God.

> We re-learn how to think, talk, and walk in life according to the ways of God as we grow up spiritually. (Ephesians 2:2–3, Colossians 3:9–10, but read Verses 5–10)

PART 2. FILLED WITH THE SPIRIT

We learned in Lesson 3 that the Holy Ghost was sent by Jesus to the earth after He rose from the dead and went back to heaven. The Holy Ghost would now do what Jesus had done for His disciples, which is teach them the things of God. He would also remind His disciples of the things Jesus had taught them (John 14:26). Jesus further explained to His disciples that the way the Holy Ghost would do this is by living inside of them and empowering them to be His witnesses on earth. Acts 1:5, 8 explained the disciples would be baptized with the Holy Ghost. Acts 2:4 described this experience as being "filled with the Holy Ghost." Ephesians 5:18 instructs the children of God to be "filled with the Spirit."

Exercise:

In John 14:17 Jesus explained that the Holy Ghost (Spirit of Truth), which was soon to come, would be given to those who already know Him. To understand this scripture, you need to know that the "world" stands for sinners or non-believers in Christ or non-followers of Christ and "ye = you" refers to the disciples or disciplined followers of Christ.

Read John 14:17 to find the below answers:

10) the world (meaning sinners) cannot _____ the Spirit,

11) because the world does not _____ the Spirit,

12) neither does the world _____ the Spirit,

BUT

13) you (meaning followers of Christ) _____ the Spirit,

14) for the Spirit dwells _____ you

15) and the Spirit shall be _____ you.

The scriptures explain that people who are sinners cannot be filled with the Holy Spirit because they do not know Him. The only way a person can know the Spirit is by being born of the Spirit.

From Part 1 of this Lesson 4 we learned that a sinner becomes born of the Spirit when they believe on Jesus and tell others that Jesus is the Lord and Savior of their life. After a person has this relationship with the Spirit, they are ready to become filled with the Spirit.

In John Chapters 14, 15 and 16, Jesus told His disciples many things to prepare them for being filled with the Holy Spirit.

Read Acts 2:1–40 to see how the Holy Ghost finally came to the disciples in fulfillment of God's promise and Jesus' explanations.

The phrase "filled with the Holy Ghost" in Acts 2:4 KJV describes the experience in which a person receives from God's Holy Spirit extra power and boldness to live and witness for God. (See Acts 1:8, 4:31.)

See "**An Example Using Peter**" on the following page.

Know His Spirit   Chapter 1   12

An Example Using Peter

To understand how being filled with the Holy Spirit can change us into stronger Christians, let us look at the example of how Jesus' disciple Peter was changed.

Less than two months before Peter was filled with the Holy Spirit, he was not bold enough to speak in defense of Jesus who he believed was Christ, the Son of the Living God. He also said he would never be offended to acknowledge Him. (Matthew 16:16–19; Matthew 26:31–35)

However, when Jesus was arrested in the Garden of Gethsemane, Peter ran away from the scene. He left Jesus to be falsely accused by His enemies and to suffer alone. Peter denied even knowing Jesus three times after it became clear that Jesus was in serious trouble. During Jesus' trial before the Jewish leaders and Roman authorities, Peter did not come forward to defend Jesus' innocence in any way. Instead, he watched what happened to Jesus from a distance, too scared to help Him at all. (Matthew 26:47–75)

After His resurrection, Jesus met with His disciples, including Peter, and assured all of them of His love. Jesus explained to them the meaning of the Old Testament scriptures concerning Him. He helped them understand the purpose for His life, death, and resurrection from the dead. Then He breathed the Holy Spirit on them so they could become born of the Spirit.[1] (John 20:21–29)

Seeing the risen Jesus Christ, hearing His explanations, and being born of the Spirit were not enough to make the disciples strong witnesses for Christ. Jesus told them to wait for the promise of receiving extra spiritual power from the Father. Once they were filled with God's Holy Spirit, then they would be ready to work for God. (Luke 24:36–49)

From Acts Chapters 2 through 4 we see how Peter became a bold witness for Jesus Christ after being filled. Through being filled with the Holy Spirit, Peter could remember important scriptures and explain deep insight about why Jesus had come to the earth the way He did. Through being filled with the Holy Spirit, Peter could endure being beaten and thrown in jail for preaching the gospel of Jesus Christ. Through being filled with the Holy Spirit, Peter performed healings and miracles boldly in the name of Jesus. (Acts 2–4:22)

Peter explained that this spiritual gift from God is for us today, too, to help us also be bold witnesses for God. (Acts 2:38–39)

You will learn more about this in future lessons.

LESSON 5.   SPEAKING IN OTHER TONGUES

PART 1. FIRST APPEARANCE!

When Peter and Jesus' disciples were first filled with the Holy Spirit, the Holy Spirit not only changed their lives but also changed their speech.

Acts 2:4 says,

And they were all filled with the Holy Ghost, and began to speak with other tongues, as the Spirit gave them utterance.

"Speak with other tongues" is the way the King James Version of the Bible describes speaking in different languages that are foreign and unknown to the speaker.

In Acts 2:5–11, we find that godly Jewish men from every nation of the world were in Jerusalem at the time of the writing. When the disciples were filled with the Holy Ghost, this event occurred noisily — with the sound of a mighty rushing wind followed by the appearance of fiery, cloven-shaped tongues that rested on each disciple and all of Jesus' followers gathered in the upper room. In response, all began to speak in other languages exuberantly. This caused the Jewish men from all over the world to come see what was going on in that upper room. These representatives from other countries became witnesses to help explain the remarkable thing the disciples had just experienced.

Exercise:

Read Acts 1:11–15 and Acts 2: 1–4. Who and how many were there to "speak with other tongues" for the first appearance? (Acts 1:14–15)

1) _____

Read Acts 2:4. How were they enabled to speak in other tongues?

2) _____

Read Acts 2:5–8. How can we tell the "other tongues" were different languages?

3) _____

Read Acts 2:11. What types of things did the foreign representatives say Jesus' disciples and followers were speaking in the different languages?

4) _____

PART 2. BEFORE FIRST APPEARANCE!

The Bible indicates that Jesus primarily spoke in the languages that were commonly understood by the Jewish people at the time He was on the earth. Jesus spoke the Hebrew/Aramaic language because He was sent to proclaim the message of the Kingdom to the Jews. (Matthew 15:21–24, Aramaic in Mark 5:41)

Jesus likely spoke the koine Greek language which was commonly understood in New Testament times by all people. He also possibly spoke the Roman language. These two languages would have enabled him to speak with persons other than the Jewish people such as the Roman centurion and Pilate. (Matthew 8:5, John 18:33–38)

After Jesus' resurrection, and before His final ascension to heaven, Jesus told His disciples that the power to speak in new languages would be given to them and other believers by the Holy Spirit.

Exercise:

Read Mark 16:9–18. Where is the reference to speaking in new tongues (languages)? **5) Verse** _____

Who did Jesus say would receive this ability? (v. 15–17); **6)** _____

Read Mark 16:20. When the disciples and other believers went everywhere preaching God's Word, then the Lord let the sign of "speaking in new tongues" (and the other signs listed in verses 17-18) follow them. These signs helped to **7)** _____ God's Word to everyone.

The Old Testament prophet Isaiah foretold the coming ability to speak in other languages. After it happened about 750 years later, Isaiah's words are referred to from the New Testament in 1 Corinthians 14:21.

Read Isaiah 28:9–12 and 1 Corinthians 14:2, 14, 21.

Here is a summary of what you just reviewed in timeline order.

- Isaiah foretold that men would speak in other languages by the power of God to represent God speaking to people in a different way.
- Jesus, before leaving earth, told His disciples that speaking in new languages would be a sign to them from God for believers in Him.
- The Holy Spirit came to earth because of Jesus sending Him. When the Holy Spirit came upon the first people, He enabled them to speak in foreign languages although they had not been taught them.
- 1 Corinthians 14:2 explains that the person who receives this new language (or languages) does not understand what they are saying. But the Holy Spirit, which fills their human spirit, is speaking to God through them, and God understands what is being said.

PART 3. MORE BIBLE FIRST TIMES!

This sign from God of "speaking in other tongues" was first given to the Gentiles (meaning non-Jewish people) at Cornelius' house. Peter was led by the Holy Spirit to go preach to them. While he was preaching, they began speaking in foreign languages. This let Peter know that they had become filled with the Holy Spirit. Read about this in Acts Chapter 10.

Other Bible verses show that observers could tell if believers were filled with the Holy Spirit, by the way they received the supernatural ability to speak in foreign languages. Let's examine these ourselves.

Exercise:

Read Acts 10:44–48. How did Peter know that Cornelius and his family (the Gentiles) had been filled with the Holy Spirit? (Verses 45–46)

8) _____

Read Acts 19:1–6. What happened after Paul laid hands on the Ephesians for them to receive the Holy Spirit? (Verse 6)

9) _____

Read Acts 8: 9–20. What do you think Simon "saw" that made him want to buy the ability to lay hands on people so they could receive the Holy Ghost? (Verse 18–19)

10) _____

The first 16 verses of Acts 9 tell the story of how Saul (before he became the Apostle Paul) persecuted the Jews that were followers of Christ. After Jesus spoke to Paul on the road to Damascus, he became blind in his eyes. Then God sent the disciple Ananias to pray for Saul.

Read Acts 9:17–18. What happened to Saul (Paul)?

11) _____

Now **Read 1 Corinthians 1:1–2 and 14:18–19.** Based on your study in this lesson, when do you think the Apostle Paul received the ability to speak in other tongues (foreign languages)?

12) _____

PART 4. THE PURPOSE FOR SPEAKING IN TONGUES

In reading Isaiah 28:7–13 we can get a sense of God's frustration in His dealings with His chosen people Israel (also known as the Jewish people). God had called the nation of Israel to be His representatives to the world, but the Israelites constantly fell short of fulfilling that calling.

In the Old Testament, God gave the Israelites specific laws so they would know His righteous way to live. He used strong spokespersons in the form of godly prophets, priests, and kings. God's representatives gave clear and understandable messages to the people. However, some leaders—also in the positions mentioned above—gave false messages. The false leaders increased. They led the people of God to increase in their sin and rebellion against the laws of God.

Finally, God sent the message to the Israelites that sometime in the future, a new relationship between God and humankind was coming. In this new relationship, God would use His Son to speak to the people of Israel. He would also put the Spirit of His law in their hearts. God also sent messages that this new relationship would also be for non-Israelite (meaning non-Jewish) people, who the Bible refers to as Gentiles.

In Isaiah 28: 9–12 God explained that He would even send strange languages to speak to the Israelites, since they did not respond to the clearly, understandable messages. If they accepted the messages that came through the different languages, their acceptance would bring a spiritual refreshment into their lives. And yet, at the end of verse 12, God let us know that even with this special sign from Him, many would still not accept His message to live righteously.

Exercise:

What do we learn about the purpose of speaking in other languages (tongues) from the following passages:

Isaiah 28:11–12   13) causes the weary to _____ and is _____

Mark 16:17   14) a sign that follows them that _____

1 Corinthians 14:2   15) speaks mysteries unto _____

1 Corinthians 14:22   16) a sign for them that _____

Look at five different ways the King James Version of the Bible describes the strange type speech (tongues or utterances) that can come from the Holy Ghost working within us.

What does **Isaiah 28:11** call the speech? **17)** _____

What does **Mark 16:17** call the speech? **18)** _____

What does **Romans 8:26** call a strange expression from the Holy Ghost? **19)** _____

What does **1 Corinthians 13:1** call two types of tongues?

20) _____ and **21)** _____

Do not get confused!

The Holy Ghost mainly uses our
native language to speak to us and through us.
But you need to understand the Holy Ghost
uses strange speech also.

Does every believer in Christ "speak in other tongues"?

No, they do not. Yet the Bible does let us know that this sign is available for all believers (Mark 16:15 – 20). The most important thing is to be filled with the Holy Spirit so you can receive additional power from God to be a witness for Him. Speaking in other tongues is one sign that the experience of being filled with the Holy Spirit has taken place.

Now is truly the time for all of God's children, young and old,
to be filled with His Holy Spirit because God needs bold representatives
for Him, in these last days of the earth, as we know it now.

In Chapter 1 of
Know His Spirit Bible Study,
you have been introduced to who the Holy Spirit is.
Please, read on to learn much more about
being filled with the Holy Spirit of God.

Chapter 2:

PURPOSE!

Chapter 2

Detailed Contents

Additional Study
- Chapter 8: Adult Bible Study Handouts
- Appendix C: Youth Lessons 1-28 Study Handouts
- Appendix H: KHS Video Lessons Synopsis

LESSON 6. THE LAW OF THE SPIRIT MAKES US FREE

PART 1. ADAM GAVE US SIN AND DEATH

The Bible says we are all born with a desire to sin (meaning we have a sinful nature).

Sin is simply the act of disobeying God's law (meaning His instructions or commandments on how to live right).

This sinful nature was passed on to all people of the earth because of the first man Adam's sin.

Let us review Adam's sin and the effect of his sin on everybody's life.

Exercise:

Read Genesis 2:7–8, 15–17.

What was Adam's job? (v. 15) **1)** _____

What was right for Adam to eat? (v. 16) **2)** _____

What was wrong for Adam to eat? (v. 17) **3)** _____

What would happen to Adam if he disobeyed God? (v. 17) **4)** _____

Read Genesis 2:18–25 for fun. Learn how the first woman was made.

Read Genesis 3:1–6. Did Adam disobey God? **5)** _____

Read Genesis 3:17–19. What punishments did God put on Adam?

6) (from v. 17–18) _____

(and from v. 19) _____

Read Genesis 3:22–24. What was another punishment God pronounced on Adam and Eve? (v. 24) **7)** _____

Read Romans 5:12. What did Adam's sin give to every human being that is born to an earthly man? **8)** _____

A. Old Testament forgiveness of sins came by the blood of animals

Since sin is against God's righteous nature (meaning a "do the right thing" nature according to God's definition of what is right), God gave laws to the Israelite nation to show people what is right and what is wrong in His eyes. Unfortunately, the Israelites did not always keep the laws of God because of the sinful nature passed on to them from Adam. That is why God instructed them to sacrifice animals.

God explained that by shedding the blood of certain animals in the way He instructed, the people would receive forgiveness for their sins temporarily. This is because their sins were "covered" or "hidden" from God's view by the blood of the animals.

Exercise:

Definition: Atonement — "to make amends for an offense or error or for an offender," or "to bring into unity."[1] When the offering of animal sacrifices was finished, God forgave the sins of the people. Their actions enabled them to have a relationship of being "at one" with God.

Read Leviticus 17:11.

What part of the animal did God say made atonement for people's sins?

9) _____ ; What did God say was in the blood? **10)** _____

Read Hebrews 9:7.

How often did the priests have to give God sin offerings of animal sacrifices to atone for people's sins? **11)** _____

Read Hebrews 9:22.

Can any sin be forgiven without the shedding of blood? **12)** _____

Definition: Remission — "pardon a sin" or "forgive an offence"

_____

You can read about the type of animals and sacrifices required in the Old Testament to atone for sins in Leviticus Chapter 9.

B. New Testament forgiveness of sin comes by the blood of Jesus

Just as revealed in God's interactions with the Israelites, the sinful nature all human beings are born with does not allow us to keep God's laws all the time. (Romans 3:23)

This same sinful nature causes us to die from the earth. It also causes us to be punished by God forever IF the blood of Jesus does not make atonement for our sins. Jesus came to the earth from heaven to become the final sacrifice for our sins. He represented a perfect offering for the sin of all human beings to God. His blood that was shed on the cross has power to atone for everyone's sins once and for all. (Romans 5: 8–11, Hebrews 9:11–12)

The only thing a person is required to do today, to receive forgiveness or sins, is:

- **A**sk God to forgive you for your sins.
- **B**elieve in what Jesus did for you when He died on the cross, in substitution for you, to pay God's penalty for your sin.
- **C**onfess the risen Jesus Christ is your personal Lord and Savior.

Exercise:

Read Romans 3:9–18. These verses describe how God sees people. How many people are "good" or "righteous" people without God's help?

13) _____

Read Romans 6:23 and **Psalm 9:17**. What can a sinner expect to get paid for his sinful lifestyle. **14)** _____

What can a believer in Jesus Christ expect to receive? **15)** _____

Read John 1:29. What animal sacrifice did Jesus represent? **16)** _____

Read John 3:16. What do we have to do to receive forgiveness for sins and to receive everlasting life? **17)** _____

Read Romans 10:9. What do we have to confess to be saved from everlasting punishment? **18)** _____

PART 2. SIN WANTS TO BOSS YOU AROUND

The sinful nature within us wants to control our actions. The desire to sin is strong even when we do not want to commit sinful acts in our hearts. In the exercise below, you will learn some important facts about sin.

Exercise:

Read 1 John 3:4. What is sin? **19** _____

(Hint: Transgress means "to disobey" or "to violate" an instruction. The "law" in the Bible refers to the instructions from God or "God's Word" on what is right and what is wrong to do.)

Read Romans 3:23. How many people have sinned? **20)** _____

When a person sins, what do they come short of. **21)** _____

(Note: Exodus 33:17–22 explains that the "glory of God" is the "goodness of God.")

Read Proverbs 13:15, 21. What type of life will a person have that sins all the time? **22)** _____

(Hint: Transgressor is a sinner; one who sins all the time.)

Read Romans 6:23. If you live a life where you sin all the time, what will you get paid at the end of your life? **23)** _____

(Hint: Wages mean payment.)

Read Hebrews 9:27. What happens after a person dies? **24)** _____

Read Psalm 9:17. What is God's judgment on those who die as sinners? **25)** _____

(Hint: The "wicked" and people who "forget God" are sinners.)

Read Mark 9:43–44. What is Hell? **26)** _____

> *Sin leads to Death*
>
> *Death leads to Judgment*
>
> *Unrepentant Sinner's Judgment leads to Hell*
>
> *Hell is a place of tormenting punishment Forever*

Read **Romans 7:7–11** to answer the next questions.

How does knowing God's law let a person know what sin is? (verse 7:7)

27) _____

> (Hint: "Covet" means to desire what someone else has in a wrong way.)

After we learn the law, how does our desire to sin become "alive" and try to control us? (verses 7:8–9)

28) _____

> (Hint: God's "laws" are also called "commandments."
> "Concupiscence" means a very intense longing to commit sin.)

How does sin cause us to die after we learn the law? (verses   7:9–11)

29) _____

Summary

- The desire to sin is so strong in us, that even after a person learns right from wrong, he or she will sin sooner or later unless they have extra help from God. This is because it is too hard to resist the desire to sin.

Sin Wants to Boss You Around!

- The desire to commit sin within you wants to control you. If the sinful nature is never changed, then you will die as a sinner and be punished by God forever.

Part 3. Did You Know You Were A Slave To Sin?

The Bible explains that sin controls the action of those who do not want to obey God. Sinners are the servants or slaves of sin. Read **Romans 6:16–17, 20– 21**.

Now let us look at a man who really wants to do the right things for God, but he keeps doing the wrong things instead. He wants to serve God with his mind and spirit, but his flesh (meaning the actions of his body) keeps him sinning. Read **Romans 7:14–25**.

Believe it or not, the man you just read about became a great Apostle for God. He went on to write most of the New Testament. In Romans 7th Chapter he describes his struggle with trying to be a man for God before he allowed the Spirit of God to guide his actions. Read Romans 1:1 to find out who this man was. The problem he had is the same problem all people have.

Exercise:

Read Romans 7:23 to answer the following questions.

What law makes us a slave? **30)** _____

(Hint: We are brought into captivity to this law)

Where is this law found? **31)** _____

Which two laws are having a war? **32)** _____, _____

Where is this war taking place? **33)** _____

Read Romans 7:24–25 to answer the next questions.

Is there any hope for the good spirit in us to win over the bad desires in us? If yes, then how? **34)** _____, _____

Summary

From the readings, we can see that even if a person wants to obey God, it is hard to do so because of a sinful flesh. Paul explained that there is a law of sin that is in operation in our body. Let us do more research on how to overcome the problem of "wanting to live right in the mind and spirit," but "not being able to do so in the body." This research will show us the main reason Christ sent the Holy Spirit to live in us, after Jesus returned to live in heaven. Read on.

PART 4. THE LAW OF THE SPIRIT
MAKES US

FREE

FROM THE

LAW OF SIN AND DEATH!

Exercise:

Read Romans 8:2.

What does this scripture say about the law of the Spirit?
35) _____

We get this new law by having life in whom?

36) _____

Read Romans 8:1. How can we get rid of being condemned (meaning to be "judged as guilty") for the sins we commit? Romans 8:1 shows us 3 ways to get rid of condemnation. **37)** _____,

_____, _____

Read Romans 8:3–4. These scriptures tell us that the law could not make people righteous before God. What does make us righteous?

(v. 4) **38)** _____

Read 8:5–10. Where does the Spirit have to be to help you live like the Spirit wants you to live? (v. 9)

39) _____

Read **Romans 8:11–15.** Once the Spirit of God is living in you, then through the Spirit's help you will be able to do three things:

(verse 13) **40)** _____

(verse 14) **41)** _____

(verse 15) **42)** _____

Summary

In your own words, summarize what the Law of the Spirit makes you free from: (**Romans 8:2, 6, 10, and 13**)

43) _____

_____

_____

In John 16:7–11, Jesus explained why His leaving the earth would be better for everyone. He would send back the Comforter to live inside of us to help us with our sinful nature problem. Jesus referred to God's Holy Spirit as the Comforter in this passage (see Table 2-1).

In verse 8, Jesus described three big jobs the Holy Spirit would do when He came. 1) The Holy Spirit would reprove the world of sin. 2) The Holy Spirit would reprove the world of righteousness. 3) The Holy Spirit would reprove the world of judgment. Reprove means "to convince, to expose, or to call attention to the remissness of your actions (meaning you are not doing something you should be doing), usually with the intent to correct you or assist you in changing." This simply means the Holy Spirit would be inside of us helping us to resist the temptation to sin and to help us to stop sinning.

In verses 9–11, Jesus explained why the Holy Spirit would work this way. Without the Holy Spirit in the world, people would not recognize their sinful actions. Also, they would not believe that God would punish them for performing sinful actions.

Bold, Living Witnesses for God!

You have already learned in Chapter 1 how God sent the Holy Spirit. Jesus sent the Holy Spirit to fill the disciples so they would have added power in their spirits, making them bold, living witnesses for God. We, too, need to be filled with the Holy Spirit so He can work in us to the fullest, transforming us into bold, living witnesses for God. With the help of the Holy Spirit, people should be able to look at Spirit-filled Christians and see God's right ways of living in their everyday actions.

LESSON 7.   HOLY SPIRIT'S NAMES

To better understand how the Holy Spirit makes us free from sin and death, we can look at some of the names Jesus and the Apostles called the Holy Spirit. These names explain the work of the Holy Spirit.

In the Bible the name of a person often tells us something important about that person's character. God had many names to describe who He was to His servants in the Old Testament. One example of this is when Abraham referred to God as "Jehovah-Jireh," which means "God will provide" (Genesis 22:8–14). Another example is when God changed Abram's name to Abraham, which means "a father of many nations" (Genesis 17:5). In the New Testament Jesus used different names to describe Himself. For example, Jesus called Himself "The Bread of Life" (John 6:35), "The Good Shepherd" (John 10:14), and "The Light of the World" (John 8:12).

In Chapter 1, Lesson 1, we learn that the Holy Spirit also has different names. Now it is time to learn the meaning of some of the Holy Spirit's names. Through doing the next exercise, you will better understand who the Holy Spirit is and what He can do for you!

Exercise:

In the first column of Table 2-1, there are scriptures listed. Under the column "Holy Spirit's Name" write down the name for the Holy Spirit found in those scriptures. In the "Lesson Learned" column, write down what the scriptures reveal about why the Holy Spirit is called by that name. The first entry shown below has been completed for you. In the other entries on the following page hints have been provided as a guide.

Table 2-1. More Names for the Holy Spirit

Scripture(s)	Holy Spirit's Name	Lesson Learned
John 14:16 John 14:26 John 15:26 John 16:7	Comforter	He will abide with us forever; He will teach us all things; He brings all things to our remembrance that Jesus tells us (this means we will be reminded of the Word of God we read, hear and study); He will testify of Jesus; Jesus had to go away so the Comforter could come. The Comforter is our spirit helper and counselor here on earth.

Table 2-1. More Names for the Holy Spirit continued

Scripture(s)	Holy Spirit's Name	Lesson Learned
John 14:17 John 16:12–15	Spirit of _ _ _ _ _	
John 16:8	_ _ (This is a two-letter word that tells the Holy Spirit's gender, whether male or female.)	
Matthew 3:16 Matthew 12:28 (Acts 10:38)	Spirit of _ _ _ (These scriptures explain how the Holy Spirit helped Jesus)	
Luke 4:18 2 Corinthians 3:17, 18	Spirit of the _ _ _ _	
Romans 8:11	Spirit of Him that raised _____ _____	
Romans 8:15–17 (Galatians 4:4–7)	Spirit of _ _ _ _ _ _ _ _	Through the work of the Spirit, we are now called the _____ of God. What does it mean to be an heir? _____
1 John 2:20	_ _ _ _ _ _ _ from the Holy One	How are you able to know all necessary things concerning salvation?
1 John 2:27	The _ _ _ _ _ _ _ _ _	Where does the teacher abide? What does He teach?

LESSON 8:   HOLY SPIRIT'S JOBS

In Lesson 7 we learn some of the names that describe the Holy Spirit. Hopefully, the Holy Spirit's identity is becoming clearer to you. Let us continue to discover the Holy Spirit's purpose on earth by studying more scriptures that talk about Him.

In this lesson you will again use a table to list things you learn about the Holy Spirit. This time more of the research work has been done for you. The first and second columns have been filled in. All you need to do is write down what you learn from the scriptures in the third column. Think carefully about what the scripture is telling you before you begin writing. You may want to have a dictionary available to look up any words whose meanings you do not know.

Exercise:

Table 2-2. Holy Spirit Jobs

Scripture(s)	Holy Spirit's Jobs or Personal Character	Lesson Learned / What does this mean to You?
John 14:18–23 Ephesians 2:11–13 Ephesians 2:14–22 (re-read verse 22)	He brings Jesus and God the Father to us and in us (Jews and Gentiles who believe in Christ)	
Ephesians 2:18 John 4:24	Jesus gives us access to God the Father by means of the Holy Spirit	Like flesh talks to flesh, spirit talks to spirit. If God is a Spirit, how can we communicate with Him?
John 16:7–11	Reproves the world of sin, righteousness and judgment	What does reprove mean?
Romans 5:5 (also read verses Romans 5:1–4)	Sheds or pours out the love of God in our hearts, giving us hope that good things can happen from God, even when bad things are happening to us	How does knowing that almighty God loves us, help us during the bad times in our lives?

Table 2-2. Holy Spirit Jobs continued

Scripture(s)	Holy Spirit's Jobs or Personal Character	Lesson Learned / What does this mean to You?
Jude verse 20 Ephesians 3:16–17 1 Corinthians 14:2, 4, 14	When we pray in the Holy Spirit our holy faith increased. Also, our spiritual self becomes stronger, even if our minds cannot understand everything completely.	What part of us do we want our spiritual self to be stronger than? Remember what you learned in Lesson 7 from Romans 7:22–23. ————————————
1 John 2:20–21 Romans 8:14 (Look at how the Holy Spirit led Jesus after His baptism in Mark 1:9–12. Look at how Paul received direction in Acts 16:6–7.)	Gives us direction from within our hearts.	
2 Corinthians 3:18 2 Corinthians 5:17 Colossians 3:10	We are changed more into the image of God, day by day, by the work of the Holy Spirit in our hearts and our lives.	Notes: Humankind was originally created in the image of God. Then God's adversary the Devil deceived the first man Adam to disobey God which caused all of humankind to lose our Godly nature. Now people are born with the nature of satan. But, when we accept Jesus as our Lord and Savior, then the Holy Spirit gives us a new Godly spiritual nature. Then the Holy Spirit begins to work in us to make us more and more like God. This occurs as we read our Bibles, pray and act upon God's words as shown to us by the Holy Spirit.

Holy Spirit's Jobs

The Holy Spirit Gives People Jesus'...

Love	Truth
Direction	Joy
Peace	Hope
Knowledge of God	Help

and so much more

Table 2-2. Holy Spirit Jobs continued

Scripture(s)	Holy Spirit's Jobs or Personal Character	Lesson Learned / What does this mean to You?
Acts 10:38 Acts 6:5, 8 Acts 8:39 1 Corinthians 12:8–10	The Holy Spirit is the one who causes miracles to work through us	When you read John 1:29–34 and John 2:1–11, you find out that Jesus did not perform any miracles until after He was filled with the Holy Spirit. If Jesus was filled with the Holy Spirit before miracles flowed through Him, then how about us?
Romans 8:13–14 Galatians 5:16–18 Galatians 5:19–25	The Holy Spirit helps you to mortify or kill or get rid of those wrong thoughts and habits in your life that are against God's nature.	
1 Corinthians 2:9–12 John 14:26 John 16:12–14	Helps us to understand spiritual things	
1 John 4:1–6 1 John 2:18–28	Helps us to know the difference between the Words from Christ and the words from the devil or anti-christ	
1 Corinthians 14:15 Romans 8:26–27	Helps us to Pray and Praise God. He helps us to pray for ourselves and for others	
Acts 10:38 1 John 2:27 2 Corinthians 1:21–22 Luke 4:18	Anoints the saints of God, meaning He gives special power to God's people to do God's work	
1 Corinthians 2:9–10	The Spirit searches our hearts and searches the deep things of God. He then gives us new ideas from God.	

Table 2-2. Holy Spirit Jobs continued

Scripture(s)	Holy Spirit's Jobs or Personal Character	Lesson Learned / What does this mean to You?
Acts 8:29 1 Timothy 4:1 Revelation 2:7	The Holy Spirit can talk to us	
John 16:13 John 15:26 John 14:26	The Holy Spirit will only talk about things that come from God the Father and God the Son (Jesus) and Word of God (Bible)	
Acts 4:31 Acts 4:8, 13	The Holy Spirit helps us to have the boldness to tell people about Jesus. He also helps us to know what is the right thing to say to people.	
Galatians 4:6	The Holy Spirit will cause us to call out and think of God as our Daddy! (A good Daddy, the best ever Father!)	Definition: "Abba" was used by the Jews to represent a loving, trusting name given to a Father by a baby.
2 Peter 1:21 1 Peter 1:10–12 1 Timothy 3:14–15	The Holy Spirit is the one that instructed men on what to write in the Bible.	
Acts 5:3–11	The Holy Spirit can be (but should not be) lied to. Ananias and Sapphira were born of the Spirit and members of the Church. They probably were filled with the Spirit, too. But they decided to lie to the Church leaders about what they had done in private.	Note: You can even be filled with the Holy Spirit and yet make an active decision to lie and deceive other Christians. But the Holy Spirit always understands what you are doing, and the price you pay for your sin may be very high.

Table 2-2. Holy Spirit Jobs continued

Scripture(s)	Holy Spirit's Jobs or Personal Character	Lesson Learned / What does this mean to You?
Acts 5:9	The Holy Spirit can tell you the secrets of people's hearts. He is very willing to do this if people are trying to deceive or hurt you, or if they are trying to hurt the work of the Church.	Ananias and his wife Sapphira tried to lie to the apostles about the amount of money they were giving for use by the Church. The Holy Spirit revealed to Peter that the couple was lying. Trying to tempt (or test) the Holy Spirit cost them their lives. We should not lie to the Holy Spirit either or it may cost us our life.
Acts 7:51	You can choose not to do what the Holy Spirit wants you to do.	
Ephesians 4:30 (read verses 17–30 to understand completely)	The Holy Spirit is hurt or grieved when we do not follow His leading.	We are never forced by the Holy Spirit to do anything. He gives us instructions, but the choice is ours to follow those instructions or not.
Matthew 12:31	You can say bad things about the Holy Spirit. But God does not want us to say bad things about Him because He sent the Holy Spirit to help us.	God considers blaspheming the Holy Spirit a sin that He will not forgive.
Acts 19:2	From the time the Holy Spirit was first given until now, some people do not know Him. Also, some people do not believe in the complete works of the Holy Spirit. The Holy Spirit is not forced on anyone.	

LESSON 9:   HOLY SPIRIT'S POWER

PART 1. THE BIBLE DESCRIBES THE HOLY SPIRIT'S POWER

Since the Holy Spirit is the Spirit of Almighty God, the Bible gives a clear description of how awesome and magnificent His power is.

Exercise:

In **Luke 1:35** the angel Gabriel was talking with Mary about how she would become pregnant with the Son of God. What kind of power did the angel describe the Holy Spirit as being? **1)** _____

There are three words used to describe this "power of the Highest." They are: 1. Omnipresent, 2. Omniscient, and 3. Omnipotent.[2] Only the word "omnipotent" is found in the Bible (Revelation 19:6), however, there are many scriptures that let us know all three words are valid in describing the power of God. Let us review these words one at a time using dictionary definitions and scriptures. Think carefully about the scriptures provided in this lesson. They will help you to understand the magnificent power of the Holy Spirit.

1. **Omnipresent** – The dictionary defines this word as meaning "present in all places at all times." There are scriptures that let us know God is everywhere through the work of the Holy Spirit.

    > *Revelation 5:6 "And I beheld, and, lo, in the midst of the throne and of the four beasts, and in the midst of the elders, stood a Lamb as it had been slain, having seven horns and seven eyes, which are the seven Spirits of God sent forth into all the earth."*

    Note:

Do not be confused by the above scripture talking about "seven Spirits of God." We know from Ephesians 4:4–6 that there is only one Spirit of God. This scripture along with Revelation 4:5 and Isaiah 11:2 gives us an idea of how the one Holy Spirit can be present in every place through its seven traits: the spirit of the Lord, of wisdom, of understanding, of counsel, of might, of knowledge, and of the fear of the Lord.

Proverbs 15:3 "The eyes of the Lord are in every place, beholding the evil and the good."

Psalm 139:7–10 "Whither shall I go from thy spirit? or whither shall I flee from thy presence? If I ascend up into heaven, thou art there: if I make my bed in hell, behold, thou art there. If I take the wings of the morning, and dwell in the uttermost parts of the sea; Even there shall thy hand lead me, and thy right hand shall hold me."

God is everywhere!

2. **Omniscient** – The dictionary defines this word as meaning, "having infinite (meaning "unlimited") awareness, understanding, and insight." There are scriptures that show us how God is able to know everything that is going on at all times through the work of the Holy Spirit.

> **Job 34:21 "For his eyes are upon the ways of man, and he seeth all his goings."**
>
> **Psalm 147:5 "Great is our Lord, and of great power: his understanding is infinite."**
>
> **Hebrews 4:13 "Neither is there any creature that is not manifest in his sight: but all things are naked and opened unto the eyes of him with whom we have to do."**

God knows, sees, and hears everything!

God can do anything!

3. **Omnipotent** – The dictionary defines this word as meaning "having virtually unlimited authority or influence." There are scriptures that let us know that God's power works through the Holy Spirit to accomplish anything He wants.

> *Zechariah 4:6 "Then he answered and spake unto me, saying. This is the word of the Lord unto Zerubbabel, saying, Not by might, nor by power, but by my spirit, saith the Lord of hosts.*

> *Romans 15:13 "Now the God of hope fill you with all joy and peace in believing, that ye may abound in hope, through the power of the Holy Ghost."*

> *Ephesians 3:20 "Now unto him that is able to do exceeding abundantly above all that we ask or think, according to the power that worketh in us"*

> *Luke 1:35–37 "…The Holy Ghost shall come upon thee, and the power of the Highest shall overshadow thee… For with God nothing shall be impossible."*

Summary Exercise:

Based on what you have learned above about the three words that describe the power of the Holy Spirit, write in your own words what you understand these words mean.

2) Omnipresent –

_____

_____

3) Omniscient –

_____

_____

4) Omnipotent –

_____

_____

PART 2.   THE HOLY SPIRIT GIVES OF ITS POWER TO PEOPLE

In John 14:15–18 Jesus promised not to leave His believers comfortless, or without help once He physically went back to heaven. Our helper from Jesus is the Holy Spirit. Once each believer is filled with the Holy Spirit, then we receive extra power to live like God wants us to live on this earth in righteousness (meaning right living), peace, and joy (Romans 14:17).

Below is a summary of the different types of power all Spirit-filled Believers have available to them through the Holy Spirit, which lives inside of them. Do not worry if you are unable to understand everything below. Try to understand the big points of what the Holy Spirit can do inside of you, if you let Him lead and guide your life.

1) **The Holy Spirit becomes our prayer partner and can lead us in praying the "right way."**

    The right way to pray is pray in agreement with the will of God. The Bible lets us know in Romans 8:26 that we as humans do not know the right things to pray about. Sometimes we are confused on what the will of God is for our lives. We need someone who knows the will of God for our lives to help us pray. The Holy Spirit is that person inside of us that can make our prayers correct.

    Romans 8:26 "Likewise the Spirit also helpeth our infirmities (meaning problems): *for we know not what we should pray for as we ought: but the Spirit itself maketh intercession for us with groanings which cannot be uttered."*

> *The Spirit itself maketh Intercession for us*

2) **Through the Holy Spirit living in us, God the Father and God the Son "Jesus Christ" are now able to also live inside of us, and we can hear them speak to our human spirits as needed.**

Just imagine it. The Holy Spirit allows God to live inside of you!

> *Ephesians 2:19, 22 "Now therefore ye are no more strangers and foreigners, but fellowcitizens with the saints, and of the household of God; ... In whom ye also are builded together for an habitation of God through the Spirit.*

> *John 14:23 "Jesus answered and said unto him, If a man love me, he will keep my words: and my Father will love him, and we will come unto him, and make our abode with him."*

> *Ye are... an habitation of God through the Spirit*

3) **The Holy Spirit pours out God's love into our hearts. This love makes us love God correctly and our fellow human beings correctly.**

> *1 John 4:8 "He that loveth not knoweth not God; for God is love."*

> *Romans 5:5 "And hope maketh not ashamed; because the love of God is shed abroad in our hearts by the Holy Ghost which is given unto us."*

> *The Love of God is shed abroad in our hearts by the Holy Ghost*

4) If the Holy Spirit is allowed to pray though the believer, then this is "praying in the Spirit." Praying in the Spirit will cause the faith of the Believer to be increased.

> Jude 20 *"But ye, beloved, building up yourselves on your most holy faith, praying in the Holy Ghost."*

> *Building up… your most holy faith,*
> *Praying in the Holy Ghost*

5) The Holy Spirit will show us how we are falling short of living as good Christians. He will give us the power to change from our bad habits to doing what is right.

In other words, our lives will become clean and holy like God wants them to be, as the Holy Spirit works with us. This will happen over a period of time and not just overnight. Scripture does explain that when we become born again, Believers receive a new nature to be like God. However, when we are born again, we are like "baby" Christians. It takes time, as we learn the Word of God, to fully become the mature people God wants us to be. The Holy Spirit will give us the power to live right, think right, and talk right according to what God calls "right."

> Romans 8:8–9a, 13 *"So then they that are in the flesh cannot please God. But ye are not in the flesh, but in the Spirit, if so be that the Spirit of God dwell in you… For if ye live after the flesh, ye shall die: but if ye through the Spirit do mortify the deeds of the body, ye shall live."*

> *Ye are not in the flesh, but in the Spirit, If…*
> *the Spirit of God dwell in You*

6) The Holy Spirit gives us boldness to be witnesses for Jesus Christ.

When Peter and the other disciples were on their own after Jesus had been crucified, they all went into hiding. Perhaps they thought that since they had been friends of Jesus, people might want to crucify them, too. However, after Jesus rose from the dead, He talked with His disciples over a 40-day period and then instructed them to go to Jerusalem and wait for the Holy Spirit.

Ten days later, when the disciples became filled with the Holy Spirit, they were no longer afraid to talk about Jesus and tell the world about the gospel; meaning to tell the good news that Jesus rose from the dead and was alive to be Savior of the world.

This new boldness to be witnesses for Jesus Christ came on them after they were filled with the Holy Spirit. Each of us who becomes filled with the Holy Spirit has this same power to be bold witnesses for Christ. We will not be ashamed to share the story of Jesus to others.

As we learn more about the Word of God, the Holy Spirit will help us to be wiser witnesses. We will have the ability to say the right thing, to the right person, at the right time, then the Holy Spirit will do the rest.

> *Acts 1:8 "But ye shall receive power, after that the Holy Ghost is come upon you: and ye shall be witnesses unto me both in Jerusalem, and in all Judea, and in Samaria, and unto the uttermost part of the earth."*

*Ye shall receive power,
After that the Holy Ghost is come upon you*

7) The Holy Spirit can show you things that will happen in the future. This information could come in answer to your prayers or just to direct your life in walking with God.

> *John 16:13 "Howbeit when he, the Spirit of truth, is come, he will guide you into all truth: for he shall not speak of himself; but whatsoever he shall hear, that shall he speak: and he will shew you things to come. He shall glorify me [Jesus]: for he shall receive of mine, and show it unto you."*

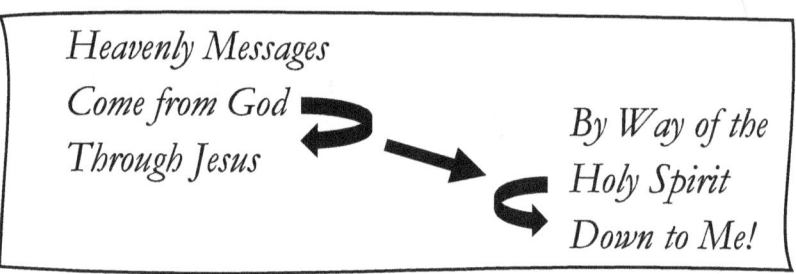

8) The Holy Spirit will give you power in the form of "gifts" to perform miracles, healings, to give insight into good and evil, to give insight into the future plans of God, and to give words of comfort to others.

> *1 Corinthians 12:1, 4, 7–11*
> *"Now concerning spiritual gifts, brethren,*
> *I would not have you ignorant…*
>
> *Now there are diversities of gifts, but the same Spirit…*
>
> *But the manifestation of the Spirit is given to every man to profit withal. For…*
>
> > *to one is given by the Spirit the word of wisdom;*
> > *to another the word of knowledge by the same Spirit;*
> > *to another faith by the same Spirit:*
> > *to another the gifts of healing by the same Spirit;*
> > *to another the working of miracles;*
> > *to another prophecy;*
> > *to another discerning of spirits;*
> > *to another divers kinds of tongues;*
> > *to another the interpretation of tongues:*
>
> *But all these worketh that one and the selfsame Spirit, dividing to every man severally as he will."*

The Holy Spirit enables you to do what Jesus did!

Summary Exercise:

Write in your own words the 8 types of power that you can receive from the Holy Spirit as described in 1) through 8) in Part 2 of this lesson.

1) _____

2) _____

3) _____

4) _____

5) _____

6) _____

7) _____

8) _____

Now, look at each of the 8 types of powers again. In the space provided below, write down how you think these powers show that God is omniscient, omnipotent, and omnipresent. There are no wrong answers, just record what you have learned.

- God is omniscient because _____

- God is omnipotent because _____

- God is omnipresent because _____

PART 3.   TEN EMBLEMS OF THE HOLY SPIRIT'S POWER

There are ten emblems that represent different messages about the Holy Spirit's power to help us, keep us and deliver us safely into God's care and protection forever[3]. An emblem is defined in the dictionary as *"an object, or the figure of an object symbolizing and suggesting another object or an idea."* The ten emblems are listed below. Scriptures that explain the idea the emblem represents are listed with the ten emblems. One of these emblems is on this book's cover.

1. Fire: zeal and refining power

Read Luke 3:16, Isaiah 4:3–4, Acts 2:3, Matthew 3:11

The idea here is that the Holy Spirit will burn off the things in our lives which are not pure or pleasing in God's eyes. The spiritual burning process will strengthen the things in our lives that are pleasing in God's eyes. This is like the process in which silver and gold are purified. All the dirt and properties that are not silver and gold are burned off in a very hot fire, while the pure silver and gold become brighter and shinier.

2. Dove: gentleness, harmlessness, and comforting power

Read Luke 3:22, John 1:32–33

The idea here is that the Holy Spirit is not an overpowering spirit that forces Himself and His power on us. He nudges us and speaks to us to try and guide us in the right direction, but He is never forceful.

3. Water: life-giving and infinite power

WATER

Read John 7:37 – 39

The idea here is that the Holy Spirit will never run out. He will be a mighty power from God available to us until the end of time. This mighty power will be in us, bubbling over the things of God to us and through us.

4. <u>Wind</u>: resurrection power

Read John 3:8, Acts 2:2, Ezekiel 37:9

The idea here is that although the Holy Spirit is real, we cannot see Him with our natural eyes. In fact, we cannot depend on any of our five senses to prove that He has changed us from sinners to children of God. The change that takes place when we are born of the Spirit is invisible, but it is just as real as the wind, which blows, yet is not seen.

5. <u>Oil</u>: consecration and anointing power

Read Isaiah 61:1–3, Luke 4:14–21, Psalm 45:6–7, Hebrews 1:8–9, James 5:14–15

The idea here is that the Holy Spirit covers us and prepares us for special service. Also, when real oil is placed on people during prayer, the oil represents the power of the Holy Spirit coming on that person to perform healings and blessings for them as they have faith in God. Oil itself does not have power without prayer and faith.

6. <u>Seal</u>: redemptive and keeping power

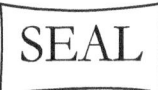

Read Ephesians 1:13, Ephesians 4:30, 1 Peter 1:5

The idea here is that the Holy Spirit is like a tight lid on a jar that has been placed there to protect or preserve what is on the inside, such as a jar filled with jelly. The lid is so tight that no air can enter the jar and spoil that jelly. The lid also keeps the taste of the jelly fresh for a really long time as long as the lid is never removed. In a similar way the Holy Spirit keeps us "saved" in the eyes of God until Jesus returns and carries us to live with Him forever.

7. Earnest: ownership and "guarantee" power
Read 2 Corinthians 1:21–22, Ephesians 1:13 – 14

The idea here is that the Holy Spirit is like earnest money you put down on a house. If someone wants to buy a house, then they must first give the seller a portion of the cost of the house. This portion is called earnest money. This lets the seller know the buyer is serious about buying. The seller will then stop advertising that the house is for sale. They will save it for the person who paid the earnest money, until they provide the rest of the payment. This earnest money makes the house almost as good as yours until you provide the rest of the money. In a similar way, the Holy Spirit makes the Kingdom of God ours now in a spiritual sense, until the Kingdom of God physically covers the earth. All the privileges and benefits of being a child of God are given to believers in Christ now, before the time of the new heaven and new earth.

8. Rain: life-giving and quickening power
Read Joel 2:23–32, Hosea 6:3, James 5:7, Hosea 10:12

The idea here is that rain can liven up dying things or revive dead things such as grass, flowers, and trees. God looks at our hearts and spiritual lives as either alive, dying or dead. Or maybe we are just baby Christians who are like seedlings in the ground that need more rain so they can become full and mature. God sends the Holy Spirit to liven up, revive, and strengthen our spiritual lives.

9. Dew: refreshing and invigorating power
Read Psalm 72:6, Hosea 14:5

The idea here is that the Holy Spirit does not come upon us one day and then leaves us later, like rain which falls for a little while and then stops. The Holy Spirit wants to stay with us like dew that sits on grass early in the morning giving it a fresh look. He wants to continuously work with us to make our lives better day by day.

10. <u>Gift</u>: joyful, gracious, and liberating power

Read Acts 2:38 – 39, Acts 4:31 – 33, 2 Corinthians 3:17 – 18

The idea here is that just like birthday or Christmas gifts make us happy, giggly and lighthearted, so does the Holy Spirit when He fills our lives. We feel better than we ever thought we could feel about life.

Exercise:

Which emblem of the Holy Spirit is used on this book cover?

9) _____

Optional Exercise:

Use the space below to draw the emblem or multiple emblems of the Holy Spirit that speak to your heart the most and write the reason why.

Exercise:

Based on what you have learned in this lesson, draw your own symbols to go along with the ideas of the Holy Spirit's power that are listed.

Table 2-3. Ten Emblems of the Holy Spirit's Power

FIRE: zeal & refining power	
DOVE: gentleness, harmlessness, & comforting power	
WATER: life-giving & infinite power	
WIND: resurrection power	
OIL: consecration & anointing power	
SEAL: redemptive & keeping power	
EARNEST: ownership & guarantee power	
RAIN: life-giving & quickening power	
DEW: Refreshing & invigorating power	
GIFT: joyful, gracious, & liberating power	

Chapter 3:

~ 4000 YEAR SPAN TIMELINE

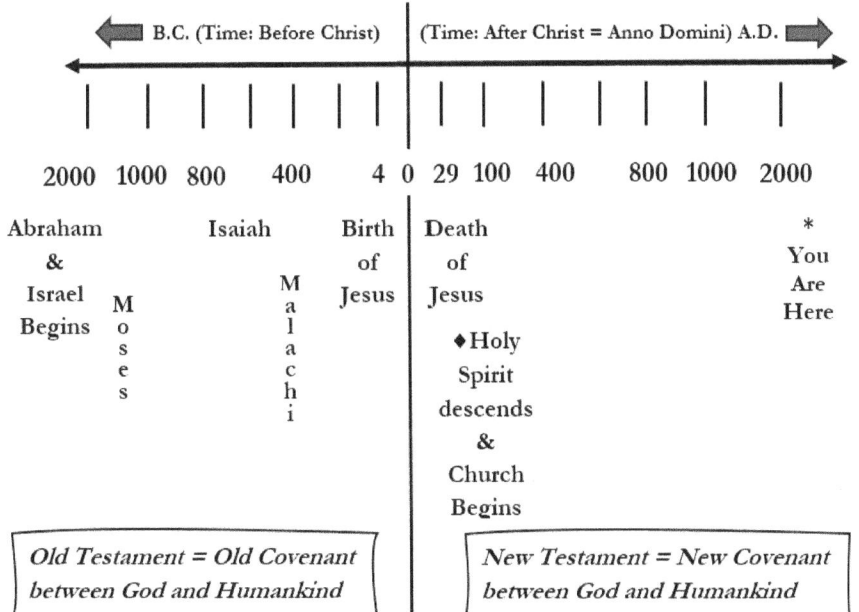

| B.C. (Time: Before Christ) | (Time: After Christ = Anno Domini) A.D. |

Old Testament = Old Covenant
between God and Humankind

New Testament = New Covenant
between God and Humankind

Bible History!

Chapter 3

Detailed Contents

Additional Study
- Chapter 8: Adult Bible Study Handouts
- Appendix C: Youth Lessons 1-28 Study Handouts

LESSON 10. HE'S COMING! (MEANING THE HOLY SPIRIT)

God spoke by the Holy Spirit to prophets in the Old Testament and told them to write about events that would take place far in the future. The ability of the prophets to foretell events (meaning to talk about something to occur before it happens) is called prophecy. For example, there were many Old Testament prophecies giving details about events that would happen at the time of Jesus' birth. When Jesus was born all the details came true just as they had been prophesied about in the Old Testament scriptures.

Hundreds of years before the coming of the Holy Spirit and "speaking in other tongues" took place, there were prophecies about their coming by two notable Old Testament prophets. Once the disciples were filled with the Holy Spirit, they remembered the prophecies. In the New Testament book of Acts Chapter 2, it explains that when Peter and the 120 disciples began speaking in other tongues after being filled with the Holy Spirit, the people who heard them thought they were drunk with alcoholic beverage early in the morning. Peter told the people that they had received the fulfillment of the Old Testament prophecy by the prophet Joel. In addition, Apostle Paul remembered a prophecy about speaking in other languages that had been written by the prophet Isaiah.

Exercise:

Read the scriptures below. Draw a line to match the Old Testament prophecy with the New Testament fulfillment of that prophecy.

Old Testament prophecy	New Testament fulfillment
Joel 2:28–32	1 Corinthians 14:21
Isaiah 28:11–12	Acts 2:14–21

There were also New Testament prophecies given by John the Baptist and Jesus, on the baptism of the Holy Spirit and the added spiritual power it would bring to our lives. Read three of these prophecies below. Write down when you think the prophecies were or will be fulfilled.

New Testament Prophecy	When Fulfilled*
Luke 3:16, John 1:32–33	1) _____
John 7:37–39	2) _____
Acts 1:8	3) _____

*Hint: Part of the answer for the time of fulfillment for all three is Acts 2:1–4. To learn the other time of fulfillment, look at Acts 2:38–39.

LESSON 11.   DAY OF PENTECOST FULLY COMES

PART 1.   THE FEAST OF PENTECOST WAS ONE OF THE ORIGINAL 7 YEARLY FEASTS

The baptism of the Holy Ghost was first given to a group of about 120 Jewish believers in Christ in the New Testament Church. This event occurred when the "day of Pentecost had fully come"! (Acts 1:15, Acts 2:1) The "Day of Pentecost" was a feast or celebration that God had instructed the Jews to gather annually, beginning in Old Testament times. Let's review this further.

In the Old Testament God selected a family to be His "chosen people." These chosen people of God were first called Israelites and Hebrews, then Jews or Jewish people. The Israelites were the descendants of one Hebrew man Abraham, his son Isaac, and his grandson Jacob. Jacob was renamed Israel by God after he won a wrestling match with God (Genesis 32:24–30).

Israel's twelve children started the Israelite nation. Once the family grew very large, God gave them instructions on how to live their everyday lives. He gave them laws and commandments (meaning rules). These laws and commandments told the Israelites how to treat God properly, how to treat each other properly, and how to treat non-Israelite people.

In addition to giving the Israelites laws and commandments, God directed them to have feasts. These feasts included activities that would honor God and allow the people to fellowship with each other.

Read Leviticus 23:1–3.

There were seven (7) feasts God directed the Israelites to celebrate on specific days of each year.[1] One of these yearly feasts of the Lord was the Feast of Pentecost.

Exercise:

List the 7 feasts of the Lord that were to occur once per year. The below verses describe the feasts, but sometimes the name of the feast is not easy to figure out. Hints are provided to help you. Note that the "Sabbath" in the Jewish religion was on Saturday, the last day of the week. This day was set aside to rest and worship God. (Leviticus 23:3)

1) **Leviticus 23:4–5** _____

    (Hint: Look in verse 5. This feast is the Lord's _____)

2) **Leviticus 23:6–8** _____

    (Hint: Look at verse 6 for the name of this feast.)

3) **Leviticus 23:9–14** _____

    (Hint: In verse 10 this feast is called by the name of what the people had to bring to the priest.)

4) **Leviticus 23:15–21**

    a. Old Testament name _____ (Deuteronomy 16:9–10)

    b. New Testament name _____ (Acts 2:1)

    (Hint: This feast has a different name in the Old Testament than in the New Testament. The New Testament name is based on the feast that occurred 50 days after the Feast of the Sheaf of Firstfruits after Passover. The New Testament name was first seen in Acts 2:1. "Pentecost" means fiftieth, such that "Day of Pentecost" means fiftieth day.)

5) **Leviticus 23:23–25** _____

    (Hint: Look at verse 24. It is named after what is "blown."

6) **Leviticus 23:26–32** _____

    (Hint: Look at verse 27. It was set aside as a day of _____)

7) **Leviticus 23:33–44** _____

    (Hint: The name of the feast is in verse 34.)

The Feast of Firstfruits happened on the "morrow after the Sabbath," which means the day after the Sabbath. What day of the week did this feast happen on?

8) **Leviticus 23:10–11** _____

Now look at the names of the feasts in Table 3-1 "Yearly Feasts of The Lord for the Nation of Israel" to see if you have the correct names.

<u>Notes for Reviewing Table 3-1</u>

- Study each section of Table 3-1 to understand God's purpose for having the Israelites celebrate each of the seven (7) feasts.

- God had the Israelites do activities in the Old Testament that symbolized events to take place after Jesus came to the earth.

- The last column explains the New Testament meaning for each of the feasts.

- The first page of the table explains how the events represented by the first four (4) feasts have been already fulfilled.

- The second page of the table shows how the events that the last three (3) feasts symbolize are to be fulfilled in the future.

TABLE 3-1. YEARLY FEASTS OF THE LORD FOR THE NATION OF ISRAEL

Feast	Old Testament Meaning[2]	Bible Reference	Month of Sacred Year	Day	Corresponding Modern Month	New Testament Meaning[3] (Already Fulfilled)
Passover	To remind Israel of how God mightily delivered them out of Egypt. God made the death angel "pass over" Israel when he saw the blood of the lamb on the outside doorposts.	Lev. 23:4–5, Ex. 12:12–14 Ex. 12:21–28	1 (Nisan or Abib)	14	March – April	Jesus became the lamb that was killed for us. His blood is used to remove our sins from God. Death cannot keep us when it comes for us and sees the blood of Jesus in our soul-spirit. Death must pass over us, letting us go to eternal life with God. This Feast symbolized death's "pass over." John 1:29; 1 Cor. 5:7
Unleavened Bread	To remind Israel of the day that God freed them from being under the bondage (sinful rule) of the Egyptians.	Lev. 23:6–8 Ex. 12:15–17	1 (Nisan or Abib)	15–21	March – April	Leaven symbolizes sin. God wants no sin to be in our lives. This Feast symbolized sinless Jesus, the Bread of Life, being broken for us during His crucifixion and death, to deliver us from sin's ruling presence over our lives. 1 Cor. 5:7–8; Matt. 26:17, 26
Firstfruits	The beginning of harvest was a time of joy, which Israel was to celebrate. They were to present to God the first sheaf of grain as a token of the harvest to come.	Lev. 23:9–14	1 (Nisan or Abib)	16	March – April	This feast symbolized the resurrection of Jesus Christ. When Jesus rose from the dead and ascended to heaven, He represented the first of many who would also be resurrected and join Him in heaven. 1 Corinthians 15:20, 23
O. T. name is "Weeks" N. T. name is "Pentecost"	Celebrate the finished product of the grain, 50 days (7 weeks + 1 day) after seeing a part of it at the feast of Firstfruits. Each family brought two loaves of bread made from their harvest of grain.	Lev. 23:15–21, Deut. 16:9–10, Acts 2:1 (also called the Feast of Harvest in Exodus 23:16)	3 (Sivan)	6 (50 days after the sabbath day before the Feast of Firstfruits)	May – June	50 Days after the resurrection of Jesus (spiritual firstfruit), the "Day of Pentecost was Fully Come," when the Holy Spirit came to finish the work Jesus began. By living inside believers, the Holy Spirit would make many people the children of God (more spiritual fruit or harvest for God) Acts 1:8; Acts 2:1, 4, 15–21

Feast	Old Testament Meaning[2]	Bible Reference	Month of Sacred Year	Day	Corresponding Modern Month	New Testament Meaning[3] (To Be Fulfilled in the Future)
Trumpets (*Rosh Hashanah*)	To blow trumpets (Ram's Horn = Shofar) announcing the 7th month of the year. The 7th month was when the Day of Atonement took place.	Leviticus 23:23–25	7 (Tishri)	1	September – October	**Symbolism:** It symbolizes the New Testament promise that one day a Divine Trumpet will sound; then all people redeemed by the blood of Jesus will rise to meet Him in the air ("the rapture"). When this trumpet sounds, the dead believers will rise first, followed by the living. 1 Cor. 15:51–52; 1 Thess. 4:16–17
Day of Atonement (*Yom Kippur*)	This was the most sacred day of Israel's year. Atonement means "to cover". Animal sacrifices were made on this day to atone or cover the sins of the people and to obtain God's forgiveness for their sins. The priest took the blood of the animals into the Most Holy Place of the Tabernacle and sprinkled it on the mercy seat before God. They asked God to accept the blood as payment for the sins of the people.	Leviticus 23:26–32	7 (Tishri)	10	September – October	For the Christian church Jesus made atonement for our sins when He was crucified, died and rose from the dead. His one-time sacrifice on our behalf put an end to the necessity for yearly animal sacrifices. He entered the Most Holy Place on high in heaven and remains there representing us before God. **Symbolism:** Some Christian Bible scholars teach that the Day of Atonement symbolizes the future time when the Jewish nation, as a whole, will accept Jesus (Yeshua) as their Messiah, repenting of their sins and accepting His atoning blood. This will occur after the rapture of the Christian church. Hebrews 9:11–12; Zechariah 12:10
Tabernacles (Booths or Ingathering)	To remind the Israelites of the tabernacles or tents they had lived in for forty years in the wilderness, as they waited to enter the Promised Land.	Leviticus 23:33–44	7 (Tishri)	15–21	September – October	**Symbolism:** This feast symbolizes for us today that this earth is our temporary home. One day all believers in Christ - Jews and Gentiles - will live with God in a new heaven and a new earth forever. Also, scholars believe when Jesus will reign as King on earth during the Millennium, this feast of tabernacles will be reestablished for all people to observe. Zech. 14:16–19

PART 2.   PASSOVER & PENTECOST FEASTS ARE IMPORTANT TO CHRISTIANS TODAY

The Jews celebrated Old Testament feasts in New Testament times also. The first three feasts of the Jewish sacred year – the Passover Feast, Feast of Unleavened Bread, and the Feast of the Sheaf of Firstfruits – were all combined to become a part of the Passover. At the time Jesus lived, the Passover feast lasted for one week and consisted of these three main events.[4] Passover began on the fourteenth day, Unleavened Bread on the fifteenth day, and the feast offering of the Firstfruits was held on the sixteenth day. The month Nisan for the Jews happened around the same time as the modern-day months of March and April. Refer to Table 3-1.

The Jews in the New Testament also celebrated the Feast of Pentecost. Read Matthew 26:1–2, 17–19 and Acts 20:16 to read accounts of Jesus and the Apostle Paul attending the Feasts of Passover and Pentecost. Significant events happened around the time of Jesus' 33rd year on earth, as it relates to these two feasts, which would change life for everyone forever.

In Hebrews 10:1 and Galatians 3:24, we learn that God's instructions to the Israelites used a lot of symbols to stand for events that would take place after Jesus came to earth. The exercises below will help you understand what the Passover and Pentecost feasts symbolize.

Exercise:

Read **John 19:13–18**. Jesus was crucified during the day of preparation for which feast? (verse 14) **9)** _____

The Jews sacrificed a lamb during the Passover feasts. They began doing this after God used Moses to deliver the Israelites from the evil Egyptian Pharaoh in the Old Testament. The Israelites had to kill a lamb and place its blood on the two side posts and the upper post on their doors. Then when the death angel came to kill the firstborn children in each home, the angel would "pass over" their houses, not killing their children, because of the blood he saw. This was the tenth plague God sent upon Egypt. Read about the first Passover in Exodus Chapter 12.

Read **John 1:29, 1 Corinthians 5:7, and 1 Peter 1:18–19.**

What animal sacrifice was Jesus a symbol of? **10)** _____

Why was Jesus sacrificed for us? **11)** _____

Exercise continued...

What Christian celebration takes place around the same time as the Jewish Feast of the Passover? **12)** _____

> (Hint: Look at Table 3-1 to see what months happen when the Feast of Passover is celebrated. Then think about what holiday Christians celebrate each year in those months.)

Here are two math problems for you...

Problem 1. Read Acts 1:1–3. After Jesus "showed himself alive after his passion" (meaning after He rose up from the dead), how long did Jesus show Himself to His disciples. **13)** _____ **days**

The Feast of Pentecost occurred 50 days after the Feast of Firstfruits. Acts 2:1 explains that the Day of Pentecost "was fully come." This means the most important Day of Pentecost occurred 50 days after the most important Feast of Firstfruits. Jesus' resurrection occurred on the Sunday morning after the combined feasts of Passover and Unleavened Bread. This was the day of the Feast of Firstfruits. Jesus' resurrection was a "spiritual Firstfruit" given to God and the most important "Firstfruit."

Read **1 Corinthians 15:22–23**. What type of "spiritual firstfruit" did Jesus represent? **14)** _____

> (Hint: Before Jesus' resurrection, the spirit of every dead person went to a place called Sheol. After Jesus rose from the dead, He was the first resurrected person who could go live with whom?)

Problem 2: If Jesus' resurrection was the true time of Firstfruits that had been symbolized by the Israelite feast, then the Day of Pentecost must have "fully come" 50 days after Jesus rose up from the dead. Based on this and your answer for question 13) above, how long did the disciples wait in Jerusalem for the Holy Ghost to come upon them?
15) _____

> (Hint: Subtract the answer to question number 13) from the number "50" to come up with the answer.)

Special Note: After the Day of Pentecost had fully come, the beginning of today's Church Age began on earth. Now, people are born into the Kingdom of God through the work of the Holy Spirit. All who believe on the risen Jesus Christ become a child of God.

Summary

The Passover and Pentecost celebrations are very important to our study of the Holy Spirit. They are symbolic of events that are the basis of all our Christian beliefs.

Jesus' crucifixion and resurrection occurred during the Passover Week, which is when Christians celebrate the remembrance of Christ's passion and resurrection *(also known as the Easter holy day)*. Jesus' resurrection occurred on the Sunday morning after Passover, which is when the Feast of Firstfruits took place. His resurrection represented the spiritual Firstfruit of the children of God. Jesus was the first child of God to be raised up from the dead to go live with God eternally.

Forty days after Jesus' resurrection, He walked and talked with His disciples on earth. On the 40th day, while preparing to go back to heaven, Jesus told His disciples to go to Jerusalem and wait for the promised Holy Spirit. Ten days later, 50 days after Jesus' resurrection, the Holy Spirit filled the disciples in the upper room in Jerusalem. The Bible describes this day as "when the Day of Pentecost was fully come."

The Pentecost feast, that was celebrated by the Jews, was representative of this time when the Holy Spirit would come after Jesus' resurrection. When the Jews celebrated this feast, they celebrated the time of the full harvest of grain. The coming of the Holy Spirit represents this time when God will use the Spirit to gather His full harvest of souls.

Precious Fruit

"Be patient therefore, brethren, unto the coming of the Lord. Behold the husbandman *[meaning God]* **waiteth for the precious fruit of the earth** *[meaning people becoming His children through the work of the Holy Spirit]*,

and

hath long patience for it, until he receive the early and latter rain" *[meaning God's complete harvest of souls, from the time Jesus and the Holy Spirit were sent over 2000 years ago, until the future time of the final judgment of all people].*

Early and Latter Rain

James 5:7

LESSON 12: DIFFERENT WAYS PEOPLE IN THE BIBLE WERE FILLED WITH THE HOLY SPIRIT.

PART 1.   JEWISH BELIEVERS WERE THE FIRST TO BE FILLED WITH THE HOLY SPIRIT

The first group to be filled with the Holy Spirit were the Jewish disciples who obeyed Jesus' instructions after He ascended on a cloud back to heaven.

Jesus told His disciples to go to Jerusalem and wait for the promise from the Father to be baptized (filled) with the Holy Spirit.

There were about 120 disciples. The group included the disciples who closely followed Jesus while He was on earth. (Acts 1:12-26)

> [Note: Matthias was chosen to replace the position Judas Iscariot held among the twelve disciples.]

The 120 also included Mary, the mother of Jesus, and Jesus' brothers.

Exercise:

Read Acts 2:1–4 and answer the following questions about the way this group was filled with the Holy Spirit.

1) They were all **with one** _____ (meaning they were all thinking alike) **in one** _____.

What type of weather events does the phrase "a sound… as of a rushing mighty wind" seem to describe? **2)** _____

What came into the room and sat on each person? **3)** _____

How many of the 120 Jewish Christians were filled with the Holy Spirit? **4)** _____

Who began to speak with other tongues? **5)** _____

Who gave each person the "utterance" for the new tongue / language (meaning who supplied the ability for speaking in the foreign language)?

6) _____

After the events in Acts 2:1–4, the apostles performed miracles, healings, and they caused 3000 people on one occasion (Acts 2:41), and 5000 people on another (Acts 4:4), to be saved at one time.

Some were arrested for preaching the gospel. **All these things occurred within a short time after the first 120 Jewish disciples were filled with the Holy Spirit.** Peter and John became bolder in preaching the gospel despite the threats from unbelieving Jewish rulers.

God also blessed the entire multitude of people gathered with the disciples to be saved and filled with the Holy Spirit. The next few exercises will identify specific stories of the Jewish believers becoming filled with the Holy Spirit.

Exercise:

Read **Acts 4:23–31. Re-read verse 31**.
What 3 things happened after the group that was assembled prayed?

7) _____, _____, _____

Philip, a man full of faith and the Holy Spirit (Acts 6:3–6), went to the city of Samaria and preached Christ to the citizens. He also performed many miracles there, which caused many of the people to accept Jesus as their Savior. Both men and women were baptized as they believed in the Lord Jesus Christ and believed the things Philip preached concerning the Kingdom of God. Now these new believers were ready to be filled with the Holy Spirit.

Let us examine how the Samaritan believers received this gift.

Read **Acts 8:4–24**. Did Philip cause the Samaritans to be filled with the Holy Spirit? (v. 14-17)

8) _____

What did Philip accomplish by preaching to the people? (v. 5-8, 12)

9) _____

How did the people receive the Holy Spirit? (v. 17)

10) _____

Re-read verses 18-19. What do you think Simon saw, to make him want to buy the ability to lay hands on people so they could receive the Spirit?

11) _____

Paul's Experience

The Apostle Paul began his interactions with the new Christian church as its enemy, at which time his name was known as Saul (Acts 8:1–3 and 9:1–2). For example, Saul would enter Christian Jew's homes and drag them off to jail.

One day, when he was on his way to hurt more Christians in the city of Damascus, Saul had a close encounter with the Lord. This experience caused Saul to change from a non-believer to a believer in Christ.

During the encounter, Saul became temporarily blind. His traveling companions had to lead him by the hand into Damascus where he stayed three days without his sight. Saul also did not eat or drink anything during the three days.

While Saul – who later became known as Paul (see Acts 13:9) – was seeking God through prayer and fasting, he became ready to be filled with God's Holy Spirit.

Let us review his story.

Exercise:

Read Acts 9:1–18.

Re-read verses 10–18. Who did the Lord send to help Saul?

12) _____

What did Ananias do to Saul to enable him to receive his sight and to be filled with the Holy Spirit? (v. 17)

13) _____

PART 2.
THE HOLY SPIRIT IS FOR GENTILES, TOO!

When the Bible refers to Gentiles in the natural sense (meaning not in the spiritual sense of the word), then it is describing the people who are not the natural descendants or offspring of Abraham, Isaac, and Jacob (who was also known as Israel).

The offspring of these three men are called Hebrews, Israelites, and Jews. Everyone else is considered a Gentile. In the early years of humankind, after Adam was banished from the Garden of Eden, God began revealing things about Himself in a special way through His relationship with the Jewish people. Even in the New Testament, when God came to walk among humans in human flesh (meaning as Jesus in His first coming to earth), He was born a Jew and spent most of His earthly life preaching and teaching among the Jews. However, there are many Old Testament passages that reveal that God always planned to extend His relationship of love and salvation to the Gentiles, too. Two such passages are Genesis 12:1–3 and Isaiah 42:5–7.

In keeping with His pattern of communicating to people, God sent the baptism of the Holy Spirit to the Christian Jews first. Then this gift from God was also passed on to Christian Gentiles. **The first Gentiles to be filled with the Holy Spirit were the household of Cornelius.**

Exercise:

Read Acts Chapter 10.

Re-read verses 44–48. How did the group at Cornelius' house become filled with the Holy Spirit?

14) _____

_____

How did the Apostle Peter and the people with him know that these Gentiles had been filled with the Holy Spirit?

15) _____

_____

Did these believers receive water baptism before or after they received the Holy Spirit?

16) _____

As the Apostle Paul became a mature believer in Christ, he preached and taught the Kingdom of God to Jews and Gentiles. His ministry work was most successful with the Gentiles instead of the Jews. Many of the Jews became hard-hearted against believing in Jesus Christ as the Savior for all people.

In Acts Chapter 19, we see Paul preaching in Ephesus to Jews and the Greeks (Gentiles). He caused many more Gentiles (and some Jews) to become disciples for Christ and to be filled with the Holy Ghost.

Exercise:

Read Acts 19:1–7.

Why had the 'certain disciples' not been filled with the Holy Spirit? (v. 2)

17) _____

What baptism had these disciples received? (verse 3)

18) _____

How did they come to receive the Holy Spirit? (verses 5-6)

19) _____

Summary

In the examples above, we find that Christians received the Holy Spirit by anointed disciples laying hands on them in prayer, by simply hearing the Word of God, or by the Spirit filling them during anointed prayer services. These Christians were Jews and Gentiles, men and women. The verses in Acts 2:17, 38–39 let us know that receiving the gift of the Holy Spirit was for children also. Several of the above scriptures show instances where entire households and multitudes were filled. This suggests that children were present receiving the Holy Spirit alongside the adults.

We can see from the scriptures that there is no set formula for being filled with the Holy Spirit. People received on the roadside, in church assemblies, in their homes, and seemingly in any place their hearts met the condition of being saved and wanting to be filled.

We, too, can receive the baptism of the Holy Spirit any time and any place our hearts are ready to receive. **"How I Can Be Filled"** will be discussed in more detail in Chapter 5, Lesson 20.

LESSON 13:   JESUS WAS FILLED WITH THE HOLY SPIRIT WITHOUT MEASURE

In John 3:25–36, John the Baptist's disciples became confused after Jesus came on the scene. Jesus quickly became more popular than John as He began preaching and teaching "**Repent ye, for the kingdom of heaven is at hand**" (compare Matthew 3:1–2 and 4:12, 17). When these disciples questioned John about what was happening, John explained, "Ye yourselves bear me witness, that I said, I am not the Christ, but that I am sent before him…

> **He must increase, but I must decrease. He that cometh from above is above all: he that is of the earth is earthly, and speaketh of the earth: he that cometh from heaven is above all… For he whom God hath sent speaketh the words of God: for God giveth not the Spirit by measure unto him. The Father loveth the Son, and hath given all things into his hand.**" (John 3:28, 30-31, 34-35)

John the Baptist knew that Jesus would have the full power of the Holy Spirit from God. In other words, Jesus did not just have a portion of the Holy Spirit's power, but He had it all. That is what the expression "for God giveth not the Spirit by measure unto him" means.

Let's look at how Jesus became filled with the Holy Spirit.

Exercise:

Read how the four gospels describe when Jesus was filled with the Spirit:

- **Matthew 3:13–17**
- **Mark 1:9–11**
- **Luke 3:21–22**
- **John 1:32–34**

> *God giveth not the Spirit by measure unto him [Jesus].*

When Jesus was filled with the Holy Spirit, did He speak in other tongues?   **1)** _____

What outward evidence did Jesus and John the Baptist see when Jesus was filled? **2)** _____

At the time Jesus was filled, who spoke and what did He say?

3) _____, _____

Read Matthew 15:21–28.

While Jesus walked the earth, to what group of people was He sent to minister? (verse 24)

4) _____

While Jesus walked the earth, what language did Jesus primarily need to speak based on the above passage?

5) **The language of the** _____ **people**

Read John 16:7.

While Jesus walked the earth, could the Holy Spirit be given to live inside of people?

6) _____

Read John 7:37–39 and Mark 16:17.

From these two passages, what did Jesus say the Holy Spirit would eventually cause to happen to the people who believe on Him?

7) _____ **(John 7:38)**

_____ **(Mark 16:17)**

Summary

Jesus was not born an offspring of Adam like all other human beings. Jesus was God before He came to the earth in human form (John 1:1 – 3, 14). He became the only begotten Son of God after the Holy Spirit placed His seed in Mary's womb, causing her to become pregnant with Him (Matthew 1:18–25). After His birth, Jesus was fully God and fully human.

Jesus grew up with the Holy Spirit leading, guiding and blessing His life until the age of 30 years old. He lived a perfect, sinless childhood because of this (Luke 2:40, 52). At the age of approximately 30 years old, God sent the greatest anointing upon Jesus (Luke 3:22–23).

God gave the full power of the Holy Spirit to fill Jesus at the time of His water baptism. From that time on Jesus lived the most impactful, powerful life ever recorded past, present or future of any human being. Jesus was truly God with us, talking and walking among us, teaching us the ways of God by His personal example, as led by the Holy Spirit.

LESSON 14. THE CHURCH IS FILLED WITH THE HOLY SPIRIT WITHOUT MEASURE

PART 1. THE HOLY SPIRIT STILL FILLS CHRIST TODAY WITHOUT MEASURE. 'THE BODY OF CHRIST TODAY IS THE CHURCH WITH CHRIST AS ITS HEAD.'

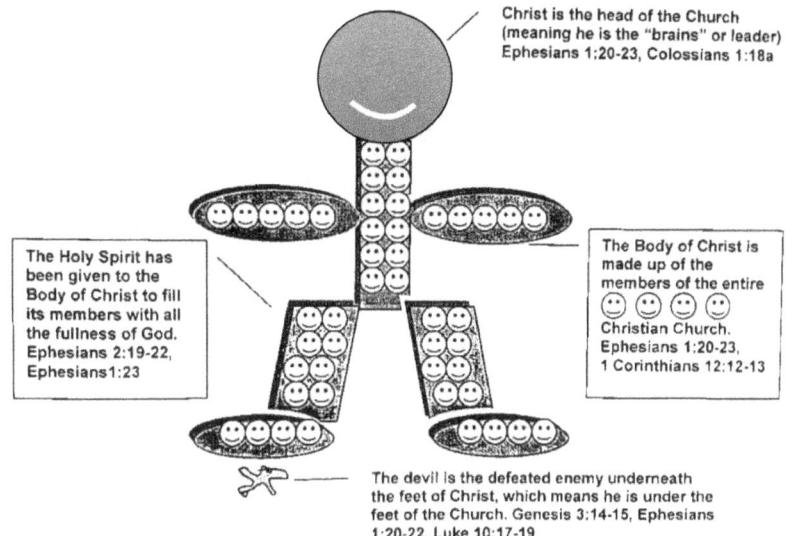

Christ is the head of the Church (meaning he is the "brains" or leader) Ephesians 1:20-23, Colossians 1:18a

The Holy Spirit has been given to the Body of Christ to fill its members with all the fullness of God. Ephesians 2:19-22, Ephesians 1:23

The Body of Christ is made up of the members of the entire Christian Church. Ephesians 1:20-23, 1 Corinthians 12:12-13

The devil is the defeated enemy underneath the feet of Christ, which means he is under the feet of the Church. Genesis 3:14-15, Ephesians 1:20-22, Luke 10:17-19

Christ Is the Head of the Body
Ephesians 1:20–23 "Which he wrought in Christ, when he raised him from the dead, and sat him at his own right hand in the heavenly places, Far above all principality, and power, that which is to come; and hath put all things under his feet, and gave him to be the head over all things to the church, Which is his body, the fullness of him that filleth all in all."

Colossians 1:18a "And he is the head of the body, the church..."

The Body is the Church
1 Corinthians 12:12–13 "For as the body is one, and hath many members, and all the members of that one body, being many, are one body: so also is Christ. For by one Spirit are we all baptized into one body, whether we be Jews or Gentiles, whether we be bond or free..."

The Devil is Under the Feet of the Body Which is the Church
Genesis 3:14a, 15 "And the Lord God said unto the serpent... And I will put enmity between thee and the woman, and between thy seed and her seed; it shall bruise thy head, and thou shalt bruise his heel."

Luke 10:19 "Behold [Jesus said] I give unto you power to tread on serpents and scorpions, and over all the power of the enemy: and nothing shall by any means hurt you."

The Holy Spirit Fills Up the Inside of The Body

Ephesians 2:19–22 "Now therefore ye are no more strangers and foreigners, but fellowcitizens with the saints, and of the household of God; and are built upon the foundation of the apostles and prophets, Jesus Christ himself being the chief corner stone... in whom ye also are builded together for an habitation of God through the Spirit."

> Born-of-the-Spirit Christian
> + Filled-with-the-Spirit
> = Empowered Spirit-Filled Christian

The Church is the body of Christ who are Jews and Gentiles born of the Spirit. Christ is the head of the Church. The Holy Spirit still fills up Christ without measure today when He fills the members of the Church.

After Jesus physically rose from the dead and ascended into heaven, He sent the Holy Spirit back to fill Christians with knowledge and power from God. Through the workings of the entire body of Christ, the true born-again members of the Church have access to all power from the Holy Spirit, to accomplish all the works that Jesus did when He walked the earth (Acts 10:38). Jesus also said the believers after Him would do greater works than He did if they would believe on Him (John 14:12).

Hebrews 13:8 says, "**Jesus Christ the same yesterday, and today, and forever**." Jesus' ministry today is the same as when He lived on the earth in New Testament times. The way He carries out His work today is through Christian believers who make up His new earthly body. The true members of the Church, who are established by their faith in Christ Jesus, are the people through whom Acts 10:38 is fulfilled "today" as it was through Jesus on "yesterday."

> "**How God anointed Jesus of Nazareth with the Holy Ghost and with power: who went about doing good, and healing all that were oppressed of the devil**." Acts 10:38

Jesus Christ directs the actions of believers who are filled with and in tune to the leading of the Holy Spirit. In this way Jewish and Gentile believers finish the work on earth that Jesus began in Luke 4:14–21.

PART 2. INDIVIDUAL MEMBERS OF THE CHURCH BODY ARE FILLED WITH A MEASURE OF FAITH AND GRACE FROM THE HOLY SPIRIT.

Each member of the Church is given a different portion or measure of faith and grace from the Holy Spirit.

> **"For I say through the grace given unto me, to every man that is among you, not to think of himself more highly than he ought to think; but to think soberly, according as God hath dealt to every man the measure of faith."** Romans 12:3

> **"But unto every one of us is given grace according to the measure of the gift of Christ."** Ephesians 4:7

These scriptures let us know there is an "interdependency" among Christians. It is necessary for Christians to work together to accomplish the entire work of Jesus Christ.

Definition: "Interdependency" means the need to depend upon one another. For example, two people equally need each other's skills to complete a job.

Exercise:

Read 1 Corinthians 12:12–30.

Based on passage above, how are the members of the body of Christ like the parts that make up our bodies? (verses 12–14)

1) _____

_____

How are the parts of our bodies interdependent on each other? (verses 15–26)

2) _____

_____

How are the members of the body of Christ interdependent on each other? (verses 27–30)

3) _____

_____

When individual Christians are filled with the Holy Spirit and experience a great anointing in their daily walk with God, God has still made it so they are dependent on others to do God's work.

Exercise continued:

In your own words, write down why you think God made the members of the Church interdependent on each other to perform His work most effectively?

> (Hint: The members of the Church must work together for the same reason the different parts of the body must work together.)

4) _____

_____

_____

_____

Chapter 4:

You In The Spirit

Chapter 4

Detailed Contents

Additional Study
- Chapter 8: Adult Bible Study Handouts
- Appendix C: Youth Lessons 1-28 Study Handouts
- Appendix H: KHS Video Lessons Synopsis

LESSON 15.   LED BY THE SPIRIT

"**But if ye be led of the Spirit, ye are not under the law**" Galatians 5:18

"**For as many as are led by the Spirit of God, they are the sons** [children] **of God**" Romans 8:14

"**But ye have an unction** [meaning anointed teacher or Holy Spirit] **from the Holy One, and ye know all things; ... The anointing** [meaning Holy Spirit] **which ye have received of him** [Jesus Christ] **abideth in you, and ye need not that any man teach you: but as the same anointing teacheth you all things, and is truth, and is no lie, and even as it hath taught you, ye shall abide in him** [Jesus Christ]." 1 John 2:20, 27

Welcome to School *(an analogy)*

Type of School: Spiritual school set up by God *(John 4:24)*

Principal: Loving heavenly Father – God *(John 14:23-26)*

Vice Principal: Jesus *(John 14:23-26)*

Teacher: Holy Spirit *(John 14:23-26)*

Student: You *(John 14:15-21, 26; John 17:20)*

Class Textbook: Scripture (Holy Bible, Word of God) *(2 Timothy 3:16-17)*

Lesson Plans: Designed to teach how to live godly in this world *(2 Timothy 3:12-17, Galatians 5:18)*

Tests: Tests *(Trials, Tribulations)* will affirm if you have learned the lessons correctly. Tests come in the form of challenging life experiences. A test is passed when you handle the challenge like the Word of God instructs. *(Romans 5:1-5; 1 Peter 4:12-19; 1 Corinthians 10:12-13)*

Grade Promotion: After each test is passed correctly, then you will get new lessons and challenges to help you grow as a child of God. *(1 Peter 1:6-16, James 5:10-11)*

Talking: Talk to teacher and principals in prayer anytime. *(Mark 11:23-25, Philippians 4:6, Hebrew 4:15-16)*

Listening: Hear the principals and teacher by reading the Bible and listening to the small voice inside you *(1 Kings 19:11-13; Jeremiah 33:3, John 10:27, 1 John 2:20, 27)*

Follow Directions: When you follow the teacher's directions daily, you are being "**Led by the Spirit**" of God. *(Isaiah 1:19, Psalm 84:11, Romans 8:14)*

The Holy Spirit is given to you to teach you what the Word of God means. He helps you understand how to apply the Bible lessons to your everyday life. Being born of the Spirit places you in the Kingdom of God as God's child. Learning the ways of God and daily living by them is what keeps you in the Kingdom. Only then will you enjoy the full benefits of being God's child.

The difference between your neighborhood schools and God's spiritual one is that the purpose for the neighborhood school is to teach you how to make a living (meaning it prepares you to get a job). God's spiritual school teaches you how to live (meaning how to act and think the right way so you can have a wonderful life).

The difference between your human teacher and the Holy Spirit teacher is that the Holy Spirit is inside you. He goes with you everywhere you go. The Holy Spirit will remind you of things you learn from the Bible, even when you do not have the Bible around. He will also protect you from going the wrong way, then an uncomfortable feeling will rise inside you. Just like an alarm clock wakes a person from sleep, this uncomfortable feeling comes to urge you to change your actions. You now have a chance to do the right thing instead of the wrong thing. If you change, then the Holy Spirit would have worked inside you to "lead you not into temptation" and "deliver you from evil." (Matthew 6:13)

Beware, There's Danger Ahead!

The Holy Spirit will never force you to do the right thing. The choice is always yours. If you choose to follow the lead of the Holy Spirit, He will cause you to have a wonderful life! Jesus said, "**I am come that they might have life, and that they might have it more abundantly**" (John 10:10b).

Jesus gives us this abundant (meaning wonderful) life as we listen to the Holy Spirit. The Bible says God is able to do "**exceeding abundantly above all that we ask or think, according to the power** [Holy Spirit power] **that worketh in us**" (Ephesians 3:20). This means that if our actions are led by the Spirit of God, then we will experience unimaginable blessings from God. Hallelujah! Amen!

Lesson 16. Living in the Spirit

The Bible tells us that as the children of God
we are to live in the Spirit and the Spirit is to live in us.

What I Do	**What the Spirit Does**
I live in the Spirit–Galatians 5:25	The Spirit lives in me–Romans 8:11

Does the Bible telling us to live in the Spirit, while at the same time telling us the Spirit should live in us sound confusing? Do you wonder if it is possible to do both?

Q: How can I live in the Spirit, when the Spirit is supposed to fill and live in me?

A: In spiritual matters both are possible. Read on.

I in the Spirit, and the Spirit in Me

**"But ye are not in the flesh, but in the Spirit,
if so be that the Spirit of God dwell in you"** Romans 8:9

Definition: "Dwell" means to live in all the time, or to "remain in."

When we accept Jesus Christ as our Lord, the Spirit comes to live inside of us. When the Spirit dwells in us, then we hear Him and do what He tells us to do all the time. However, He will not remain in us if we continue to live sinful lives. If we listen to the Spirit as He guides us to quit our sins, then He will live in us all the time. As a result, the Spirit of God will dwell in us. When the Spirit dwells in us, this means we are "in the Spirit" (Romans 8:9).

Exercise: An Object Lesson

This exercise uses the objects of glass and water in a demonstration to help you better understand the idea of "I am living in the Spirit when the Spirit is living in me." See actions on the next page.

Materials: You will need an empty glass next to a sink filled with water. (You can use a cup in place of the glass, and a punch bowl of water or some other container filled with water in place of the sink.) You will also need a utensil such as a ladle to scoop water out of the sink/container.

Materials Represent: The glass represents a person. The sink filled with water represents the Holy Spirit of God, which is the generator of life and salvation for all people through their faith in Jesus Christ.

1. Action: Sit the empty glass near the sink of water.

Explanation: The empty glass is filled with air.
This represents a person whose spirit is controlled
by the prince of the power of the air, which is the devil.
(Ephesians 2:2)

2. Action: Scoop some water from the sink and fill the glass with it

Explanation: When the glass is filled with water, this represents a person who now has their human spirit directed by the Holy Spirit. This change took place in their life when they received salvation from God by accepting Jesus Christ as their Lord and Savior. (Ephesians 5:25–26, Titus 3:5, Isaiah 12:3) Because of their faith in Jesus, the Holy Spirit came to live inside of them so that they were "born of the Spirit." The old sinful spiritual nature was replaced.

3. Action: Tilt the glass over and let some water spill out, leaving the glass partially filled with water and partially filled with air.

Explanation: Your hand pulling the glass over to the side to let water spill represents the pull of sin on the life of a person who has been born of the Spirit. If the person gives in to this desire to sin, then their spiritual self becomes weakened. Attitudes and actions, which are not Christian-like, creep back into their life. The portion of air in the glass represents the ways of the devil creeping back into the life of this Christian. (Hebrews 12:1, 1 Corinthians 3:16–17)

4. Action: Finally, take the glass of water and place it completely in the sink that is filled with water.

Explanation: When the glass filled with water is placed in the sink filled water, this represents what happens when a person becomes filled with the Spirit and lives in obedience to the Holy Spirit's guidance every day. Just like the water is in the glass and the glass is in the water, the Spirit-filled person has the Spirit in them, around them, and surrounding them with His helpful presence. The person is in the Spirit while the Spirit is also in them. God wants us to live in the Spirit all the time by reading our Bibles, praying and doing what the Spirit directs us to do daily.

LESSON 17. WALKING IN THE SPIRIT

PART 1. INTRODUCTION TO WALKING IN THE SPIRIT

"If we live in the Spirit, let us also walk in the Spirit"
Galatians 5:25

"Walk in the Spirit, and ye shall not fulfill the lust of the flesh."
Galatians 5:16

This lesson will help you learn specific actions God describes as the right behavior for someone who lives in the Spirit. This right behavior should be seen in your everyday "walk" in life.

Our human body (also called the "flesh" and "carnal man" in the King James Version of the Bible) naturally desires to do the wrong things, which are actions that God defines as sin.

The wrong desires of the body are still present after our human spirit has been born again with a new godly nature. The challenge for the Spirit-filled Christian is to let the Spirit help you:

 a) NOT do things the way the flesh wants you to, while

 b) DOING the things the way God wants you to

In other words,

 The FLESH MUST LOSE

and

THE SPIRIT RULE!

Exercise:

Read Galatians 5:16, 17.

What two contrary or opposing things are fighting to rule your actions?

1) _____, _____

PART 2.   THE FLESH MUST LOSE...

Exercise:

Read Galatians 5:19–21.

What 17 actions of the flesh are called out as "No, No's" for Christians?

2) _____, _____, _____

_____, _____, _____

_____, _____, _____

_____, _____, _____

_____, _____, _____

_____, _____

Stop. Think about it.

Take the time to review and think about all the actions of the flesh that hurt you as a Christian. Use a dictionary to look up definitions of words you do not know or look at the definitions that are provided in Appendix A with the Answers.

> Consider your own personal life. Write down which of the 17 actions of the flesh you need to get rid of below.
>
> _____

Read Colossians 3:5–7.

What 5 actions of the flesh are Christ's followers to stop doing?

3) _____, _____, _____

_____, _____

> Consider your life against this list. Write down more "fleshly" actions you need to get rid of. _____

Read Colossians 3:8–9. Write down 6 more fleshly acts that are not to be part of the Christian life.

4) _____, _____, _____

_____, _____, _____

> Consider your life against this list also. Write down any additional fleshly acts you must get rid of. _____

Stop and pray. Ask God to help you get rid of these works of the flesh out of your life. Read Psalm 51 and 1 John 1:5-10 to help you pray.

PART 3.   ... AND **THE SPIRIT RULE!**

Exercise:

In the spaces next to the scriptures below, write down what the Christian should do to the fleshly actions that comes in their mind to commit.

Read   Galatians 5:24   5) _____

Colossians 3:5   6) _____

Colossians 3:9b   7) _____

Romans 8:13b   8) _____

What do you think these scriptures tell you about how to handle fleshly desires? (Hint: Mortify and crucify mean to "kill.")

9) _____

_____

Read Galatians 5:22–23.

What **9 things should be produced** in a Christian's life?

10) _____, _____, _____

_____, _____, _____

_____, _____, _____

Read Colossians 3:12–14.

What **8 things** do these scriptures say **should be in a Christian's life?**

11) _____ , _____

_____ , _____

_____ , _____

_____ , _____

Stop and pray. Ask the Holy Spirit to help you become more the child of God in your daily walk in life, as described by these passages containing the "don'ts" and the "do's." Read Psalm 32, 1 Corinthians 10:12-13, Ephesians Chapter 5, and 1 John 3:1-12 to help you pray. Note: More detail on the Fruit of the Spirit is covered in Chapter 7.

LESSON 18.   PRAYING IN THE SPIRIT

PART 1.   THE SPIRIT HELPS US TO PRAY CORRECTLY.

> **Likewise the Spirit also helpeth our infirmities** [meaning problems]: **for we know not what we should pray for as we ought: but the Spirit itself maketh intercession for us with groanings which cannot be uttered.**
>
> **And he that searcheth the hearts knoweth what is the mind of the Spirit, because he** [the Holy Spirit] **maketh intercession for the saints according to the will of God.**   Romans 8:26–27

> Please help me, Lord!
> I just do not know what to do!

Prayer is absolutely necessary in our lives.

Simple prayers are great to pray at any time, such as:

> "The Lord's Prayer," "Help me, Lord!", "Forgive me, Lord!" and "I need you to lead and guide me, Lord!"

Yet sometimes we want our prayers to have deeper thoughts in them, and we just cannot think of the right words to say. It is as if something on the inside of us wants to speak in a clearer way, but the words that come into our minds are not good enough. They do not satisfy the longing in our hearts to talk to God about our real needs.

The difficulty in our ability to think of the right words may be better understood when we consider Scriptures a) and b) below:

a) **"For my thoughts are not your thoughts, neither are your ways my ways, saith the Lord. For as the heavens are higher than the earth, so are my ways higher than your ways, and my thoughts than your thoughts."** Isaiah 55:8–9

b) **Ye lust, and have not: ye kill, and desire to have, and cannot obtain: ye fight and war, yet ye have not, because ye ask not. Ye ask, and receive not, because ye ask amiss, that ye may consume it upon your lusts.** James 4:2–3

Scripture a) explains why the Spirit, who knows the will of God, may be uncomfortable with some of our prayers. He knows we do not always understand the right way to pray about things in our life.

Scripture b) explains why we do not get answers to some of our prayers. We sometimes pray for certain things for wrong reasons. To "ask amiss" means to ask from an imperfect motivation in our heart.

Overall, when we pray, one set of words comes into our heads to say, but the Spirit within us knows whether those words are right or not from God's viewpoint. For the Spirit-filled Christian, the Holy Spirit can help us to pray correctly according to God's will for our lives.

Romans 8:26–27 explains how the Spirit helps us to pray

- ◆ The Spirit knows our real problems and helps us to get God's help in solving our problems, by working from inside of us.
- ◆ We do not know how to pray correctly on our own.
- ◆ The Spirit wants to pray through us, for us, correctly.
- ◆ When we allow the Holy Spirit to lead our prayers, sometimes we may not understand the words that come forth out of our mouths or the sounds we make, such as a deep moaning or groaning.

God understands and agrees with the prayers by the Holy Spirit

- ◆ The Holy Spirit is completely in tune to God's will for our lives.
- ◆ The Holy Spirit designs our prayers to be in line with God's will.
- ◆ When we pray in line with God's will for our lives, then our prayers produce great results (our problems are helped).
- ◆ The Holy Spirit also helps us to pray for others correctly.

PART 2. **YOU MAY OR MAY NOT UNDERSTAND WHAT THE SPIRIT IS SAYING WHEN HE PRAYS THROUGH YOU, FOR YOU!**

There are several scriptures that describe how the Holy Spirit intercedes for us. To "intercede" means to be an in-between person who helps two other persons or groups, with different points of view, come to an agreement or view that is best for all. Let us look at some scriptures to find out how the Holy Spirit intercedes (meaning to pray or communicate with God) on our behalf to God. We will discuss:
A. How He speaks and B. What He is saying and doing when He speaks

A. How He speaks

1. **Ephesians 6:18** This passage lets us know that the Holy Spirit uses all types of prayers and pleadings to God for our personal benefit and for other believers. This means the Holy Spirit uses every speaking manner He knows how to talk to God on your behalf. He will use clearly understandable speech and other forms of speech as described below. He will also use private, public, church and family prayer.

2. **Romans 8:26** This passage describes the Holy Spirit's intercession (His pleading speech on our behalf) as being "with groanings which can not be uttered." The picture that comes to mind from reading this scripture is of a person who is moaning because of a great struggle in their heart. They do not even have understandable words to say because of the sadness or heaviness in their human spirit as it speaks to God.

3. **1 Corinthians 14:4, 13–16** This passage explains that the "unknown tongue" or foreign language that the Holy Spirit can give, can also be used by the Holy Spirit during our prayer. When we pray in the Spirit using the foreign language from Him, then our natural mind does not understand what is being said. We are told in these scriptures that we should ask God to tell us what the Holy Spirit is saying so we can understand what He is praying about. We are also instructed that when our prayer includes using the foreign language, we should also pray in our regular language, so that our mind and spirit are both benefited.

B. What He is Saying and Doing When He Speaks

4. The Holy Spirit causes our prayers
    to line up with the will of God.
    (Romans 8:26–27)

    > *Dear Lord,*
    > *Not my will, but your*
    > *will be done in my life…*

5. The Holy Spirit causes our prayers
    for others to be the best they can be,
    really meeting their needs.
    (Romans 8:27, Ephesians 6:18)

    > *Dear Lord,*
    > *Please help my*
    > *family and friends…*

6. The Holy Spirit always gives
    praise to God, even when we
    do not know what He is saying.
    (1 Corinthians 14:16–17,
    Acts 2:6–11)

    > *Oh God,*
    > *You are so Awesome,*
    > *so Powerful, so Good,*
    > *and…*

7. When the Holy Spirit prays through us,
    for us, then our inner spiritual person
    becomes stronger, causing us to
    become stronger Christians.
    We become better able to resist
    the desire of our flesh to commit sin.
    (Jude 20, 1 Corinthians 14:4)

    > *My Lord,*
    > *I thank you for*
    > *taking that desire away*
    > *from me to do…*

8. Praying in the Holy Spirit helps to
    increase our faith in God.
    (Jude 20)

    > *Oh God,*
    > *I know you can help*
    > *me to…*

PART 3. PRAYING IN THE SPIRIT WITHOUT LEARNING THE WORD OF GOD IS NOT ENOUGH TO CHANGE YOU INTO A STRONG CHRISTIAN

The Holy Spirit works with the Word of God to bring the greatest benefits from God's Word into our lives. Let us review some of Jesus' words describing how the Holy Spirit would work after He was sent to us.

John 14:26

"But the Comforter, which is the Holy Ghost, whom the Father will send in my name, he shall teach you all things, and bring all things to your remembrance, whatsoever I have said unto you."

Jesus was telling His disciples that the Holy Spirit would remind them of the things He taught them when He walked the earth. For us today, the lessons that Jesus and God the Father want to teach us are all recorded in the Holy Bible for us to learn. When Jesus walked the earth, He was the Word of God turned into human flesh (John 1:1, 14). Since that time, God used holy men to record the Word of God in a written book for our use – the Holy Bible. God will never use the Holy Spirit to tell us or pray for anything that is not based on the written words in the Bible.

John 7:38–39

"He that believeth on me, as the scripture hath said, out of his belly shall flow rivers of living water. (But this spake he of the Spirit, which they that believe on him should receive…)"

In this scripture Jesus explains how a good understanding of the Word of God gives a continuous, abundant flow of the Spirit to the believer.

Matthew 22:29

"Jesus answered and said unto them, Ye do err, not knowing the scriptures, nor the power of God."

Jesus tells us again that a good knowledge of the Word of God must be combined with the power received from the Holy Spirit for a person to serve God correctly.

From the above scriptures you can see that the more you know the Word of God, the more helpful your praying in the Spirit will be to you.

♦ **More Word, More Power!** versus **Less Word, Less Power!**

We do not want to be like the people in the New Testament Corinthian church who misunderstood how the Holy Spirit works. They confused "speaking in unknown tongues" as being the most important part of the Holy Spirit's power. They thought people who spoke often in foreign languages, given by the Holy Spirit, were more spiritual and more important than people who did not. Apostle Paul corrected their thinking in letters he wrote to the church. His messages are important to us to understand today.

Key points are summarized below:

1   **You can speak in foreign languages by the Spirit and still sin.** This is wrong. If you are not living the right way according to the Bible's description of living right, then "speaking in unknown tongues" in public does not please God. **(1 Corinthians Chapter 5 and Chapter 14)**

2   **Praying in foreign languages is one way to "pray in the Spirit."** Praying in the Spirit includes praying in your own understandable language and / or praying in a foreign language by the wisdom of the Holy Spirit. **(Ephesians 6:18, 1 Corinthians 14:14–15)**

3   **When "praying in the Spirit" in a foreign language by the Holy Spirit, your mind does not benefit from what you are saying.** This is because you have never learned the foreign language being spoken. You should pray and ask God to give you the interpretation of what the Holy Spirit is speaking through you. In this way the time of praying in the Spirit will benefit both your spirit and your mind. **(1 Corinthians 14:13–17)**

4   **When "praying in the Spirit" in a foreign language, your spiritual self is built up or strengthened through the prayer.** That is what the word "edify" means as used in 1 Corinthians 14:4. However, this type of prayer does not benefit others like it does you. Therefore, when in the presence of others, it is best to pray so everyone can understand you and primarily pray in the foreign language(s) during private prayer. **(1 Corinthians 14:4, 16–19)**

5   **There is a correct time and place for doing everything the Holy Spirit wants us to do.** The Bible says that everything that comes from the Lord is done "decently and in order." **(1 Cor. 14:40)** This also applies to determining when and how we pray.

PART 4. PRAYING IN THE SPIRIT WITHOUT THE LOVE OF GOD FILLING YOUR HEART IS NOT ENOUGH TO DEVELOP YOU INTO A STRONG CHRISTIAN.

Read 1 Corinthians Chapter 13 below.

In the King James Version (KJV) Bible, the word "charity" is the theme word used in 1 Corinthians 13. In other Bible translations, the word charity has been changed to the word which represents the essence of what charity means in this passage, which is the word "love."

Keep "love" in mind as you read the word "charity."

Though I speak with the tongues of men and of angels, and have not charity, I am become as sounding brass, or a tinkling cymbal.

And though I have the gift of prophecy, and understand all mysteries, and all knowledge; and though I have all faith, so that I could remove mountains, and have not charity, I am nothing.

And though I bestow all my goods to feed the poor, and though I give my body to be burned, and have not charity, it profiteth me nothing.

Charity suffereth long, and is kind; charity envieth not; charity vaunteth not itself, is not puffed up,

Doth not behave itself unseemly, seeketh not her own, is not easily provoked, thinketh no evil; Rejoiceth not in iniquity, but rejoiceth in the truth;

Beareth all things, believeth all things, hopeth all things, endureth all things.

Charity never faileth: but whether there be prophecies, they shall fail; whether there be tongues, they shall cease; whether there be knowledge, it shall vanish away.

For we know in part, and we prophesy in part. But when that which is perfect is come, then that which is in part shall be done away.

When I was a child, I spake as a child, I understood as a child, I thought as a child: but when I became a man, I put away childish things.

For now we see through a glass, darkly; but then face to face: now I know in part; but then shall I know even as also I am known.

And now abideth faith, hope, charity, these three; but the greatest of these is charity.

Chapter 5:

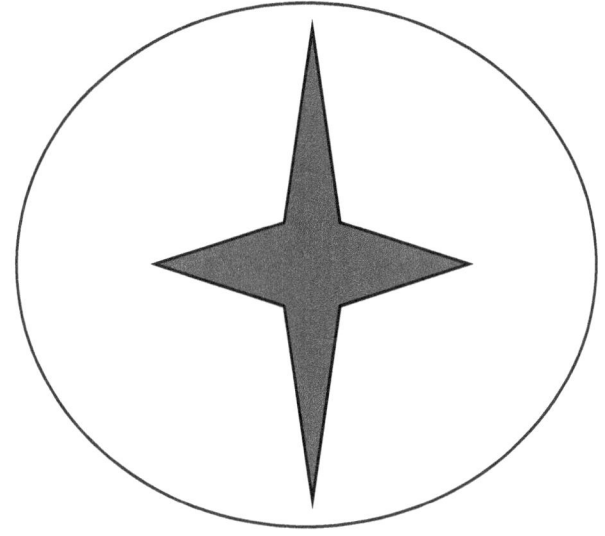

The Spirit In You

Chapter 5

Detailed Contents

Additional Study
- Chapter 8: Adult Bible Study Handouts
- Appendix C: Youth Lessons 1-28 Study Handouts
- Appendix H: KHS Video Lessons Synopsis

LESSON 19. WHY I NEED TO BE FILLED

I need to be filled with the Holy Spirit so I can...

♦ Obey the command from the Lord. Ephesians 5:18
♦ Receive power from on high to be a dynamic witness for the Lord.
  Acts 1:8, Acts 2:38–39, Galatians 3:13–14, John 7:37–39
♦ Receive from God all the things that will help me have "life and
  godliness." 2 Peter 1:3
♦ Experience the fullness of God. Ephesians 3:16–20
♦ Make my worship of God seem more real. John 4:24, John 14:17

Exercise:

♦ **Obey the command from the Lord.**

Read Ephesians 5:18. There are two commands (or instructions) given
in this verse. One is a negative command which is a "Do Not" type
command. The other is a positive "Do" type command.

Write the negative command. **1)** _____

Write the positive command. **2)** _____

♦ **Receive power from on high to be a dynamic witness for the
  Lord.**

Read Acts 1:8. How far did Jesus say disciples would go to witness to
others about Him, after the Holy Spirit came upon them?

3) _____

Read Acts 2:38–39. Re-read verse 39. Who is the gift and the promise
of the Holy Spirit for? **4)** _____

Read Galatians 3:14. This verse says that the promise of the Holy Spirit
is for whom? **5)** _____

Read John 7:37–39. Who did Jesus say would receive the Holy Spirit?
6) _____

**Do you believe that the gift of the Holy Spirit is for you, to fill and
strengthen your Christian life? Yes _____ or No _____**

♦ **Receive from God all the things that will help me have "life and godliness." (2 Peter 1:3.)**

Read 2 Peter 1:3.

What gives us all things that "pertain to life and godliness" (meaning a wonderful life, and a life of living right according to God's way).

7) _____

What does God's divine power have to work "through" to give us this wonderful life, and to help us live pleasing to God?

8) _____

Who has to have this knowledge? Circle one answer.

9) a. My Mama   b. My Father   c. My Preacher   d. Me

How is the divine power of God given to us in the first place?
         (Hint: Re-read Acts 2:38, Galatians 3:14 and Acts 1:8)

10) _____

♦ **Experience the fullness of God.**

Read Ephesians 3:14–20.

These scriptures represent a prayer by the Apostle Paul for the saints at the church in Ephesus and to all the saints (meaning Christians) of God (Ephesians 1:1).

Re-read verses 16–19. In Paul's prayer for us, he asks God to increase the strength of our inner spiritual self by helping us to receive more power from God's Spirit within us. He also prayed that our faith in Christ would increase and our understanding of God's love for us would increase. Finally, he lets us know that if we have more of the Spirit, we can be filled with all the fullness of God.

Re-read verse 20. Depending on how much power we have working in our lives from the Holy Spirit, what is God able to do for us?

11) _____

♦ **Make my worship of God seem more real.**

Read John 4:24.

How must we worship God? **12)** _____

Read John 14:17.

What is the Holy Spirit called in this verse? **13)** _____

If you become filled with the Spirit of Truth, how do you think He will help your ability to worship God? (Hint: Consider your answer to 12) above.)

14) _____

_____

The Holy Spirit

Puts the

Real Church

In Our Hearts!

LESSON 20. HOW I CAN BE FILLED

STEP 1.	BE BORN AGAIN
STEP 2.	ASK
STEP 3.	SEEK
STEP 4.	KNOCK
STEP 5.	RECEIVE
STEP 6.	FILL UP
STEP 7.	REFRESH

STEP 1.

Be Born Again

Jesus answered, "Verily, verily, I say unto thee, except a man be born of water and of the Spirit, he cannot enter into the kingdom of God. That which is born of the flesh is flesh; and that which is born of the Spirit is spirit. Marvel not that I said unto thee, Ye must be born again. [See Appendix E for Endnote explaining "born of water"] **John 3:5–7**

Even the Spirit of truth; whom the world cannot receive, because it seeth him not, neither knoweth him: but ye know him; for he dwelleth with you, and shall be in you. **John 14:17**

And it came to pass, that while Apollos was at Corinth, Paul having passed through the upper coasts came to Ephesus: and finding certain disciples, He said unto them, Have ye received the Holy Ghost since ye believed? And they said unto him, We have not so much as heard whether there be any Holy Ghost. And he said unto them, Unto what then were ye baptized? And they said, Unto John's baptism. Then said Paul, John verily baptized with the baptism of repentance, saying unto the people, that they should believe on him which should come after him, that is, on Christ Jesus. When they heard this, they were baptized in the name of the Lord Jesus. And when Paul had laid his hands upon them, the Holy Ghost came on them; and they spake with tongues, and prophesied. **Acts 19:1–6**

Be Born Again continued…

The ability to become "filled with the Holy Spirit" can only happen after one believes on Jesus Christ, accepting Him as their Lord and Savior. Then Jesus births you into His spiritual kingdom = born again.

According to John 3:5–7, a sinner can be born of the Spirit. According to John 14:17, a sinner (called the world in that scripture) cannot receive the Spirit of Truth, which is the Holy Spirit. This means a sinner cannot be filled with the Holy Spirit. John 14:17 explains that the reason a sinner cannot receive the Holy Spirit is because the Holy Spirit is not "with" the sinner, so that the sinner does not "know" Him. In other words, there is no relationship between the sinner and the Holy Spirit. You cannot be filled with the Spirit you do not know.

When a sinner is born again spiritually, they ask Jesus Christ to become the Lord and Savior of their life (see Chapter 1, Lesson 4). Jesus becomes Lord of the person's human spirit through the work of the Holy Spirit. The Holy Spirit regenerates the person's spirit (Titus 3:4–7) and translates the person spiritually into the Kingdom of God through Jesus Christ (Colossians 1:12–14). This process is called being "born of the Spirit." After a sinner is born of the Spirit, then he or she now has the Holy Spirit "with" them. This rebirth makes them a Christian who is "related" to the Holy Spirit. Now the born-again / born of the Spirit Christian, having the Spirit "with them," can become filled with the Spirit.

In Acts 19:1–6, we find that the Apostle Paul knew only believers in Christ could become filled with the Holy Spirit. When he met some disciples in Ephesus, he asked if they had been filled with the Holy Spirit. He knew how important it was for them to have this special power from God. These disciples responded that they had not heard about the Holy Spirit. Also, it turned out that they had not been taught to believe on the risen Jesus Christ yet. They had only repented of their sins based on John the Baptist's preaching in the wilderness before Jesus had been crucified and resurrected. After learning this, Paul first led them to accept Jesus Christ as their Lord. Then, he baptized them in the name of the Lord Jesus. Next, he prayed for them to receive the Holy Spirit. The Holy Spirit fell upon them immediately, and they spoke in tongues and prophesied.

Complete this sentence

Before you can be filled with the Spirit, you must be _____.

And I say unto you,

**Ask, and it shall be given you;
seek, and ye shall find;
knock, and it shall be opened unto you.**

**For every one that asketh receiveth;
and he that seeketh findeth; and
to him that knocketh it shall be opened.**

If a son shall ask bread of any of you
that is a father, will he give him a stone?
or if he ask a fish,
will he for a fish give him a serpent?

Or if he shall ask an egg,
will he offer him a scorpion?

If ye then, being evil,
know how to give good gifts
unto your children:

**how much more shall your heavenly
Father give the Holy Spirit
to them that ask him?**

Luke 11: 9–13

Ask

Jesus said in Luke 11:11–13,

**"If a son shall ask bread of any of you
that is a father will he give him a stone?
Or if he ask a fish, will he for a fish give him a serpent?
Or if he shall ask an egg, will he offer him a scorpion?
If ye then, being evil know how
to give good gifts unto your children:
<u>how much more shall your heavenly Father
give the Holy Spirit to them that ask him?"</u>**

Jesus also said in Luke 11:9,

"Ask, and it shall be given you."

The picture Jesus draws in our minds with these scriptures is one based on a person having the right to ask for things from another person because of their relationship to each other.

For example, if someone's young son or daughter was hungry, and they were too small to get food for themselves, then the parent is responsible for giving the child food when they ask for it. This is because the child needs it, he or she is dependent on their adult parent, and the parent is required to provide for the child's needs.

In this same way, God knows we need to be filled with the Holy Spirit. He is our heavenly Father and the only one who can help us receive the Holy Spirit to fill us with His power.

Therefore, He is required to provide for our needs. Most of all, since this is a good gift that God has already provided for us, He is very happy to help us receive the Holy Spirit when we ask Him.

STEP 3.

Seek

Jesus said,

"Blessed are they which do hunger and thirst after righteousness: for they shall be filled."

Matthew 5:6

Jesus said,

"... seek, and ye shall find..."

Luke 11:9b

"... for he that cometh to God must believe that he is, and that he is a rewarder of them that diligently seek him."

Hebrews 11:6b

'If you want it, and you search for it, and you go after it, then you are going to get it. But you have got to want it!'

God has diligently done everything He can to get our attention and draw us to Him. God loves us, wants us and desires us. He has great plans for us. He has patiently worked to win us over to His loving care. His love for us is like a man who loves a woman and does special things for her until he convinces her to marry him. God loves us even greater than this.

When we finally begin to give God our attention, He loves it. God immediately wants us to get to know Him better. He knows we need to be filled with His Holy Spirit, so the Spirit can help us comprehend God's great love and plans for our lives. This is the why He made the Holy Spirit available for all on the full Day of Pentecost in the New Testament.

Because we do not fully understand God and the way He works, we can cause our own delay in being filled with His Holy Spirit. When this happens, we should continue to seek the Lord by reading our Bibles and praying regularly, until we are filled with the Holy Spirit.

Knock

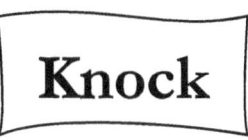

... "knock and it shall be opened unto you."

Luke 11:9c

**"And ye shall seek me, and find me,
when ye shall search for me with all your heart."**

Jeremiah 29:13

**"Blessed is the man that walketh not in the counsel of the ungodly,
nor standeth in the way of sinners,
nor sitteth in the seat of the scornful.
But his delight is in the law of the Lord;
and in his law doth he meditate day and night.
And he shall be like a tree planted by the rivers of water,
that bringeth forth his fruit in his season;
his leaf also shall not wither;
and whatsoever he doeth shall prosper."**

Psalm 1:1–3

The idea of "knocking," as used by Jesus in the first scripture above, is based on there being a "need" on the part of the knocker. The needy person will not stop knocking until the door has been opened and their need has been met. Spiritually speaking this means spending lots of time seeking God's powerful presence in your life until your soul is completely satisfied.

The people who realize they need the Lord will read their Bibles more often. They will listen to God's word through godly preachers, teachers, music and other Christian media more often. They will also talk to God about every area of their life regularly, asking for His presence, guidance and blessing.

STEP 5.

Receive

Christ hath redeemed us from the curse of the law, being made a curse for us: for it is written, Cursed is every one that hangeth on a tree: That the blessing of Abraham might come on the Gentiles, through Jesus Christ; that we might receive the promise of the Spirit through faith. Galatians 3:13–14

But without faith it is impossible to please him: for he that cometh to God must believe that he is, and that he is a rewarder of them that diligently seek him. Hebrews 11:6

If any of you lack wisdom, let him ask of God, that giveth to all men liberally, and upbraideth not; and it shall be given him. But let him ask in faith, nothing wavering. For he that wavereth is like a wave of the sea driven with the wind and tossed. For let not that man think that he shall receive any thing of the Lord. A double minded man is unstable in all his ways. James 1:5–8

And all things, whatsoever ye shall ask in prayer, believing, ye shall receive. Matthew 21:22

A. Receive the Holy Spirit by Faith

Anything we receive from the Lord; we receive by faith. We receive being born of the Spirit by faith. We cannot look directly at our human spirits for proof that the new lordship of God has taken place. Instead, we hear the Word of God, believe it, and then begin telling others that Jesus is the new Lord of our life.

Similarly, we receive being filled with the Holy Spirit by faith. As you ask, seek, and knock, God has already promised that you will receive, find, and have an open door in answer to your request to be filled with the Holy Spirit.

'God poured out the Holy Spirit to fill everyone when the Day of Pentecost was fully come. Now, everyone just must receive the fullness of the Holy Spirit, into their inner spirit, by faith! And it's done!'

According to Romans 10:8 and 10, there are two activities that show a person has faith in God.

A person that has faith in God:

1) **Believes the Word of God in his or her heart and**

2) **Confesses to other people the Word of God that he or she believes.** (This means you communicate to others your belief.)

◆ It is not enough to believe God in your heart only,

But

◆ You must also have enough confidence in God's Word to tell others what you believe to be rightfully yours from His Word.

Then,

◆ When you confess what you believe in your heart to be rightfully yours by the Word of God, your belief and confession are what causes the belief to come to pass in the earth.

Finally, to God, if your faith is based on His Word, then you have already received what you are believing Him for spiritually, even when you may not have received it naturally. (Hebrews 11:1)

To reiterate again, it is your belief and your confession of what you are believing God for that will make what you are believing to take place in the natural, on earth.

_____

'After you wholeheartedly seek God to fill you with His Holy Spirit, and you receive His fullness into your spirit by a prayer of faith, then begin thanking God for filling you with His Holy Spirit.

As you praise God for filling you with His Holy Spirit, then the signs of your having been filled will soon manifest in your life.'

_____

B. Signs are Evidence that You Have Received the Holy Spirit

**God has provided signs to comfort the believer,
and as evidence to the unbeliever,
that the believer has been filled with the Holy Spirit.**

In the book of Acts the sign of speaking in other tongues was associated with almost all the stories of believers being filled with the Holy Spirit.

Prophesying was also mentioned in several of these stories, which is another sign that a person is filled with the Spirit.

There are other signs that the Bible says would be a part of the Spirit-filled believer's life.

Sign of Speaking in Tongues

The sign of "speaking in tongues" is discussed in detail in Chapter 1, Lesson 5. Now let us look at the other signs.

Exercise:

From Joel 2:28, list the three (3) signs that were foretold to happen when God would pour out His Spirit upon all flesh.

1) _____

2) _____

3) _____

In Mark 16:17–18, Jesus also listed signs that would be a part of the life of believers. List the five (5) signs.

4) _____

5) _____

6) _____

7) _____

8) _____

Sign of Prophesying

Prophesying is explained in 1 Corinthians 14:3–25. It is clear from these scriptures that prophesying uses the common language of the speaker and not a foreign language, unless the foreign language is interpreted.

In verse 3, prophesying is described as having three purposes – to edify, exhort and comfort.

- **Edify** means to build up a person spiritually through speaking uplifting words.
- **Exhort** means to encourage someone with words.
- **Comfort** means to soothe and cheer up people who are downhearted and discouraged.

To accomplish these three purposes, the speaker receives the uplifting, encouraging, and soothing words to share from God. These words lift up or magnify God's name and power, and they lift the individual or group being spoken to through sharing spiritual insight.

Sign of Spiritual Dreams

Spiritual dreams and visions, given by the Holy Spirit, are not like the regular dreams people have when they sleep.

Spiritual dreams are like the ones Joseph interpreted in Genesis Chapters 40 and 41. Those dreams from God used symbols that no one could understand on their own. God had to explain the meaning.

Sign of Spiritual Visions

Spiritual visions also come from God. The person having them does not think of them alone. He or she does not have to sleep to have these visions. It is as if God unfolds a plan to their mind so that the person could begin working on God's plan for their life. Or the visions could show the person things that they did not know from the past, present, or future.

For example, the book of Revelation in the Bible is a group of visions that were given to the Apostle John on the Isle of Patmos. In those visions, God revealed spiritual insight on churches that were current to John's time and revealed spiritual insight on future events that will affect the whole world.

In **Mark 16:17–18**, Jesus listed the following signs that were to follow any believer in Him:

> **"And these signs shall follow them that believe;**
> **In my name** [meaning in the Name of Jesus]
> - **they shall cast out devils;**
> - **they shall speak with new tongues;**
> - **they shall take up serpents;**
> - **and if they drink any deadly thing, it shall not hurt them;**
> - **they shall lay hands on the sick, and they shall recover"**

Then in **Mark 16:20**, it says that the following happened to the disciples with whom Jesus shared the above words.

> **"And they went forth, and preached every where,**
> **the Lord working with them, and confirming the word**
> **with signs following. Amen."**

In earlier lessons from studying Acts 1:8 and Acts Chapter 2, we learned the disciples did not begin their new lives as preachers, apostles, miracle workers and teachers, until after they were filled with the Holy Spirit.

We found that these supernatural signs began operating in the disciples' lives after they were filled with the Holy Spirit. We have also learned that the Holy Spirit is a gift from God sent in fulfillment of His promise to give His children help to live holy and abundant lives on the earth.

Warning! Do NOT Seek After A Sign!

God does not want us to seek after signs to show up in our lives. We are not to focus on speaking in tongues or being able to handle a snake and not die. This is NOT what God wants us to seek after.

We ARE to seek to know God through being filled with His Holy Spirit. Then signs will show up in our lives to confirm God's Word in us as we co-labor with the Lord in ministering to people (1 Corinthians 3:9-13).

In Acts 8:9–24, read the story of how Apostle Peter rebuked a man named Simon for having the wrong pursuit of seeking after a sign. Simon was more excited about the foreign tongues supernaturally given to people by the Holy Spirit, than receiving power and wisdom from God through the Holy Spirit.

TO BE FILLED WITH THE HOLY SPIRIT
WITH
THE SIGNS OF EVIDENCE IN YOUR LIFE,
YOU
SHOULD DO THE FOLLOWING:

1   Desire to be filled with God's Holy Spirit. Desire this because you want to have all the help God has provided for you to live a victorious, abundant life in this world. Also, desire this because you want to be the best witness you can be for God.

2   In a prayer of thanksgiving, thank God for sending the Holy Spirit to be your personal, daily helper in this life. Then, ask God to help you receive His gift of the Holy Spirit that He has already sent to you from heaven.

3   Now believe God's Word when He says that you shall receive the Holy Spirit after asking for Him. Then, because you believe God, receive the Holy Spirit into your life by faith. Do this even if you do not feel different or have signs appearing immediately.

4   After you have asked and received the Holy Spirit by faith, the rest is up to God. You have done your part. God will send the signs as evidence into your life.

5   Finally, continue to seek God for all the benefits of being filled with the Holy Spirit daily. Expect God to give you added help and strength because He is a faithful God. God will provide for the needs of those who believe in Him and diligently seek Him.

**Read the next section, C,
to learn of other ways you can
Receive the Holy Spirit.**

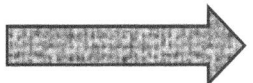

C. Methods of Receiving the Holy Spirit

In Chapter 1, Lesson 5, Part 2, we looked at examples of how people in the Bible became filled with the Holy Spirit. Through studying their experiences, we learn that a person can be filled in different ways and in different places, but all must receive by faith.

In the table below, scriptures are referenced from the early Church's experiences. Fill in the blanks with the number of people filled and the places they were filled. Keep in mind that the same experiences the early Christians had are available for you today.

Exercise:

For some of the answers, you may have to use words like "many" for the number and "in the city" for the location.

Table 5.1 Methods of Receiving the Holy Spirit

How Filled	Reference Scriptures	Number of People	Where Filled (Location)
A believer, who has the ability from God, can lay his or her hands on your head and pray that you are filled with the Holy Spirit, and you will immediately be filled.	Acts 8:5–6, 12, 14–17 Acts 9:17 Acts 19:1–7	_____ _____ _____	_____ _____ _____
You can be with a group of people who all have the same desire to be filled. As you all pray and ask God to fill you, then all will receive Him.	Acts 1:13–15, Acts 2:1–4 Acts 4:31–33	_____ _____	_____ _____
You can be filled with the Holy Spirit immediately after you are born again.	Acts 19:1–7	_____	_____

Table 5.1 Methods of Receiving the Holy Spirit continued

How Filled	Reference Scriptures	Number of People	Where Filled (Location)
Some unknown amount of time can pass between when you are born again and when you become filled with the Holy Spirit	Acts 8:12-17	_____	_____
You can just be listening to the wonderful Gospel message and become filled with the Holy Spirit.	Acts 10:1–8, 19 –48	_____	_____
You can be alone, seeking God to be filled with the Holy Spirit and be filled.	Mark 16:17, Luke 11:9–13	——————— ———————	——————— ———————
While you are expressing your love to God by giving Him praise and thanksgiving; and worshipping God from deep within your heart, you can become filled with the Holy Spirit.	Ephesians 5:18–21	_____	_____

STEP 6.

Fill Up

**"And be not drunk with wine wherein is excess;
but be filled with the Spirit;**

**speaking to yourselves in psalms and hymns and spiritual songs,
singing and making melody in your heart to the Lord;**

**giving thanks always for all things unto God and the Father
in the name of our Lord Jesus Christ;**

**submitting yourselves one to another,
in the fear of God."**

Ephesians 5:18–21

**To understand the concept of "filling up" with the Holy Spirit,
let us do an exercise in comparison and contrast.**

We will compare and contrast the two types of people described in Ephesians 5:18.

One person is drunk with wine, excessively. The other person is filled with the Holy Spirit of God.

> For the comparison part of our exercise, we will see where these two types of people have similar actions or attitudes.

> For the contrast part of the exercise we will see where these people have different actions and attitudes.

In order to do this exercise, you must think back on movies where you have seen drunken people in action. Or maybe you know of people who have drunken alcoholic beverage in excess and have observed their behavior.

If you have never seen a person who has had too much alcoholic beverage to drink, you will need to get help doing these exercises from someone who has seen someone drunk.

Comparison Exercise:

In the space provided below, write down how a person who is drunk with an excess of alcoholic beverage acts similarly to the person that is filled with the Spirit as described in Ephesians 5:19–21.

One who acts like this is Filled with the Holy Spirit	One who acts like this is Drunk with an excess of wine
Merrily speaks to themself and to others as inspired by words from psalms, hymns, and spiritual songs (v. 19)	9)
Melodiously sings to themself and in the presence of others (v. 19)	10)
Gives thanks to God all the time for all things (v. 20) *(this means even during times when disappointing things occur)*	11)
Submitting to others in a way that shows a love and reverence for God (v. 21) *(this means engaging with people in a way that pleases God)*	12)

Contrast Exercise:

In the space provided below, write down how a person who is drunk with an excess of alcoholic beverage acts differently to the person that is filled with the Spirit as described in Ephesians 5:19–21.

They speak and sing **psalms, hymns,** and **spiritual songs** (v. 19)	13)
The melody in their heart comes from songs that **lift up God's name and power** (v. 19–20)	14)
Submitting themselves to others is done **in the fear of the Lord**. (No submission to another goes against the Word and Will of God.) (v. 21)	15)

Summary

DO!

Fill Up on the Holy Spirit

The experience of a person becoming filled with the Holy Spirit could be considered like a person who fills up on an alcoholic beverage. A drunk person is sometimes thought of as a carefree, merry type person.

God wants us to drink excessively of His Holy Spirit by speaking and singing His Words from the Bible all the time.

When we do this, we become carefree, thankful and merry in our hearts, especially as we understand God's promises of blessings and deliverance from trouble. Finally, God wants us to love and treat each other the way the Bible describes.

DON'T!

Fill Up on Wine
(Alcoholic Beverage)

Unfortunately, Satan has made a counterfeit or phony experience for every good experience from God.

Sadly, some stores that sell alcoholic beverages will use the word "spirits" to refer to wine and other alcoholic drinks. Many people think that filling up with the alcoholic spirits can help ease hurtful experiences or just help them to have a good time for fun. But filling up with alcohol (drinking it in excess) will often lead to regretful, shameful, and empty experiences. (Prov. 20:1, 23:20– 21; Luke 21:34–35; 1 Cor. 5:11– 13)

A night of alcoholic fun can become a night you wish had never happened. Or an empty night of wine-drinking foolishness will not satisfy your heart's desire to have lasting joy after it is all over.

Filling up with alcoholic beverages is not the type of "spirit" experience God intended for us to have. Instead, God instructs us to fill up with His Holy Spirit. Think of it as getting "drunk" with the Holy Spirit.

This Holy Spirit-filled experience occurs as we meditate on God's goodness, praising and worshiping Him in good times and bad. It also occurs as we treat others the way God wants us to treat them, giving ourselves to them in the fear of the Lord, even when we do not want to.

Below, I,
Author of **Know His Spirit Bible Study**,
share with you my rewrite of Ephesians 5:18–21
using today's language, to help explain its meaning.

'Don't get drunk from drinking a lot of alcoholic beverages but

Do get drunk from drinking a lot of God's Holy Spirit.

*The way to do this is by speaking and singing
the wonderful words of God from the Bible
when you are alone and when you are with others.*

*Especially sing the psalms a lot, as well as hymns
and spiritual songs based on the mighty Word of God.*

*Also, give praise and thanks to God all the time,
no matter what is happening in your life.
This, too, will cause you to get drunk on the Holy Spirit.*

*This praise is done in the name of our Lord Jesus Christ,
because the name of Jesus gives us power to
look past our problems and look to
the magnificence of our God, the problem solver.*

*Finally,
become drunk with the Holy Spirit by
loving and serving people the way God wants us to,
and not the way our mind or our flesh wants.'*

Refresh

"And I am sure that, when I come unto you,
I shall come in the fulness of the blessing of the gospel of Christ.

Now I beseech you, brethren, for the Lord Jesus Christ's sake,
and for the love of the Spirit, that ye strive together with me
in your prayers to God for me; that I may be delivered from them
that do not believe in Judea; and that my service
which I have for Jerusalem may be accepted of the saints;
that I may come unto you with joy by the will of God,
and may with you be refreshed."

Romans 15:29–32

"For with stammering lips and another tongue
will he [God] speak to this people. To whom he [God] said,
This is the rest wherewith ye may cause the weary to rest;
and this is the refreshing..."

Isaiah 28:11–12

Spirit-filled Christians still have problems in their lives and will sometimes need Spiritual ...

- Sometime people who are not Christians do mean things to Christians.
- Sometimes Christians do things to hurt each other's feelings.
- Sometimes Christians do things that weaken their relationship with God.
- Sometimes Christians wrongfully think they are better than others which weakens their relationship with people
- Sometimes Christians get tired of actively doing God's work.
- Sometimes Christians do not understand some things God allows to happen, such as the death of someone they love. This can cause them to be upset with God.

When Christians have these types of problems, they need to have a special experience with God which brings them back to feeling His closeness, forgiveness, love, and special care. This experience provides for a time of spiritual "refreshing."

... Refreshing!

In Romans 15:32, the Apostle Paul expressed a need to be refreshed.

Paul was very much a Spirit-filled Christian. In fact, in Romans 15:29, he speaks about experiencing the full blessing of the gospel of Christ. Yet at the end of the passage in Romans 15:29–32, Paul speaks of a hope to be refreshed when he visits the people in the church in Rome. The reason he needed this refreshing is because of the problems he was having with non-Christians in Judea. He was also concerned whether the Christians in Judea would accept his work for God despite the trouble the non-believers were giving him.

Isaiah 28:11–12 reveals that one of the purposes of speaking in tongues (being filled with the Spirit) **is to refresh people.**

Through the Holy Spirit's presence coming upon us in a special way, He can give us a new attitude about the problems we are experiencing. This new attitude comes to strengthen our walk with God.

Spirit-filled Christians can experience a new out-pouring of God's Spirit, which refreshes their outlook on life. It is as if the Spirit-filled Christians receive the Holy Spirit afresh!

'Just like the rain comes to refresh the green, green grass, the Holy Spirit comes to refresh the Spirit-filled soul!'

After You Become Born As A Christan,

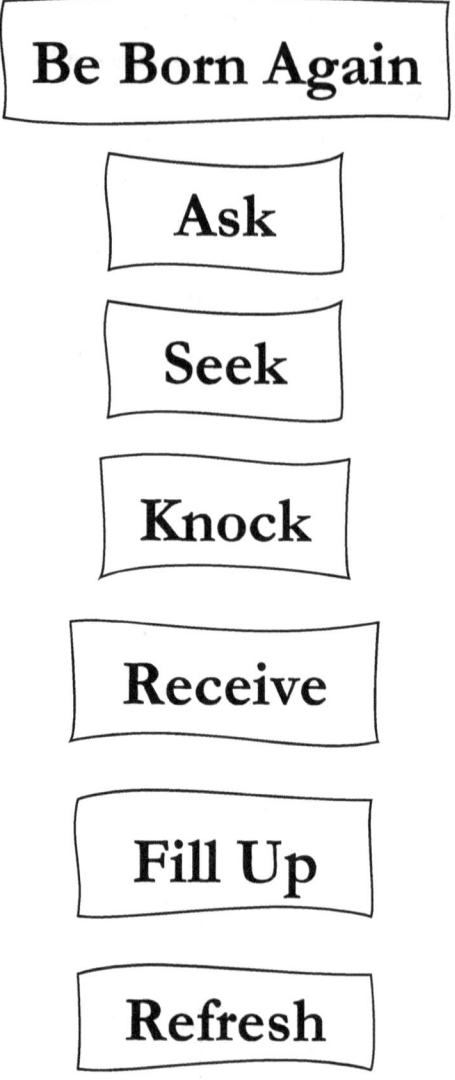

Be Born Again

Ask

Seek

Knock

Receive

Fill Up

Refresh

Then,

You Must Grow Up As A Christan!

GROW UP!

LESSON 21.   WHAT TO DO AFTER I AM FILLED!

Question: After I am filled with the Holy Spriit, what do I do next?

Answer: Grow Up!

Becoming filled with the Holy Spirit begins a new experience in your relationship with God. It does not matter whether you are 5 years old or 105 years old. Your inner spirit must learn how to hear from God with this new spiritual listening device that you have just received.

It is as if you have a new telephone system that gives you a clearer connection to talk and listen to God. Now you must learn to walk with God in a new way, by the leading of the Holy Spirit, one day at a time. Each day you will grow as a Christian, having a better understanding of how to communicate with God.

There are things you need to do privately, when you are all alone, to grow up as a Christian. There are also things you should do publicly, when you are around others.

Below are some specific instructions on what you should do.

Privately, Develop Your Inner Spiritual Self

- Become more Christ-like in how you act.
- Continue to read your Bible and pray every day.
- Seek God for your purpose for living.
- Desire Spiritual Gifts to work in your life.

Publicly, Share the Message of God's Love

- Be a witness for the Lord.
- Do what the Bible says for you to do.
- Be peaceful, loving and caring.
- Share your Spiritual Gifts with others.

'**When you are all alone,**

you should read your Bible daily
to learn how to think and act like Jesus did.

When you are all alone

and not reading your Bible,
your thoughts and actions
should be like Christ's.

When you are reading the Bible
and praying,

you should ask God
"for what purpose did
He bring you into the world."

As you keep reading
and talking to God,

God will reveal to you why you were born.'

PART 1.   PRIVATELY, DEVELOP YOUR INNER SPIRITUAL SELF

- **Become More Like Christ in How You Act.**

  In Matthew 16:24–27 and Luke 6:40, Jesus explains that following him includes denying yourself and doing God's Word. As you seek to do God's will daily, through praying and reading your Bible, the Holy Spirit will reveal to you how to think and act like a Christian in your daily actions. Review what you learned in Chapter 4 about being led by, living, walking and praying in the Spirit.

- **Continue to Read Your Bible and Pray Every Day.**

  The Holy Spirit brings new abilities into your life as you continue to seek God. This happens when you read the Bible and think about what it is saying to you. You also need to pray about everything in your life. Then the Holy Spirit can help you to grow up in Christ. Receiving the Holy Spirit in your life is not enough to make you a strong Christian. If you do not study God's word and talk to God regularly, it is difficult for the Holy Spirit to help you. John 14:23–26 lets us know that the Holy Spirit works for God the Father and Jesus, who primarily speak to us through God's Word in the Bible.

- **Seek God for Your Purpose for Living.**

  You were born for a reason. God has a work for you to do. He also has a time that is right for you to do that work. No one knows your purpose except God. Each of us must find out our purpose from Him (Ecclesiastes 3:1–11). [Note: God will use people to affirm our purpose.] As your personal helper, the Holy Spirit can guide you in the direction that God wants you to go in life (1 Corinthians 2:9–10). When you choose to follow God's plan for your life, then you will be positioned to experience your best life on earth. So, ask God what He wants you to do at each phase of your life. Then, listen daily for the Holy Spirit to bring God's answer.

- **Desire Spiritual Gifts to Work in Your Life.**

  The scriptures in 1 Corinthians 14:1 and 1 Corinthians 12:7 let us know that the Holy Spirit has spiritual gifts that are desirable and profitable for our Christian walk with God. Ask the Holy Spirit which spiritual gifts He wants to work in your life. Then ask Him to teach you how to use them.

PART 2.   PUBLICLY, SHARE THE MESSAGE OF GOD'S LOVE

- **Be A Witness for the Lord.**

  You do not have to make people upset with you because all you do is talk about the Lord. You do not have to wear Christian clothing all the time so people can know you are a Christian. But you can, as the Holy Spirit leads you, share the love of God with your friends who are hurting, confused and lonely. The Holy Spirit can help you to share the message of God's love in such a way that you will be helpful, instead of dreadful. (Acts 1:8)

- **Do What the Bible Tells You To Do.**

  It is not enough to talk like a Christian. It is not enough to know the right things to do in your mind. The Holy Spirit will help you to be a "doer" of the instructions in the Bible. Sometimes, it is hard to do all the right things all the time. That is why you need to be filled with the Holy Spirit. Then, the Holy Spirit gives you greater inner strength to "do the right thing!" (James 1:22–25, 4:17; Ephesians 3:14–19)

- **Be Peaceful, Loving, and Caring.**

  The Bible warns us that in the last days many people will increasingly become cold-hearted and evil (read Matthew 24:3–14, 2 Timothy 3:1–5, 12–13). They will also increase in being violent, disrespectful, and selfish, caring more about themselves and less about others. For Christians, one of the jobs of the Holy Spirit is to shed the love of God in the hearts of people (Romans 5:5). Through the Holy Spirit working in your heart, you can be a peaceful, loving, caring person whether other people around you act that way or not. Ask the Holy Spirit to help you with this. It will not always be easy, but these good qualities are the true mark of a Christian.

- **Share Your Spiritual Gifts with Others.**

  God's gifts are to be shared (1 Corinthians 12:7). In Chapter 6 you will learn how God has given gifts such as encouraging words, special healings, special faith, special wisdom, and special knowledge. The purposes for these gifts are to help people know God's supernatural power and love here on earth. Spiritual gifts are not needed in heaven. The time for using these gifts is now to assist in spreading the gospel message. Share your gifts with others as the Holy Spirit leads you to do.

Whether you
are at
Work or Play,
Home or School,
or with
Family or Friends,

**You should always
show Christian
Love and Behavior
to others!**

LESSON 22. CONDUCT: DECENT AND IN ORDER

In the next Chapter (Chapter 6), you will read about the different spiritual gifts that become available to you after you have been filled with the Holy Spirit. The purpose of these gifts is to strengthen your relationship with God, and to increase your ability to share the love of God with others.

Two very strong emotions can come with receiving spiritual gifts. You will probably feel both fear and excitement. The feeling of fear happens when you are concerned that you may act the wrong way when you try to use your gift or gifts. This happens because you do not fully understand how the gifts work at first. You will learn as you use them. You may also feel very excited at which gift or gifts the Holy Spirit decided to give you. There is one other feeling you could have. You could feel disappointment at which gift the Holy Spirit chose for you. This negative feeling would also be a result of not fully understanding the gift you have received. Every gift from God is good and perfect, and worth having (James 1:17, 1 Corinthians 12:7).

The best way to handle your gift is to pray for direction on how to use your gift. Then, look for instructions in the Bible on how to use it. Also, look for examples of how people used them in the Bible. Finally, listen carefully to the small inner voice of the Holy Spirit that will guide you on when to use your gift. Remember, no voice you hear will ever tell you to do anything that does not have an instruction or example from the Bible.

Sometimes you will make mistakes in using your spiritual gift. Having this new ability can be compared to a baby learning how to walk. Just like that child falls down sometimes because they try to walk too fast, or because they stumble over something they did not notice was in their way, you will probably miss acting the right way sometimes because you are learning.

There are some guidelines you can follow to help you not make too many mistakes.

Three of these guidelines are discussed in the next exercise.

Exercise:

Guideline #1.

Read 1 Corinthians 14:40.

Write down what you believe this scripture is telling you about how you should act.

_____

_____

    'Think about this—
    There are rules to follow even when doing a work for the Lord!'

Guideline #2.

Read 1 Corinthians 14:33.

Write down what you believe this scripture is telling you about how you should act.

_____

_____

    'Think about this—
    God is not a troublemaker!'

Guideline #3.

Read 1 Corinthians 12:31 and all of Chapter 13.

What are these passages saying is the best gift to share with others?

_____

_____

    'Think about this—
    Charity means "love."
    Sharing God's love with others is greater than faith and hope!'

The First Order of God's Business is God's LOVE!

For God so loved the world that he gave his only begotten Son, that whosoever believeth on him, should not perish but have everlasting life.
John 3:16

But God commendeth his love toward us, in that, while we were yet sinners, Christ died for us.
Romans 5:8

The Lord hath appeared of old unto me, saying, Yea, I have loved thee with an everlasting love: therefore with lovingkindness have I drawn thee.
Jeremiah 31:3

As many as I [Jesus] love, I [Jesus] rebuke and chasten: be zealous therefore and repent.
Revelation 3:19

Greater love hath no man than this, that a man lay down his life for his friends.
John 15:13

Behold, what manner of love hath the Father bestowed upon us, that we should be called the sons of God
1 John 3:1

What is the First Order of Your Business!

Chapter 6:

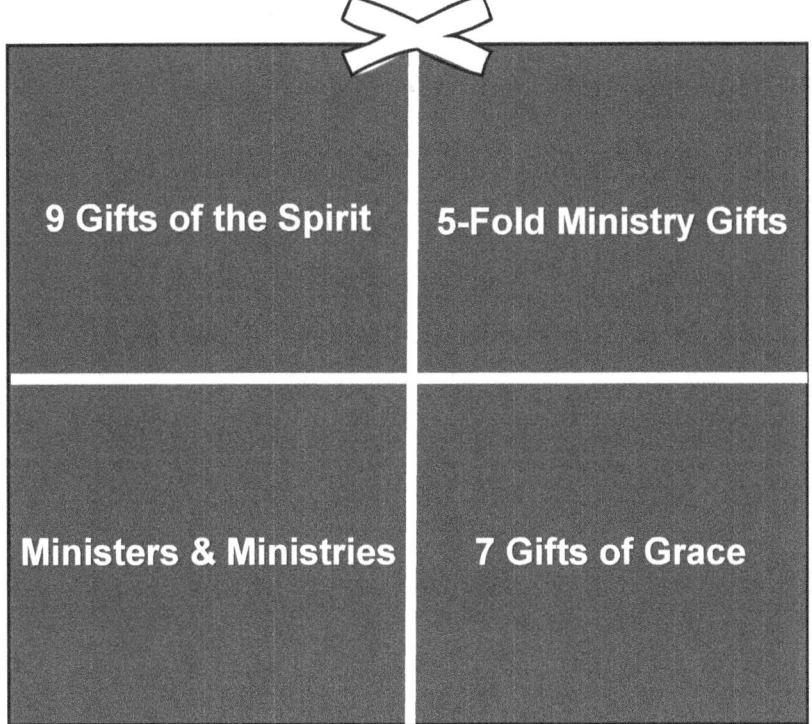

9 Gifts of the Spirit | 5-Fold Ministry Gifts

Ministers & Ministries | 7 Gifts of Grace

Spiritual Gifts

Chapter 6

Detailed Contents

Additional Study
- Chapter 8: Adult Bible Study Handouts
- Appendix C: Youth Lessons 1-28 Study Handouts
- Appendix H: KHS Video Lessons Synopsis

LESSON 23. OPERATIONS, ADMINISTRATIONS AND GIFTS

"Now there are diversities of gifts, but the same Spirit. And there are differences of administrations, but the same Lord. And there are diversities of operations, but it is the same God which worketh all in all." 1 Corinthians 12:4–6

GOD THE FATHER IS OVER ALL THE WORKINGS OR OPERATIONS IN THE CHURCH!
(1 Corinthians 11:3, 12:6)

THE LORD JESUS CHRIST SETS UP ADMINISTRATIONS OR MINISTRIES OR OFFICES IN THE CHURCH TO DO GOD'S WORK. (1 Corinthians 12:5)

THE HOLY SPIRIT GIVES SPIRITUAL GIFTS TO CHURCH WORKERS TO HELP THEM DO GOD'S WORK.
(1 Corinthians 12:7–11)

THE TRIUNE GOD *(God the Father, God the Son-Jesus Christ, and God the Holy Spirit)* **WORKED AND WORK TOGETHER TO ORGANIZE CHURCH OPERATIONS AND ADMINISTRATIONS, GIVING GIFTS TO CHURCH WORKERS TO PERFORM THEM.**

The Church is designed to be an organized group of Christian believers who work together to do God's work in God's way. God the Father is the head of the Lord Jesus Christ (1 Corinthians 11:3). The Lord Jesus Christ is the head of the Church (Ephesians 5:23). The Holy Spirit implements the Father and Son's directions which glorify the Son (John 16:13-15).

God has established the operations or activities that He expects the Church to do. The Lord Jesus Christ heads the Church in doing those activities. Christ sets up ministries or administrations to accomplish God's work. He selects ministers to head up the Church ministries.

The Holy Spirit gives the ministers spiritual gifts.[1] He is the Church's helper, helping Church workers to be successful in following God's instructions. (1 Corinthians 3:9–17)

The Holy Spirit also gives spiritual gifts to all believers. He helps all to be good followers of Christ and Christ's ministers.

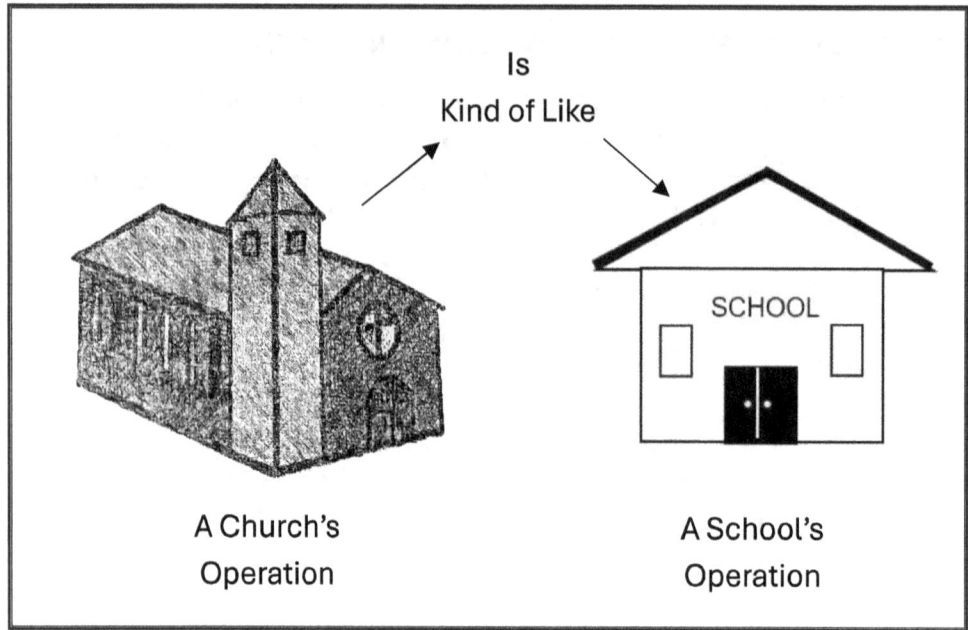

Is
Kind of Like

A Church's
Operation

A School's
Operation

**In a way, you can think of the Church's operation
the same way you think of how a school operates.**

Look at Figure 1 on the next page to review the basic way a school operates, meaning the way the school's organization is set up.

For illustration purposes only, let us make some comparisons between a school's organization and a Church's organization, using the following simple analogies:

Principal has a role like God the Father. Vice-Principal has a role like the Lord Jesus Christ. Teachers have a role like the Holy Spirit. The Student Council is like the Ministries or Offices that the Lord Jesus has set up to help the whole Church do God's work. Other student clubs are like the many different Church ministries. Student Leaders of these clubs are like the leaders of the Church ministries. The rest of the student body are like the rest of the Church members. Members of the church body do God's work by following the instructions of the Lord Jesus Christ, as given them by the Holy Spirit and Church ministry leaders. This is similar to how the student body follows the instructions of the Principal, through following the directions of the Vice-Principal, Teachers and Student Leaders.

Look at Figure 2 for a comparison between the school's organization and the Church's organization using the analogies above.

Figure 1. A School's Organization Basic Set Up

Principal
The head of the school. This position approves of the teaching plans the teachers will use. They also approve of the extra-curricular school activities the student body can have, such as sports, art and music departments.

Vice-Principal
After the Principal approves of the school's activities, the Vice-Principal works with teachers to put together plans and programs that agree with the Principal's instructions.

Teachers
Next, teachers decide how to accomplish the activities. Class teachers develop details on how to instruct their students. Sports coaches organize their teams. Art and music teachers organize their groups.

Student Council
Specially selected students are given the ability to make decisions for all students. For example, the student council may work details for school-wide events, with the help of Teacher Advisors.

Student Clubs
Student clubs are available for students with similar interests or talents, such as the yearbook staff or history club. Each has Student Leaders. Teacher Advisors also help to guide their activities. The Teacher Advisors ensure that the activities align with the Principal's instructions.

Student Body
The rest of the student body participates in school activities as approved by the Principal, as overseen by the Vice Principal, as directed by Teachers and Student Leaders.

Figure 2. A Church's Organization is Kind of Like a School's

The Trinity or Triune God is **ONE GOD** consisting of 3 divine persons

Principal
God the Father
He decides
all the workings
in the Church and
approves or
disapproves of
all activities.

Vice-Principal
God the Son
Jesus Christ
sets up plans
in the Church
to do God's work
and watches over
everything.

Teacher
God the Holy Spirit
The Holy Spirit is
present in all Church
activities. He guides
the members of the
Church body in
doing God's work
God's way, helping
every person and
every activity.

This is like how
Teachers are not
only in the
classroom, but they
are also advisors to
the student leaders.

Student Council
5-Fold Ministry Gifts
Jesus selects special
people from the Church
body who He gives as
Ministry Gifts to the
Church. Through
(1) Apostles,
(2) Prophets,
(3) Evangelists,
(4) Pastors, and
(5) Teachers,
Jesus directs the Church
in doing God's work.

Student Clubs
Ministry of Governments and Ministry of Helps
The Church has many
Ministries such as
Deacons, Administrators,
Choir, Prayer Groups,
Youth Ministry, and Prison
Ministry. Each has Church
leaders, but the Holy Spirit
should lead the leaders
and all group activities.

Student Body
Church Body
The Holy Spirit
has special gifts
for each
member of the
Church body to
help them do
God's work, as
the Lord Jesus
and His Church
leaders direct.

LESSON 24. NINE SPIRITUAL GIFTS

**"Now concerning spiritual gifts, brethren,
I would not have you ignorant."**

1 Corinthians 12:1

The Apostle Paul spoke the above words as he prepared to explain the gifts of the Holy Spirit to the members of the Corinthian Church. Paul also gave instructions on spiritual gifts to churches in Rome and Ephesus.

When we study Paul's life, we can find examples of how he used the gifts of the Spirit.[2] Therefore, Paul was able to teach the churches back then, and teach us today, by his words and his example.

We will use the Apostle Paul as our main human teacher for this introduction on the nine spiritual gifts. Let us first take a moment to get to know Paul, then we will get right into our lesson.

Let's Go!

PART 1.   PAUL, OUR MAIN HUMAN TEACHER

Before becoming a Christian, Paul was known as Saul, one of the greatest enemies of early New Testament Christians. Saul was a very educated man in his time. He was well educated in the Jewish religion, having made it to the office of a Pharisee. He was trained in the Hebrew language, which was the dominant language among the Jews. He was also trained in the Greek and Roman languages, which were the dominant languages spoken among the Gentile people in his part of the world. However, despite his great education, he had a wrong understanding of God. He thought that believing in Christ was against God's will, so he hurt Christians for their belief in Jesus Christ.

Then one day, Jesus appeared to Saul in a vision. Through this experience, Saul accepted Jesus Christ as his Lord and Savior, thereby becoming a Christian. From that time on God used Saul, who became known as Paul, to become the biggest promoter of the Christian faith. For example, Paul is the author of 14 of the 27 books in the New Testament Bible. Also, he did the most to spread the gospel message of Christ to the Gentiles (non-Jewish people) in his day.

Paul suffered a lot for the cause of spreading the gospel. But God gave Paul full use of all the spiritual gifts to do His work. We will use many examples from Paul's life to explain how the gifts of the Spirit work. Also, Paul wrote instructions on the proper use of these gifts, which we will also reference. Other Bible heroes will be used in our discussion, but Paul will be our main human instructor and example.

Paul is a perfect example of how a regular person can walk in the fullness of God, by the power of the Holy Spirit. Especially since Paul, like us, never walked and talked with Jesus when He was on earth as a human being. Paul had to believe and receive Jesus as his Lord and receive the Holy Spirit with all the benefits working in his life, just like you and me – by faith. And, since God is no respecter of persons, we can have confidence that God is willing to work in us just like he worked in Paul, if we dedicate our lives to God the way Paul gave his to God.

See scripture references for Paul's background on the following page.

Exercise:

Take a little time to get to know Paul.

1. **Read Acts 7:57–60, 8:1–3** to see…

   Saul consenting to a disciple being stoned to death for his faith in Christ, throwing male and female Christians in prison, and creating havoc against the church.

2. **Read Acts 9:1–22** to find out…

   Why and how Saul became a Christian.

3. **Read Acts 9:23–31** to see how…

   Saul, who once hunted and hurt Christians, was being hunted after he became a Christian.

4. **Read Acts 13:9** to see…

   Saul's name changed to Paul.

5. **Read Acts 21:37–40, 22:1–21** to learn…

   Paul's personal testimony to the Jewish mob about why and how he became a Christian.

6. **Read Acts 26:1–20** to see…

   Apostle Paul tell the story of his conversion to Christianity to King Agrippa.

7. **Read 2 Corinthians 11:21–12:21** to learn…

   Some of the suffering Paul went through as he worked to spread the gospel to Jews and Gentiles.

8. **Read Galatians 1:13-24** to see…

   Paul's written testimony on how God called him to preach to the heathens, and how he conferred with God on his calling.

PART 2. NINE SPIRITUAL GIFTS DEFINED

"Now concerning spiritual gifts, brethren,

I would not have you ignorant...

Now there are diversities of gifts, but the same Spirit...

But the manifestation of the Spirit is given to
every man to profit withal. For

to one is given by the Spirit the word of wisdom;
to another the word of knowledge by the same Spirit;
to another faith by the same Spirit;
to another the gifts of healing by the same Spirit:
to another the working of miracles;
to another prophecy;
to another discerning of spirits;
to another divers kinds of tongues;
to another the interpretation of tongues;
but all these worketh that selfsame Spirit,

dividing to every man severally as he will."

1 Corinthians 12:1, 4, 7–11

When Christians talk about spiritual gifts or the gifts of the Spirit, many times they are talking about the 9 spiritual gifts presented in 1 Corinthians 12:7-11. Below, these spiritual gifts are classified into three different groups based on their overall purpose. For example, discerning of spirits is included with the gifts of revelation and working of miracles precedes the gifts of healing. Definitions for each gift are provided in Table 6-1. The table includes scriptures with examples of how the gifts were used in the Old Testament, Jesus' life, and Paul's life.

Classification of the 9 Spiritual Gifts[3]

- **Gifts of revelation** – mind gifts (supernatural thoughts from God)
  1) word of wisdom, 2) word of knowledge, 3) discerning of spirits

- **Gifts of power** – working gifts (supernatural power from God)
  4) faith, 5) working of miracles, 6) gifts of healing

- **Gifts of inspiration** – vocal gifts (supernatural speech from God)
  7) prophecy, 8) divers kinds of tongues, 9) interpretation of tongues

Definition: Supernatural – something that occurs outside of natural laws; it cannot be performed by normal human activity

TABLE 6-1. NINE SPIRITUAL GIFTS DEFINED (1 Corinthians 12:7-11)

Gifts Defined[4]	Example from Old Testament[5]	Example from Jesus' earthly life[6]	Example from New Testament, from Paul's life[7]
Gifts of Revelation – mind gifts (one receives supernatural thoughts or insight from God)			
Word of Wisdom: Through this gift, God reveals a "word" or "portion" of His divine mind or plans on an event(s) that will occur in the FUTURE. The revelation comes from God's supernatural wisdom and omniscience. The insight could not be "predicted" by anyone through any natural means of reasoning or deduction. This is NOT the gift of God's wisdom but the gift of a "word" of wisdom from God.	**Genesis 6:12, 13; Genesis 37:5–11** God revealed to Noah the coming of the flood and to Joseph insight on his future. (Genesis 42:1–9, 45:1–9)	**Matthew 24:1–42** Jesus described the earthly events that will take place leading up to the time for His second coming to earth.	**Acts 27:10-25** Apostle Paul foretold of the danger that would greatly damage a ship he was sailing on. He also foretold how all lives would be saved despite the dangerous storm.
Word of Knowledge: Through this gift, God reveals a "word" or "portion" of His divine mind or insight on facts or events that occurred in the PAST or PRESENT, that were previously or presently unknown to the person by any human effort. This is NOT the gift of all God's knowledge. It is NOT the gift of man's knowledge. It IS a "word" from God's omniscience.	**2 Kings 5:15–27** God showed Elisha the sin his servant Gehazi committed, although Elisha was not a witness to the sin.	**John 4:13–18, 28–29** Jesus knew the whole truth of the woman at the well's love life.	**Acts 5:1–5** (Note: This example uses Peter instead of Paul.) The Spirit revealed to Peter the truth about a man and his wife's contribution to the church.
Discerning of Spirits: Through this gift, God reveals the spirit that is motivating a person's actions, whether a godly spirit, an evil spirit, or the nature of their human spirit. God reveals this from His supernatural omniscience on people's hearts and spirits (Acts 1:24, Hebrews 4:13). This has nothing to do with the realm of the human mind; NOT by any metaphysical operation, palm reading, psychoanalysis, extrasensory perception projection, suspicion or discernment of things.	**Exodus 33:20–23** Moses was able to see into the spirit world to view God's likeness. He could not have done this normally on his own. God gave Moses this special ability.	**Luke 10:17–18** Jesus could see into the spirit realm to behold Satan falling from heaven.	**Acts 16:16–18** Although a young girl said some things that were true, Paul discerned that a wrong spirit from the devil was giving her the words to say for the wrong purpose.

TABLE 6-1. NINE SPIRITUAL GIFTS DEFINED (1 Corinthians 12:7-11)

Gifts Defined[8]	Example from Old Testament[9]	Example from Jesus' earthly life[10]	Example from New Testament, from Paul's life[11]
Gifts of Power – working gifts (one receives supernatural actions from God)			
Faith: Through this gift, God's supernatural power is working FOR US, so that we passively RECEIVE a miracle, primarily for divine protection and provision, and sometimes to impart a divine blessing. The miraculous, supernatural exploit cannot be accomplished by any human effort. The gift of faith is NOT the same as saving faith (Acts 16:30, 31; Romans 10:17) or the measure of faith available to everyone (Romans 12:3). The gift of faith demonstrates God's omnipotent power.	**Daniel 3:16–18; Daniel 6:10–23** Special faith caused the Hebrew boys to not be afraid to be thrown in the fiery furnace and Daniel not to be afraid to be thrown in the lion's den.	**Mark 4:35–38** Jesus' special faith was the reason he could sleep during the storm when the disciples were afraid that they would die in that storm.	**Acts 28:3–5** Paul's special faith caused him to shake off a deadly poisonous snake from his arm after it bit him. Paul was not harmed after the bite.
Working of Miracles: Through this gift, God's supernatural power is working THROUGH US to actively PERFORM a miracle that altars natural laws of what a person, place, or thing can do. The Spirit enables a person to perform actions that are impossible by natural earthly laws. Based on 1 Cor. 12:28, this gift is listed ahead of the gifts of healing.	**Exodus Chps. 7–14** Through this gift Moses and Aaron performed miracles to gain freedom for the Hebrew children.	**John 6:5–14** Through this gift Jesus fed over 5000 people with five loaves of bread and two fish.	**Acts 20:9–12** Through this gift Paul caused a man to be raised from the dead who had fallen asleep and died after he fell from a high loft.
Gifts of Healing: Through this gift, God's supernatural power is working THROUGH US to actively PERFORM a miracle of healing of a person with a sickness, disease or infirmity. Note: The word "GIFTS" of Healing means the Spirit can allow a person to heal a select category(ies) of sickness. No one person will heal all types of sickness like Jesus.	**2 Kings 5:1–14** This gift was at work when Naaman followed the Word of God spoken to him by the prophet Elisha.	**Matthew 15:30–31** Through this gift, Jesus was able to heal every type of sickness & disease of people who believed in Him.	**Acts 14:8–10** Because of this gift, Paul was able to tell a man to walk who had never walked before. The man immediately jumped up and walked.

TABLE 6-1. NINE SPIRITUAL GIFTS DEFINED (1 Corinthians 12:7-11)

Gifts Defined[12]	Example from Old Testament[13]	Example from Jesus' earthly life[14]	Example from New Testament, from Paul's life[15]
Gifts of Inspiration – vocal gifts (one receives supernatural speech from God)			
Prophecy: A supernatural message from God that comes in the form of the speaker and hearer's (hearers') understandable language. Prophecy from God will edify (build up), exhort (encourage), and comfort (console) the hearers. Prophecy profitably inspires like 2 Tim. 3:16; not condemn-Rom. 8:1	**Psalm 23** Wonderful words of comfort come from the Lord through David.	**Matthew 5:1–12** Jesus comforted the people who were poor and sad with special words from God.	**1 Corinthians 14:3–4** Paul explains that prophecy helps to lift the whole church congregation.
Divers Kinds of Tongues: A supernatural message from God that comes in the form of foreign language(s) to the speaker. The speaker does not understand any part of the message from natural effort or training. Through this gift, God's omnipresence is demonstrated as the Spirit can cause a person to speak a language from anywhere on earth or the angelic language.	**Isaiah 28:11** Isaiah foretold that God would speak to people in "stammering lips" and "another tongue" in the future.	**Mark 16:17** Jesus said that those who believe in Him would be able to speak in "new tongues" as a sign of their belief.	**1 Corinthians 14:18–19** Paul spoke in other tongues (languages) often in his private prayer time. **1 Corinthians 13:1** Different languages exist for humans and angels.
Interpretation of tongues: A supernatural interpretation of the message spoken in foreign languages by a person who spoke by the spiritual gift of divers kinds of tongues. The person speaking the interpretation does not use any natural means or training to interpret the message. The interpreted message is Prophecy that edifies, exhorts, and comforts the hearers. Prophesy should not be despised (1 Thessalonians 5:20-21). Prophecy should be judged. (I Cor. 14:26-32)	**Not Applicable** This gift was not needed in the Old Testament because the gift of "divers kinds of tongues" was not given in the Old Testament.	**Matthew 15:24** Jesus did not need this gift since His primary mission on earth during His first coming was to minister to the Jewish nation.	**1 Corinthians 14:5, 13–15, 26–32** Paul explains the message God sends, as an interpretation of tongues, is a word of prophecy which will edify, exhort, and/or comfort the hearer, and provides instruction.

Every Good and Perfect Gift

comes from the Lord

for our Blessing,

**Every good gift and every perfect gift
IS from above,
and cometh down from the Father of lights,
with whom is no variableness,
neither shadow of turning.**
James 1:17

But every package

from the Devil

is always meant to destroy us.

**The thief cometh not,
but for to steal,
and to kill,
and to destroy**
John 10:10a

LESSON 25.   PHONY SPIRIT EXPERIENCES

The nine gifts of the Spirit are good and perfect gifts from God the
Father and God the Son, Jesus Christ, as assigned to us by God the
Holy Spirit. But the devil offers a counterfeit (meaning a phony and
destructive experience) for every real experience from God that is
intended for our benefit. Review **Table 6-2 God's Perfect Spiritual Gift
compared to the Devil's Phony Spirit Experience**.

Table 6-2.
God's Perfect Spiritual Gift Compared to
the Devil's Phony Spirit Experience[16]

God's Perfect Spiritual Gift
The Word of Wisdom
God reveals to a person an event that will occur in the future.

Devil's Phony spirit experience
Witches, soothsayers, sorcerers, astrologers and psychics seek to know the future and the unknown by supernatural sources other than from God. Their supernatural source is the devil. Through the devil's evil powers, they think they can know the truth about things that will happen in the future.
The truth is that the devil can not tell the truth about anything (John 8:44). He can use portions of truth to deceive people into believing that he has the power to know the whole truth. (Notice his partial knowledge in Matthew 4:5–7) All of Satan's powers are meant to bring about a person's destruction.
The Bible also talks about false prophets and false apostles (1 John 4:1, 2 Corinthians 11:13–15). The devil will use such persons to tell people wrong information about future events.
The Bible explains that we can recognize phony preachers by the type of lives they live (Matthew 12:33). Also, we can tell if someone is a true prophet of God, if the thing they say will occur in the future really comes to pass without human intervention to make it happen. (Deuteronomy 18:20–22)
Most importantly you need to judge your Christian experiences by the Word of God. The true and living God will never do anything, using supernatural powers, that is not based on His written Word.

TABLE 6-2. GOD'S PERFECT SPIRITUAL GIFT COMPARED TO THE DEVIL'S PHONY SPIRIT EXPERIENCE[16]

God's Perfect Spiritual Gift	Devil's Phony spirit experience
The Word of Knowledge God reveals to a person something that happened in current times or in the past that the individual did not know or find out through natural means.	Palm readers, fortune-tellers, Ouija boards, seances, and all manner of occult groups use demonic powers to try and find out what is happening now or in the past, without using natural senses. The devil has some limited knowledge which he uses to try and trick people into destroying their lives and the lives of others, through these ungodly activities. God hates these practices and tells us to avoid them. The Bible's instructions are clear on telling us to stay away from seeking answers through the devil's resources: **"There shall not be found among you any one that maketh his son or his daughter to pass through the fire, or that useth divination, or an observer of times, or an enchanter, or a witch, or a charmer, or a consulter with familiar spirits, or a wizard, or a necromancer. For all that do these things are an abomination unto the Lord; and because of these abominations the Lord thy God doth drive them out..."** Deuteronomy 18:10–12 **"Ye shall not eat any thing with the blood: neither shall ye use enchantment, nor observe times. Ye shall not round the corners of your heads, neither shalt thou mar the corners of thy beard. Ye shall not make any cuttings in your flesh for the dead, nor print any marks upon you: I am the Lord... Regard not them that have familiar spirits, neither seek after wizards, to be defiled by them: I am the Lord your God."** Leviticus 19:26–28, 31

TABLE 6-2. GOD'S PERFECT SPIRITUAL GIFT COMPARED TO THE DEVIL'S PHONY SPIRIT EXPERIENCE[16]

God's Perfect Spiritual Gift

Discerning of Spirits

God reveals to a person the presence and activity of the spirit that influences a person's actions, whether that spirit is good or evil.

Devil's Phony spirit experience

Any human attempt to know what another person's thoughts are, such as through using extra-sensory perception (ESP) or hypnosis or phony spirit experiences. Also, human efforts at trying to make your spirit go outside of yourself so you can be one with nature or find deeper knowledge through meditation programs, mind readers, gurus, metaphysical groups, and any similar groups are phony spirit experiences.

The Bible instructs us: **"Beware lest any man spoil you through philosophy and vain deceit, after the tradition of men, after the rudiments of the world, and not after Christ."** Colossians 2:8

God's Perfect Spiritual Gift

Gift of Faith

There are many kinds of faith, and every person has some faith. There is no human energy or effort involved in the operation of this Spiritual Gift of Faith. Through this gift, God gives a person the supernatural ability to believe Him for something supernatural to happen.

Devil's Phony spirit experience

Witchcraft uses things like magic spells, curses, and incantations, which a person is supposed to believe in to bring something they want to come to pass. However, these actions attempt to use the devil's power or human power to make "wishes" come true. This is not from God. (Acts 8:9–11)

Sidenote: God wants us to seek Him for His will for our lives. He will reveal His will to us through His written Word. Then, we use simple faith that everyone has a little of, not "wishes," to enable God's will to happen. All faith from God works in agreement with God's written Word. God will never lead us to believe for anything that is not based on His Word. Also of note, God will confirm any special word that He has spoken to you through two or three other witnesses. (2 Corinthians 13:1)

TABLE 6-2. GOD'S PERFECT SPIRITUAL GIFT COMPARED TO THE DEVIL'S PHONY SPIRIT EXPERIENCE[16]

God's Perfect Spiritual Gift

The Working of Miracles

God gives a person the ability to cause a supernatural change in the normal flow of natural events, causing something to happen that is not possible in the natural sense. This person is only able to do this by the power of the Holy Spirit working through them.

Devil's Phony spirit experience

The Bible contains stories of people who possessed some demonic power to cause supernatural type events to occur. For example, in Moses' day, Pharaoh's evil wise men, sorcerers and magicians could turn their sticks into snakes. They could turn water into blood and cause frogs to come on the dry land at their command. But when Moses, by the power of God, caused lice to come on the Egyptian people and animals, the magicians could not copy that miracle (Exodus 8:1–19).

The devil has limited powers, which he wants to use to trick people into following him, because they believe he is so powerful. However, the devil is not as powerful as God. And the devil's purpose is to destroy your life and your soul.

The instructions of the Lord are clear concerning following His Holy Spirit alone:

"Beloved, believe not every spirit, but try the spirits whether they are of God: because many false prophets are gone out into the world. Hereby know ye the Spirit of God: Every spirit that confesseth that Jesus Christ is come in the flesh is of God: and every spirit that confesseth not that Jesus Christ is come in the flesh is not of God: and this is that spirit of antichrist, whereof ye have heard that it should come; and even now already is it in the world. Ye are of God, little children, and have overcome them: because greater is he that is in you, than he that is in the world."
1 John 4:1–4

TABLE 6-2. GOD'S PERFECT SPIRITUAL GIFT COMPARED TO THE DEVIL'S PHONY SPIRIT EXPERIENCE[16]

God's Perfect Spiritual Gift
Gifts of Healing

A person is used by God to supernaturally cause the healing of sickness and disease without any natural source or ability. When healing is brought about by this gift, it is perfect and can be verified. Medical science and medical records will confirm that a healing miracle has taken place.

Devil's Phony spirit experience

False healers that present themselves in the church world and in the cult world hope to fool people into believing they have been healed when they are not. Most of these people want to make money from those who are sick and vulnerable for their own personal gain. They do not intend to help the Kingdom of God at all. There are people selling cloths and handkerchiefs that are supposed to bring about healing. There are people selling holy water and other gimmicks that are supposed to heal. But God's gifts are free money-wise. If you give your monies to the work of God in gratitude for what He has done for you, this should be your own free will offering. Also, witchcraft and mystical healings are not from God. (Acts 19:11–20)

God's Perfect Spiritual Gift
Prophecy

A person, through this gift, builds up the spirit of others through sharing encouraging, comforting, and uplifting words that come directly from God.

Devil's Phony spirit experience

An example of the wrong spirit delivering a phony message of "prophecy" can be found in Acts 16:16–19. A young girl had a demonic spirit of divination controlling her actions. Through this evil spirit, she knew partial truths that other people did not know. Her wicked bosses used her to make money from people who preferred to seek getting answers for their problems from her, rather than seeking God. When Paul came to town, she correctly told everyone that Paul and his companions were **"the servants of the most high God, which shew unto us the way of salvation."** While those specific words from the girl were true, they grieved Paul. Eventually Paul commanded the demonic spirit come out of the girl in Jesus Name, which it did within the hour.

TABLE 6-2. GOD'S PERFECT SPIRITUAL GIFT COMPARED TO THE DEVIL'S PHONY SPIRIT EXPERIENCE[16]

God's Perfect Spiritual Gift

Divers Kinds of Tongues

The ability given to a person to speak in different languages without have learned the languages. This ability is given by the Holy Spirit. The speaker does not know what they are saying in these languages unless the Holy Spirit gives the interpretation.

Devil's Phony spirit experience

Incantations or non-understandable phrases that witches, or sorcerers speak in magic spells are one type of counterfeit tongues. Or the devil may use someone to make nonsensical utterances in Church to make people believe they are speaking in tongues. If someone's utterances make you feel uncomfortable in your spirit, then pray and ask God why you feel uncomfortable. It may be that God will reveal to you that the person is not speaking by the Holy Spirit but instead a demonic spirit is influencing that person's behavior. Be led by the Spirit of God who will reveal whether another's action is of God or not. If needed, you should consult with the Pastor, or a Pastor-approved mature Believer in Christ.

God's Perfect Spiritual Gift

Interpretation of Tongues

The ability given to a person to "interpret" – not translate – the message given through a person speaking in the foreign language(s) that are also given by God. Neither the speaker nor interpreter know the foreign language(s) but all messages come by inspiration of the Holy Spirit. The interpreted message is also a word of prophecy that edifies, exhorts, and comforts the hearers.

Devil's Phony spirit experience

Some persons who have been deceived or confused by the devil will tell people things that they say is a word of prophecy from the Lord, but instead the words they speak are made up from their own mind or influenced by demonic motives.

1 Corinthians 14:5 explains that when tongues are interpreted the message that comes forth serves to edify the church. Prophetic messages should build up, comfort and uplift a Christian. Phony messages will do just the opposite. One of the best protections against believing false prophecies is to know God's Word. This is because God will only send words of prophecy that are based on the foundation of His written Word. Finally, a true Word from the God is established by 2 or 3 witnesses. (2 Corinthians 13:1)

LESSON 26.   SEVEN GIFTS OF GRACE

"For I say through the grace given unto me, to every man that is among you, not to think of himself more highly than he ought to think; but to think soberly, according as God hath dealt to every man the measure of faith. For as we have many members in one body, and all members have not the same office: so we, being many, are one body in Christ, and every one members one of another. Having then gifts differing according to the grace that is given to us,..." (Romans 12:3–6a)

The Apostle Paul gave the above instructions to the Christians in the Roman Church, which also apply to Christians today. All of Romans Chapter 12 gives simple but practical rules for daily Christian living:

- Verses 1–2 explain how Christians should serve God.
- Verses 3–8 describe what types of gifts of grace God has given to believers and the right attitude Christians should have about possessing those gifts.
- Verses 9–16 tell Christians how they should treat each other.
- Verses 17–21 describe how Christians should treat non-Christians.

Before listing the "gifts of grace," Paul wrote the words in verses 3–6a shown above. Paul warned everyone to watch how they think of a person who has these gifts. The Holy Spirit gives every believer gifts (1 Corinthians 12:7). Because He does not give all the same gift or gifts, it is easy for people to think that another person's gift(s) is better than theirs. Paul explains that everyone's gift(s) is given because of God's grace, for the purpose of helping others. God's grace can be defined as His "unmerited favor." This means there is no work a Christian can do to deserve God's gift. No gift has been given to a person because they are better than anyone else. God wants each person to see themselves as an important member of Christ's body (meaning the Church).

Exercise:

List the seven (7) "gifts differing according to the grace that is given to us" from Romans 12:6–8. Then study details on each gift in Table 6-3.

1) _____, 2) _____, 3) _____, 4) _____

5) _____, 6) _____, 7) _____

TABLE 6-3. SEVEN GIFTS OF GRACE

Gifts Defined	Example	Special Instructions v. 6-8	Comments
1. Prophecy/Prophesy A person with this gift speaks to people special messages from God regarding their personal life or their circumstances. The messages edify the people (meaning strengthens them spiritually), exhorts them (meaning encourages them in their Christian walk), and comforts them (meaning to soothe their hearts concerning experiences they are having). The message could also provide insight on God's guidance.	<u>Acts 21:8–9</u> The four daughters of Philip the evangelist had a continuous flow of the gift of prophecy working in their lives.	***"prophesy according to the proportion of faith"*** These instructions let us know that the words a person speaks in the name of the Lord are based on his or her faith that God is giving them the words. You will need to be careful not to say words that come into your own mind and thoughts. It may take time and experience for someone with this gift to learn whether what they desire to say is from God, from their own mind, or from the devil. The more you meditate on the Word of God, the better you will be able to tell if what you think you should say is from God. God will only give words to people to say that are based on the godly counsel found in God's Word in the Bible.	In the Old Testament book of Joel, it explains that in the last days God would pour out His Spirit upon all flesh and that sons and daughters would prophesy. See Joel 2:28. This passage lets us know that even children could have this gift operating in their lives while they are still under the care of their parents.

TABLE 6-3. SEVEN GIFTS OF GRACE

Gifts Defined	Example	Special Instructions v. 6-8	Comments
2. Ministering This person delivers the Bible message effectively, by precept and example. A person with this gift serves believers through good works as well as with words. The works of service help to demonstrate the ministry in word and deeds. For example, this person might use their ministry platform to provide resources for food, clothing, and shelter to widows, orphans, the poor, or to meet the special needs of the sick, seniors, or those in prison. This person may have many of the gifts of the Spirit working in their life to help them in performing their ministerial works. Acts 6:1–8	**Matthew 20:25–28** Jesus **1 Timothy 3:8–13 and Acts 6:1–6** Deacons **Romans 15:25–28** Paul	**"wait on ministering"** There is a certain time in a minister's life when their ministry work is ready for full public service. When one is first called to be a minister, they need to be trained before working alone in this calling. The person needs to learn who to serve and the proper way to serve. They also need to be trained on how to properly deliver God's message. If you believe God has given you this gift, then you should pray and ask God to give you someone to learn from. Then, let God lead you as to the proper time for you to take on a leadership position in performing this gift.	At the age of 12, Jesus knew that He was to minister to the whole world. He also knew that it was not the right time in His life then, to fully operate as a minister. The Bible says that Jesus stayed at home with His parents and followed their instructions. He used that time to learn more about God's Word and will for His life, how to work with people, and to just grow up. Luke 2:42–52 Jesus did not begin His public ministry work until He became 30 years old. Luke 3:21–23, Luke 4:1–2, 14 Just like Jesus, as a child or new Christian you may know that you are to be a minister. But first you must learn all you can, obey your parents and spiritual leaders, and let God show you the right time to begin your ministry work.

TABLE 6-3. SEVEN GIFTS OF GRACE

Gifts Defined	Example	Special Instructions v. 6-8	Comments
3. Teaching A person with this gift can help others understand Bible scriptures. God uses gifted teachers to explain the word of God to people, so they can know how to live for God daily. Jeremiah 3:15, Acts 18:9–11 True teachers of God teach by their own example as well as with their words. They live what they teach about. This benefits their students who learn by hearing their words and by watching how they apply the teaching to their lives.	**John 3:2, Matthew 4:23** Jesus **Acts 13:1** Barnabas and Paul (Saul) and others	**"wait on teaching"** A person should not want to teach the wrong thing to others who are looking to them to explain God's Word. Therefore, a person who believes they are called to teach needs to study God's Word diligently. (2 Timothy 2:15) God can use teachers at different levels of understanding. Teachers can begin by instructing children with the basic truths from God's Word, even if they do not feel they know a lot. Then, as they learn more, they will be able to teach older students if that is God's calling. Overall, a teacher must wait on God's direction before beginning to instruct others in the ways of God.	The Holy Spirit can help you understand the Word of God with or without a human teacher, when you keep praying and seeking God for answers (John 14:26, 1 John 2:27, 1 Corinthians 2:9–13). The Holy Spirit will use people with the gift of teaching to provide you some answers. Teachers have been given to the Church to help us understand God's Word. (Matthew 28:19–20) Teachers in Sunday School, Children's Church, Bible Study, Bible Colleges, and Pastors with the teaching gift, have been gifted to help Christians grow up in Christ through understanding the truth in God's Word. Then it is every believer's responsibility to live out the lessons they learn.

TABLE 6-3. SEVEN GIFTS OF GRACE

Gifts Defined	Example	Special Instructions v. 6-8	Comments
4. Exhortation A person with this gift is an "encourager." This person knows how to say and do things to lift the spirits, hopes and dreams of another. They perform encouraging acts through saying kind words and by doing kind deeds. This person sees the good in people that others may not be able to see. The encourager sees the potential of what another person can become, more than they see what that person is right now. This helps them not focus on a person's current faults or past experiences in life. Instead, they focus on helping others become the people they are meant to be.	**Acts 4:36–37** Barnabas is considered a person who gives consolation by the disciples. **Acts 9:26–28** Through the gift of exhortation, Barnabas could see in Paul what others could not see at first. The disciples did not believe that Paul (Saul) had really become a Christian until Barnabas defended him. Because of Barnabas, Paul became accepted. **Acts 15:35–39** **2 Timothy 4:11** Through this gift, Barnabas could see what Apostle Paul could not see in John Mark. Through the good that Barnabas saw, eventually Paul learned to see the good in John Mark also.	**"wait on exhortation"** From the examples discussed with Barnabas, Paul, and John Mark, we can see that the Spirit used Barnabas to encourage certain people at different times. It is as if Barnabas was called to focus his encouragement on one person or one ministry for a period. The people, ministry and timing are all determined by God. The instructions to "wait on exhortation" could mean that the person with the gift will be given a dedicated assignment for a designated time. The exhorter should be led by the Holy Spirit on who, what or when they should minister.	One of the names of the Holy Spirit is "Comforter." Even if no one is around to say uplifting words to you when you need them, the Holy Spirit can speak comforting words. You hear Him in your inner spirit, or you hear Him as you read the Bible. God knows how much we as human beings desire to receive consolation or comfort from another person. Providing this comfort could be done by a person sharing a hug, or saying kind words, or other kind deeds. This is why the Holy Spirit will anoint people with this gift of exhortation.

TABLE 6-3. SEVEN GIFTS OF GRACE

Gifts Defined	Example	Special Instructions v. 6-8	Comments
5. Giving A person, group, or Church with this gift is inspired by the Holy Spirit to give their money or things to meet the needs of others. It may look to others like the giver needs the money or things as much as the people they want to help. But this gift is not just assigned to those with an abundance. Even if you have needs, this gift makes you feel compassion for the needs of others. This gift does not replace the giver's responsibility to pay tithes and offerings to their Church or slack in taking care of their families. But because this giving is done with a right spirit, God will meet the needs of all.	2 Corinthians 8:1–5 Several Churches in the Macedonia area had this gift of grace at a time when they were experiencing a great trial of affliction (meaning problems). The passage lets us know that they gave monies joyfully to help other saints (meaning Christians) who were in need. They felt the needs of their fellow Christians in another town were greater than their own. 2 Corinthians 8:9 Jesus gave up His rich place in heaven, as Creator of the universe, to become a poor man on earth. He knew that giving up His life, to pay for our sins, was the only way to meet our need for salvation. John 3:16. Thank you Jesus for your excellent gift!	"give with simplicity" What this gift is NOT The person with this gift of grace does not decide to give their money to God's work by using "human wisdom" or "logic" to determine the best amount and the best time to give. Also, a person with this gift does not give because a speaker makes them feel guilty into giving to help others or for a cause. What this gift IS This "giving according to grace" is a simple act of following the leading of the Holy Spirit in your heart. This giver does so cheerfully and willingly because they know God will bless both the "gift" and the "giver." 2 Corinthians 9:7–11	People who do not believe they have this "gift of giving" should have a desire to be good givers to the work of God. God requires that every Christian pay their tithes and offerings to their home Church. God also encourages all Christians to be good givers to meet the needs of others. This giving is done in addition to contributing to their home Church. Read the scriptures below to get an idea of the rewards of being a "giver." **2 Corinthians 9:6** **Luke 6:38** **Proverbs 28:27** **Proverbs 11:24** **Ecclesiastes 11:1–6**

TABLE 6-3. SEVEN GIFTS OF GRACE

Gifts Defined	Example	Special Instructions v. 6-8	Comments
6. Ruling The Holy Spirit gives a person great wisdom on how to conduct the business of the Church. This person knows how to handle the people and plans of God in a smart business way. This leadership gift is not just for Pastors and Bishops, but to any member within the congregation as gifted by the Holy Spirit. Often these people become the ones assigned to work in leadership roles within the Church.	**Matthew 17:24–27,** **Mark 6:34–46** Jesus with His disciples was a leader of people and business. He divided up responsibilities to His disciples. For example, He used Peter to pay taxes and the disciples to pass out food to the multitudes. By dividing up the ministry responsibilities, Jesus could use His time to teach, preach, and pray for everyone. This also gave Him time to rest. **John 16:12, Luke 22:31–32** Trainer of Ministers—Jesus had a lot to tell His disciples. He exercised wisdom to know how much they could learn at their different levels of growth. So, He taught them in stages. He also prayed for their different needs. **Acts 6:1–6** Business Elders or Deacons	**"rule with diligence"** Definition: Diligence means "constant and earnest effort to accomplish what is undertaken." This definition lets us know that the person with this "ruling" gift needs to constantly pray and listen to the Holy Spirit's instructions on how to lead others. God can give a person the wisdom to do something, but they must still act on that wisdom. The high priest Eli is an example of a person who knew how to rule well, but he chose not to do so. He let his sons work in the temple although they were very sinful. Read about this bad example in 1 Samuel 2:22–36. When God gives this ruling knowledge, He expects the person to use it diligently in all His work.	Everyone who is in a leadership position in the Church may or may not have this gift. Here are some examples: 1) A Pastor may not be a good businessman. God can send him someone who is good in dealing with business matters to be his helper in this area. 2) God may not have chosen some of the people who are in positions of leadership in the Church. Unfortunately, these people can turn out to be bad leaders. 3) Good leaders can become bad leaders when they are not diligent in acting upon God's instructions. God has given us one way to judge whether a person will be a good Bishop, Elder or Deacon in the Church. Read 1 Timothy 3:1–12 and Titus 1:5–9. Note how they are all expected to rule well.

TABLE 6-3. SEVEN GIFTS OF GRACE

Gifts Defined	Example	Special Instructions v. 6-8	Comments
7. Mercy The person with this gift has a great desire to meet the differing needs of those who are unable to help themselves. This includes providing such things as clothes, shelter, food, educational and medical supplies without expecting any payment from the people they give the provisions to. Their gift is given freely and cheerfully with the purpose of helping others to improve their life situations.	**Acts 9:36–41** Dorcas (also known as Tabitha) gave her own time and ability to sew and give away clothes to those who needed them. The reference passage of scripture says she did many good works. When "alms deeds" are mentioned, this means Dorcas likely helped by giving away food, clothing, financial assistance and other such donations to those in need. Dorcas spent her life doing kind acts and works of charity. She was full of the love of God and full of God's love for people, which caused her to do many good works.	**"show mercy with cheerfulness"** A person with the true gift of mercy will exercise this gift sincerely with a heart of love and generosity. Their joy comes from seeing the people they help receive the benefits. Even more so, their joy comes from knowing they are doing the will of God when helping others. Anyone who gives to others for the purpose of having people brag about their charitable contributions, or for monetary gain, does not truly have this gift. Jesus explains the right way to help others in Matthew 6:1 –4.	Some well-known organizations were formed to serve the poor hurting, lost and those with broken spirits. The people that started these organizations had great hearts of mercy for those who were in need. These people went beyond feeling sorry for others to do something specific to help. Below is a list of some of these service organizations and the people that started them. You may want to do research to find others. 1. William Booth started the Salvation Army. 2. Clara Barton started the American Red Cross. 3. President J.F. Kennedy started the Peace Corps.

LESSON 27.   FIVE-FOLD MINISTRY GIFTS

PART 1.   INTRODUCING THE FIVE-FOLD MINISTRY GIFTS

PART 2.   EACH FIVE-FOLD MINISTRY GIFT DEFINED

PART 3.   FALSE MINISTRIES

PART 4.   MINISTERS AND MINISTRIES

The Five-Fold Ministry Gifts are Special People Chosen by the Lord Jesus Christ to be His Gifts to the Church!

[8]Wherefore he saith, **When he ascended up on high,
he** led captivity captive, and **gave gifts unto men.**

[9](Now that he ascended, what is it but that he also descended first into
the lower parts of the earth?

[10]He that descended is the same also that ascended up far above all
heavens, that he might fill all things.)

[11]**And he gave some, apostles; and some, prophets; and
some, evangelists; and some, pastors and teachers;**

[12]**For the perfecting of the saints**, for the work of the ministry,
for the edifying of the body of Christ:

[13]Till we all come in the unity of the faith,
and of the knowledge of the Son of God, unto a perfect man,
unto the measure of the stature of the fulness of Christ:

[14]**That we henceforth be no more children, tossed to and fro,**
and carried about with every wind of doctrine, by the sleight of men,
and cunning craftiness, whereby they lie in wait to deceive;

[15]**But speaking the truth in love, may grow up into him in all things,
which is the head, even Christ:**

[16]From whom the whole body fitly joined together
and compacted by that which every joint supplieth,
according to the effectual working in the measure of every part,
maketh increase of the body unto the edifying of itself in love.

Ephesians 4:8–16

**Wherefore he saith, When he ascended up on high,
he led captivity captive, and gave gifts unto men…
And he gave some, apostles; and some, prophets;
and some, evangelists; and some, pastors and teachers**
Ephesians 4:8, 11

Jesus physically ascended (meaning rose up) from the earth and went back to heaven. His disciples watched Him lift off the ground and ride up on a cloud high into the sky. He kept rising until they could no longer see Him with their eyes. (Luke 24:50–51, Acts 1:9–11)

However,

Jesus continues to help us while He is in heaven in the following ways:

1) He stays at the right hand of God praying for us all the time and,

2) He represents us before God when we make mistakes, just like a lawyer represents defendants in a courtroom, if we repent of our sins. (Romans 8:34, Hebrews 7:25, 1 John 2:1–2, 1 John 1:8–9)

And,

Jesus also gives us Himself on earth in different ways. Two of the ways are mentioned below:

1) After we accept Jesus Christ as our Lord and Savior, then Jesus and God the Father come to live inside of us by the power of the Holy Spirit. This is a result of us being born of the Spirit. (Romans 10:9 and John 14:23)

2) When we are filled with the Holy Spirit, we have the same power that Jesus was filled with to help Him do God's work when He was on earth. The Holy Spirit then enables us to hear from Christ more clearly so we can know what Christ wants us to do. He also helps us do God's work effectively. (Acts 10:38, Acts 1:8, John 14:26)

And also,

Jesus understands our human need to touch and talk to other human beings that can lead us in doing God's work. Jesus gave us special people who are His special gifts to us. Some Bible Teachers refer to these special people as the Five-fold Ministry Gifts.[17]

Exercise:

Re-read Ephesians 4:8, 11.

Write the 5 special groups of people that Christ has gifted to the Church.

1) _____, **2)** _____, **3)** _____

4) _____, **5)** _____

Read Ephesians 4:12. What three purposes does this verse say these special group of people have?

6) _____

7) _____

8) _____

Read Ephesians 4:13. Write down four additional purposes for these special people that is described in this verse.

9) _____

10) _____

11) _____

12) _____

Read Ephesians 4:14. In this verse we are told what will no longer happen to Christians when the special group of people are successful in helping Christians as described in verses 11, 12 and 13. Use verse 14 to help you fill in the blanks below:

> We, as Christians, will no more be **13)** _____ in our understanding of things, nor tossed **14)** _____ and **15)** _____ and carried about with **16)** _____ by the **17)** _____ and **18)** _____, whereby these crafty men lie in wait to **19)** _____ Christians.

Read Ephesians 4:15. Finally, in this verse we find what Christians will be able to do after the Holy Spirit and the special group of people have taught them. Fill in the blanks below with the two things this verse says the Christian can do:

> Christians will be able to speak **20)** _____ and grow **21)** _____

A. Apostles

The highest ministry position in the earthly Church is an Apostle. The Apostles in the New Testament were fully empowered by the Holy Spirit to carry out Christ's plan in building up the Kingdom of God on earth through setting up Churches. They set up Church governments, programs and ministers to Pastor over Churches.

New Testament Apostles also suffered for the sake of spreading the gospel. God gave them His special grace to endure their suffering. Multiple gifts of the Spirit worked through the Apostles to perform signs, wonders and mighty deeds for the sake of spreading the gospel.

Once a Church was established, God used the Apostles as His special messengers to keep the Church on the right path in performing God's kingdom work. Apostles also helped settle disputes over Church issues as they arose. Reference: 2 Corinthians 1:1, 12:12, 8:23, 11:23–28.

Exercise:

22) List the 24 Apostles that are named in the scriptures below.

Find 12 of them in Matthew 10:2–4.

_____, _____, _____, _____

_____, _____, _____, _____

_____, _____, _____, _____

Find #13 in Acts 1:26 _____

Find #14 and #15 in Acts 14:14 _____ , _____

Find #16 and #17 in Romans 16:7 _____, _____

Find #18 in 1 Corinthians 4:6–9 _____

Find #19 in Galatians 1:19 _____

Find #20 and #21 in 1 Thessalonians 1:1, 2:6 _____, _____

Find #22 in 2 Corinthians 8:23 _____
    (Hint: The word "messengers" in this verse means apostle)

Find #23 in Philippians 2:25 _____ (Hint: same hint as for #22)

Find #24 in Hebrews 3:1 _____

B. Prophets

Prophet is the second highest ministry position in the earthly Church.

In the Old Testament, the purpose of the prophet was to be a divine guide for the people of God. In Old Testament times, God's written Word was not available for all to read because it was in the process of being written. God used the Prophets as His primary way of delivering His messages to people. Through visions and special messages, God revealed to the prophet or prophetess specific insight on current and future events. Then they would tell the people exactly what God wanted them to know and do. Some examples of Old Testament Prophets are Moses, Elijah and Isaiah. Some examples of Old Testament Prophetesses are Isaiah's wife and the Judge Deborah.

In the New Testament, the role of the Prophet changed after Jesus' ministry on earth. Jesus was God on earth fulfilling the role of God's Prophet for all people. (Hebrews 1:1–2, John 6:14, John 7:16) The New Testament Prophet speaks the words of Jesus as revealed to them through the operation of the spiritual gifts. (John 16:8-15, 1 Corinthians 12:7-11).

All prophesies spoken by Believers in Christ must align with information already presented in the written Word of God. (1 Corinthians 14:37-40)

**"Quench not the Spirit. Despise not prophesyings.
Prove all things; hold fast that which is good."**
1 Thessalonians 5:19–21

Exercise:

23) Write the names of New Testament Prophets from the below scriptures:

Acts 3:22-26 with Deuteronomy 18:15-19 _____

Acts 21:10-11 _____

Acts 13:1 _____

24) Write the names of the New Testament Prophetesses:

Luke 2:36–37 _____

Acts 21:8–9 _____

C. Evangelists

The Evangelist is a messenger of the Good News of the Gospel "preaching the things concerning the kingdom of God, and the name of Jesus Christ" (Acts 8:12). Evangelists are empowered by the Holy Spirit to present the story of God's love, forgiveness and plan of salvation through Christ in a compelling manner. The result is that the hearers of their messages are moved to give their lives to Christ.

Exercise:

25) Write the name of the New Testament Evangelists found in the below scriptures:

- Acts 8:5–8, 12-13; Acts 21:8 _____
- 2 Timothy 1:2, 4:5 _____
- Luke 4:14, 18–19 _____

D. Pastors

The Pastor is the caretaker or overseer of the people of God within a Church fellowship. If you think of people as sheep, then the Pastor can be thought of as a Shepherd over God's flock of sheep in a certain place. The Pastor feeds the sheep with spiritual food, meaning the Word of God. He is responsible for the spiritual growth of the members. He demonstrates God's care for his members on a regular basis such as ministering to them when they are sick or grieving.

Overall, the Pastor's primary responsibility is to stay close by his Church and help the members continuously. In addition, the ministry of the local Pastor includes finding and restoring people who have left God to bring them back into the Church family. (Acts 20:28)

Exercise:

Read John 10:7–14. Write the name of this New Testament Pastor.
26) _____ (**Hint:** He is the Good Shepherd.)

Read Acts 14:22–23, Acts 20:17, 25, 28. Write one title that New Testament Pastors or overseers may have been called.
27) _____

Write the Name of the Pastor at your Church. _____

E. Teachers

"And God hath set some in the church,
first apostles,
secondarily prophets,
thirdly teachers…"
1 Corinthians 12:28

In Ephesians 4:11 "Teacher" is the last of the five-fold Ministry gifts listed. In 1 Corinthians 12:28 the position of Teacher is listed as being "thirdly" of the positions God has set in the church as His gifts to help the Church grow. (1 Corinthians 12:28–31) This lets us know that the Teacher is very important in helping Church members become mature Believers.

The Teacher has a special ability to help people understand God's Word. Some have been gifted to make the messages within the Bible so clear, that even a child can understand them.

Exercise:

28) Write the names of the Teachers in the New Testament identified in the below scriptures.

- **Acts 13:1** _____, _____

  _____, _____, _____

- **John 3:2** _____

- **1 Timothy 2:7** _____

  (Hint: See 1 Timothy 1:1 to find out who is speaking.)

Write the names of people in your Church who are Teachers that help you to understand the Word of God.

_____, _____, _____

PART 3.   FALSE MINISTERS

There are some people who say they are Apostles, or Prophets, or Evangelists, or Pastors, or Teachers, but their ministries do not reflect the true work of the Kingdom of God. Instead, their ministries hurt God's work and God's people.

The purpose of this section is to share scriptures and things to consider when assessing if a ministry leader is true or false.

- False leaders have wrong motives and/or unrepentant sin in their lives. Judas Iscariot is an example of an apostle called by Jesus whose wrong motives and unrepentant sin eventually led him to betray Christ. (Matthew 10:1–8, Matthew 26:14–16)

- False leaders want to exercise control over people. They crave the attention and praise of people. Some want to collect people's money to use for selfish purposes. (2 Corinthians 11:20, Luke 20:45–47)

- Novice leaders do not possess the wisdom to lead God's people. They need more training under the guidance of a mature leader in the ministry, and they need more life experiences. With proper training, novices could become God's true leaders. Without it, novices will be "lifted up with pride", "fall into the condemnation of the devil" and "fall into reproach and the snare of the devil." (1 Timothy 3:6–7)

Exercise:

Read the below scriptures to see more of what the Bible says about False Ministries and False Ministers.[18]

- **False Apostles**	**2 Corinthians 11:13 – 15**
- **False Prophets**	**1 John 4:1**
- **False Evangelists** (Ministers)	**2 Corinthians 11:15**
- **False Pastors** (Hirelings)	**Jeremiah 23:1–2, John 10:12–13**
- **False Teachers**	**2 Peter 2:1**

PART 4.   MINISTERS AND MINISTRIES

A. Ministers

The New Testament identifies three types of ministers that work in unity with the Ministry Gifts. They are Bishops, Elders, and Deacons.[19]

Bishops and Elders

The qualifications for selecting a minister for the office of Bishop and Elder are described in 1 Timothy 3:1–7 and Titus 1:5–9.

Bishops and Elders are the overseers for the people and work of God in the churches. They are empowered to preach to; pray for; and care for the needs of Church members. The New Testament Apostles ordained Bishops and Elders in every Church and city, they established during New Testament times.

Reference: Acts 14:21–23, Acts 16:4

Deacons

The qualifications for selecting a person for the office of a Deacon are described in 1 Timothy 3:8–13.

Read the story of the first deacons chosen in the Bible and why they were selected in **Acts 6:1–6**. In general, Deacons help to meet the natural needs of the Church members as compared with ministers meeting the spiritual needs. For example, in the reference passage from the book of Acts, the first Deacons were selected to make sure the daily distribution of resources was done fairly to the widows in the Church. Deacons also help oversee the upkeep of the Church facility. They know God's Word and are full of God's Spirit. (Acts 8)

Take heed therefore unto yourselves,
and to all the flock,
over the which the Holy Ghost hath made you overseers,
to feed the church of God,
which he hath purchased with his own blood.
Acts 20:28

B. Ministries

Two general terms are used in the New Testament to refer to many individual ministries within the Church. We find these terms in 1 Corinthians 12:28, which are "helps" and "governments."[20]

Ministry of Helps

The word help means "to aid" or "to assist." The Ministry of "Helps" is a group of ministries in the Church that aid or assist the Five-Fold Ministry Gifts in accomplishing God's work in the Church. There is no way to list all the Ministries of Helps. This is because whatever help is needed in the body of Christ will be provided for by the leading of the Holy Spirit.

Here are a **few examples** of the types of Ministries of Helps that can be found within a Church fellowship: Music Ministry, Youth Ministry, Men's Ministry, Women's Ministry, Outreach Ministries, Usher and Greeter Ministry, Custodial Services, Bus Ministry, Media Ministry, Pastor's Aid, Church Administration, Parking Safety, and Fine Arts Ministry.

Exercise:

Read the following scriptures to find out what "Helps" were given in the New Testament and who the Helpers were:

Romans 16:1–2   **Who helped? 29** _____

                         What service did she give? 30 _____
(Note: see answer in the Appendix for definition)

Romans 16:3–4   **Who helped? 31)** _____

                         What service did they provide? 32) _____

Romans 16:6   **Who helped? 33)** _____

                         What service did she give? 34) _____

1 Corinthians 16:15–16   **Who helped? 35)** _____

                         What service did they provide? 36) _____

2 Cor. 1:1, 11   **Who helped? (v. 1) 37)** _____

           What service did they provide? (v. 11) 38) _____

       "**Helpers**" will receive great rewards in heaven for their sincere and consistent support to the larger ministries of the Church. Helpers are not usually the most well-known church members. Often, they give their service quietly in the background. Yet consider what Jesus said about those who help God's ministry leaders in **Matthew 10:40–41**.

Ministry of Governments

The word <u>government</u> refers to a subset group of people who are given the authority to govern an organized larger community of people. In the Church, the Ministry of Governments generally refers to a group of people who have been given the authority by God and their Church fellowship to represent the entire Church in handling the spiritual and business affairs of the Church.

Here are a **few examples** of the types of Ministry of Governments that can be found in a Church fellowship:

> Committees that help the Church Overseer with implementing the spiritual direction of the Church: Council of Bishops, Pastor's Board, Ministerial Alliances, and a group established to guide the Church in handling spiritual issues that may arise.

> Committees that help the Pastor conduct the business affairs of the Church: Trustee and Board of Directors, Finance Committee, and Building Committee.

In the following scriptures, observe how Church business and spiritual disputes (meaning arguments or disagreements) were handled in the New Testament Church:

Acts 6:1–6

> A dispute among the Church members was settled by selecting seven (7) men to fairly handle the business of distributing food and supplies to meet the needs of the widows.

Acts 15:1–31

> The Apostles and Elders called a special council to settle the dispute on if the new Gentile believers needed to be circumcised. Once the decision was made, the Apostles and Elders wrote a letter documenting the final decision on this spiritual matter. The letter was delivered by special representatives to the Gentiles to give them definitive guidance. In this sense, the Apostles and Elders that assembled served as a type of "Ministerial Alliance" that made the spiritual decision that applied to the whole Church.

"But this is that which was spoken by the prophet Joel;

And it shall come to pass in the last days, saith God,
I will pour out of my Spirit upon all flesh:

and your sons and your daughters shall prophesy,
and your young men shall see visions,
and your old men shall dream dreams:
and on my servants and on my handmaidens

I will pour out in those days of my Spirit;
and they shall prophesy"
Acts 2:16–18

God has made available to us the ability to do more than what our natural minds and our natural abilities can do.

God has given our natural abilities to us. We can develop them to the best of our human capability. But God has more to offer us than just improving our natural ability to do things. God has a flow of His supernatural powers that He wants to operate in our lives.

In Acts 1:8 Jesus explains, "**But ye shall receive power, after that the Holy Ghost is come upon you.**" The word power in this verse is a translation of the Greek word "dunamis" which refers to a dynamite-like power. This Holy Spirit power enables us to do greater works for God than our natural abilities could do. As the scripture says, we receive this power "**after that the Holy Ghost is come upon you.**"

Read Acts 19:1–6. Now I ask YOU to answer the same question that Paul asked the believers in this passage from Ephesus, because he knew how important being filled with the Holy Spirit is,

Have YOU Received the Holy Ghost Since You Believed?

The response of those believers was that they had not heard of the Holy Ghost. They also had not heard of salvation by Jesus Christ. Paul first helped them to be born of the Spirit by accepting Jesus Christ as their Lord and Savior. But Paul did not leave them in that state of being born again. He laid his hands on them so they could be filled with the Holy Spirit, which fell on them immediately. They began to speak in other tongues as the Spirit gave them utterance, and they prophesied.

You may be a Christian already. As a believer in Christ, you are born of the Spirit and ready to go to heaven when you die. Yet as a Spirit-filled believer, God can give you power to do greater Kingdom-building work for Him, while you are still living on the earth.

If you are not a Christian, then the first step for you is to become one by accepting Jesus Christ as your Lord and Savior. Then, I encourage you, as my fellow believer in Christ, to be filled with the Holy Spirit. Next, seek God for His spiritual gifts to flow in your life. God wants His spiritual gifts to flow through you for the benefit of others and for your own benefit.

God Needs You to Help Save His Most Valuable Earthly Treasure —PEOPLE!

Some believe we are living in the last days of this present earth that will precede Jesus's second coming to the earth based on the description of last days events. (Reference Matthew Chapter 24, Mark Chapter 13, Luke 21:5-36, Acts 2:14-21).

In these times God wants His people to be empowered to do His last days work on the earth.

† Sons and daughters, Men and Women, God needs you to prophesy.
† Senior men, God needs you to receive and share the dreams He gives you. Young men, God needs you to receive and do His visions.
† Men and women who have a servant's heart, God needs you to receive the full work of His Spirit in your life so you can bless others.

It is time for everyone to receive the outpouring of God's Spirit.
The harvest of people who would receive Christ as their Lord is plentiful,
but the fully prepared laborers,
that God needs to bring in the harvest, are few.
(Matthew 9:35–38, Luke 10:2)

God needs ALL of us to be fully equipped to help bring in His final crop of souls before the end of the age and He pours out His final judgment over the whole earth. God Bless You! AMEN!

Who is the wise man?

Ane who knoweth the interpretation of a thing?

A man's wisdom maketh his face to shine

And the boldness of his face shall be changed.

I counsel thee to keep the king's commandment,

And that in regard of the oath of God.

Where the word of a king is, there is power:

And who may say unto him, What doest thou?

Whoso keepeth the commandment
shall feel no evil thing:

And a wise man's heart discerneth
both time and judgment.

Ecclesiastes 8:1, 2, 4, 5

Chapter 7:

Fruit of the Spirit

Chapter 7

Detailed Contents

Additional Study

- Appendix H: KHS Video Lessons Synopsis

ONE FRUIT, NINE PARTS

There are many "fruit" talked about in the Bible.

Some examples are:

the "fruit of the womb" (Psalm 127:3),

the "fruit in old age" (Psalm 92:14),

the "fruit of our lips" (Hebrews 13:15),

the "fruit of their [sinners] own way" (Proverbs 1:31),

the "fruit of the righteous" (Proverbs 11:30), and

the "people fruit" of causing more people to believe in Jesus (John 15:5).

However, the Bible only describes one <u>fruit of the Spirit</u>, and this fruit has nine parts.

The fruit of the Spirit is listed in Galatians 5:22–23. Below these scriptures are listed as written in the King James Version (KJV) of the Bible and the New Living Translation (NLT) version of the Bible.

Galatians 5:22–23 KJV	**Galatians 5:22–23 NLT**
But the fruit of the Spirit is	But the Holy Spirit produces this kind of fruit in our lives:
love,	love,
joy,	joy,
peace,	peace,
longsuffering,	patience,
gentleness,	kindness,
goodness,	goodness,
faith,	faithfulness,
meekness,	gentleness, and
temperance:	self-control.
against such there is no law.	There is no law against these things!

This scripture lets us know that we must follow the Holy Spirit's instructions on how to live to become the people God wants us to be. Romans 8:1 says it this way,

"There is therefore now no condemnation
(meaning judgment for wrongdoing) **to them which are in Christ Jesus, who walk not after the flesh, but after the Spirit."**

STRANGE (PECULIAR), HARD AND SOFT PARTS OF THE FRUIT OF THE SPIRIT

A person could think of the parts of the fruit of the Spirit as:

Strange (Peculiar)	Hard	Soft
love	longsuffering	gentleness
joy	faith	goodness
peace	temperance	meekness

Strange or Peculiar Part of the Fruit of the Spirit

The first grouping above could be thought of as the strange or peculiar part of the fruit. This group includes love, joy and peace. Love could be called "peculiar" because God expects Christians to do things like love their enemies. Joy could be called "strange" because the Bible reveals that God expects Christians to have joy even during sad or stressful times in their lives. Peace could be called a "strange" part because God expects Christians to remain peaceful when things happen to them that would disturb anyone's peace.

Hard Part of the Fruit of the Spirit

The second grouping could be considered the hard part of the fruit. This group includes longsuffering, faith and temperance. Longsuffering could be considered a hard part because nobody wants to suffer, and no one wants to suffer for a long time. Also, based on typical human nature, no one wants to wait for what they want in their lives. Yet Psalm 37:9 says, "those that wait upon the Lord shall inherit the earth." Faith could be considered a hard part because God expects Christians to believe and confess things they cannot see and may not feel. Christians are told to "calleth those things which **be not** as though **they were**" (Romans 4:17). Temperance could also be considered a hard part as the Spirit guides Christians to temper or deny fleshly cravings and habits. This requires discipline in all behaviors.

Soft Part of the Fruit of the Spirit

Gentleness, goodness and meekness could be considered the soft part of the fruit because people with these qualities are sometimes thought of as being weak. For example, God instructs Christians to do good to those who do evil things to them.

Read on to find out how the...

- Soft part of the fruit is the strong part
- Hard part is the easiest way to get what you want in life
- Strange part will keep you from heartbreak and depression

LOVE, THE PECULIAR PART OF THE FRUIT

When most people think of loving someone, they think of this strong, pleasant emotion they have for someone who is very special to them. Either this love comes from a positive relationship they have with a person such as a mother, father, or grandparent. Or these loving emotions develop as a person's five senses (meaning their sense of sight, hearing, smell, feeling and taste) cause them to desire a relationship with another person.

On the other hand, it is very natural for a person to dislike or even hate someone who makes them feel very uncomfortable. This dislike could be based on negative feelings about how another person looks, acts, smells, talks and so on. Naturally, a person wants to stay as far away as possible from someone they dislike. Or if they come near the person that offends them, they are likely to treat them in a mean, rude, or even hurtful manner.

But GOD...

... instructs us to act differently from the way we naturally feel. God's Word tells us to love others even when it is difficult for us to do so. For example, God's Word shows us we should have God's True Love to:

- ♥ Love our enemies
- ♥ Love strangers
- ♥ Love people who are in need
- ♥ Love and care about all human beings
- ♥ Love people for real *(not in a phony way just for show)*

God's love will cause you to love others in three peculiar ways, meaning in three ways that are different from the way you naturally want to act.

God's love is a peculiar way of thinking.

God's love is a peculiar way of acting.

God's love is a peculiar way of talking.

Study the following tables to understand what it means to have God's kind of love in our heart and to demonstrate it in our actions:

"True Love" and God's Peculiar 3-Way Love.

TRUE LOVE

The Love Commandment – Matthew 22:37–40 – means:

1) Love God for real – John 14:15, Mark 12:29–30

2) Love yourself – Psalm 139:14, Mark 12:31

3) Love others like you love yourself – Mark 12:31, Matthew 22:39

Four Main Greek Words translated to describe People Love:

1) **Agape** (a-ga'-pe) – God's divine love for all people, which is unconditional and sacrificial. God's divine love expressed through people. Scripture examples – John 3:16, 13:34-35; 1 Cor. 13

2) **Phileo** – love people feel for close friends. Scripture examples – Hebrews 13:1, 1 Thessalonians 4:9

3) **Storge** – love between family members who share a strong bond – this word is sometimes combined with the word Phileo. Scripture example – Romans 12:10

4) **Eros** – love expressed in romantic relationships. God has designed this love to be fully experienced between a monogamous married male (husband) and female (wife) couple. Scripture examples – Song of Solomon 1:2–4; God's design is described in Hebrews 13:4 and 1 Corinthians 7

Get Rid of Hindrances to Having God's True Love in Your Heart:

1) **Hate**: Leviticus 19:17, 1 John 4:20–21

2) **Revenge**: Leviticus 19:18, Romans 12:18 – 21

3) **Unforgiveness**: Matthew 18:21–22 (explains how often to forgive), Matthew 18:23–35 (parable of unforgiving servant), Matthew 6:12, 14–15

4) **Lover of things more than God**: 1 Timothy 6:10 (money), 1 John 2:15–17 (this world), James 4:1–6 (worldly friends)

5) **Lust / Sinful**: Matthew 5:28, Galatians 5:16, 19–21

He that loveth not knoweth not God;
for God IS Love!
1 John 4:8

GOD'S PECULIAR 3-WAY LOVE

God's Love, that is given to us by the fruit of the Spirit, wants us to Love people like this:

God's Love… Is a Peculiar way of Thinking	God's Love… Is a Peculiar way of Acting	God's Love… Is a Peculiar way of Talking	There is Power that Comes From Walking in God's Love
Matthew 22:37-40 Love God first, yourself and other people.	**Romans 13:10** Do no ill or evil actions to other people.	**James 3:1-13** Do not curse people or offend them with your words.	**Proverbs 10:12** Your love covers or forgives all kinds of sins.
1 Cor. 13:4-7 Do not be envious or high-minded. Think no evil. Believe in and hope for all good things.	**1 Cor. 13:4-7** Expect to suffer sometimes. Do not be selfish. Do not act "better than" others.	**Colossians 4:6** Let your speech always be kind, gracious and helpful.	**Phil. 2:15** You are blameless sons of God without rebuke in a crooked nation. You shine as lights on earth.
Romans 12:9-21 Do not be phony. Do not think of yourself as "better than" others. Do not be overwise.	**Rom. 12:9-21** Love all people for real. **Eph. 6:2**, **Rom. 13** Respect parents and people in authority.	**Romans 12:14** Bless those who persecute you; bless and do not curse them.	**Isaiah 54:17** No weapon formed against you shall prosper. You shall condemn those who judge you
Titus 3:1-7 Think about how you were once a sinner, to make you patient in dealing with sinners.	**Titus 3:1-11** – be nice to everyone, do not argue about the laws of God, do good works all the time.	**Titus 3:2** Speak evil of no one. Do not be a person who likes to argue.	**2 Corinthians 10:3-4** God's Love is a weapon that destroys the strongholds or problems in life.
Philippians 4:8 Think pure, good, just thoughts about others.	**Philippians 2:14-16** Do not be a troublemaker or difficult person.	**Philippians 2:14** Do not be argumentative or a complainer.	**2 Peter 1:8-11** You will always be knowledgeable in God's Word
1 Peter 3:8-9 Have a considerate mind when thinking of others.	**1 Thessalonians 4:1-12** In no way hurt, abuse or use others.	**1 Peter 3:9-10** Keep your tongue from saying bad things.	**Exodus 23:25-26** God will take sickness and barrenness away.
1 Thessalonians 5:14-15 Have a patient attitude with all people.	**1 Thessalonians 5:14-15** Comfort the feeble and support the weak.	**1 Thessalonians 5:14** Warn the unruly.	**Deuteronomy 28:1-14** Your family, job & monies are blessed.
James 5:9 Do not hold grudges	**James 5:9** Endure wrong actions.	**James 5:12** Do not swear/promise.	**Heb. 8:6** Better promises are yours.
Gal. 5:26 Do not desire vainglory.	**James 1:19** Be quick to listen.	**Rev. 3:8** Do not deny Christ.	**1 Pet. 3:13** No one can harm you.
James 1:19-20 Be slow to get angry.	**1 Tim. 1:5** Love with a pure heart.	**James 1:19** Be slow to speak out.	**Romans 13:10** When God's Love is working in you, it satisfies all the law of God that is required of you.
2 Corinthians 10:5 Get rid of thoughts against God's ways.	**Matt. 5:44-48 & Luke 6:31-35** Love and Do Good to your Enemies.	**Ephesians 4:15** Speak the truth in love to others.	
	1 John 3:10-18 Show actions of love to those in need.	**Matthew 5:25** Agree with your adversary (enemy) quickly.	
	Hebrews 13:1, 1 John 4:12 Love fellow Christians and strangers.	**Ephesians 5:4** Do not use foolish talking. Do not tease people.	
God's Love Is a Peculiar Thought, Walk & Talk			*God's Love is Strange, But in a Good Way!*

GOD'S PECULIAR 3-WAY LOVE

God's Love is a Peculiar THOUGHT

Think Evil of No One
Hope for the Best Always
Pure, Clean, Good Thoughts

God's Love is a Peculiar WALK

Love Your Enemies
Care about Strangers
Help the Needy
Be Extra Kind to Fellow Christians

God's Love is a Peculiar TALK

Do Not Use Bad or Shameful Language
Use Kind, Uplifting Words
Speak the Truth in Love
NEVER DENY GOD!

JOY, The Strange Part of the Fruit

A person is said to be "Happy" when they are delighted, pleased or glad because a particular thing has occurred.

A person is said to have "Joy" when they feel a great delight as a part of having deep, inner happiness.

The Bible explains that a person can still have joy, even when events in their lives bring them unhappy experiences, because of that person's trust and hope in Jesus Christ. They believe that Jesus Christ can work everything out for their good. This includes Him using sad, unhappy experiences to produce some positive, happy result for their life.

A happy face is present when a person is feeling happy.

Joy is present **deep in a person's heart**. It can be present although a person may be crying outside. A Christian can have tears rolling down their cheeks, while singing praises to God deep down in their heart.

When a person has God's abundant JOY because of "good things" happening in their life, then their joy may look like this:

- Joy can be displayed in the form of a Holy Dance.
  Psalm 149:3, Acts 3:8–11

- Joy can be displayed in the form of praise songs and new songs suddenly being sung by the joyous person.
  Psalm 40:3, Psalm 98:1

- Joy can be displayed in the form of a person having strange utterances come forth out of their mouth.
  Acts 2:4, 11; Acts 10:46

- Joy can be displayed in the form of inspired musicians playing wonderful melodies of praise on their instruments.
  Psalm 98:4–9, Psalm 150:3–5

JOY, THE STRANGE PART OF THE FRUIT

†

When a person has God's JOY when "bad things" happen in their life, then their joy may look like this:

† **Joy for "sad times"** is present when a person cries for a whole night, but in the morning, they are filled with the joy of the Lord. The joy comes because of God's comfort that came to them through their sad night. Psalm 30:5

† **Joy for "sorrowful times"** is present when a person is Godly sorrowful for some wrong deed they committed against God. After the person repents, God's Word says to stop feeling regret over their past mistakes and to rejoice because God has forgiven them. Nehemiah 8:9–10

† **Joy for "afflicted times"** is present when a person understands that their affliction (sickness, mistreatment, or other wrong condition) will last for a short time. The affliction cannot be compared to the eternal benefit they will receive as they keep their faith in God. 2 Corinthians 4:16–18, Romans 8:18, 28

† **Joy for "tested times"** is present when a person knows they are being treated badly because they are followers of Christ. If a person shares in the rejection that Jesus had to go through on earth, they will also share in the glory that Jesus now has. 1 Peter 4:14–16

† **Joy for "tempted times"** is present when a person's faith is challenged in many ways. In the end the person will be blessed to receive the desires of their heart when they keep the faith. James 1:2-17, Romans 5:3-5

† **Joy for "trying times"** is present when a person has many tests of their faith in God. They are filled with unspeakable joy when they do not give up on trusting God no matter the type and number of tests. God promises a flow of His goodness for this person after they pass the tests. 1 Peter 1:6–9; 4:12–13

† **Joy for "embarrassing, chastened times"** is present when a Christian understands that some problems in their life happen because they are not following God's instructions. Once they repent, God will heal their heart and turn their situation from "bad" to "good." Hebrews 12:2–11

† **Joy for "worrisome times"** is present when a person understands that they should stop worrying and start believing in God's ability to turn any experience into a positive experience. Their joy comes when instead of worry, they have hope in God. Romans 5:1–5, Psalm 112

JOY, THE STRANGE PART OF THE FRUIT

JOY – The Strange Fruit of the Spirit

Happy goes away when circumstances change
from "Happy to "Sad"

BUT

JOY remains even in sad, sorrowful, afflicted, tested, tempted,
trying, embarrassing, worrisome, "UNHAPPY" times.

The fruit of the Spirit "JOY" enables us to have

JOY for sad times	Psalm 30:5
JOY for sorrowful times	Nehemiah 8:9–10
JOY for afflicted times	2 Cor. 4:14-16; Romans 8:18, 28
JOY for tested times	1 Peter 4:14 – 16
JOY for tempted times	James 1:2-17, Romans 5:3-5
JOY for trying times	1 Peter 1:6–9; 4:12–13
JOY for embarrassing, chastened times	Hebrews 12:2-11
JOY for worrisome times	Roman 5:1–5, Psalm 112

JOY is the Great Christian 'CURE ALL!'

A merry heart doeth good
like a medicine
Proverbs 17:22a

Rejoice in the Lord alway:
and again I say, Rejoice.
Philippians 4:4

For the JOY of the Lord
is your strength.
Nehemiah 8:10c

PEACE, THE REALLY STRANGE PART OF THE FRUIT

The Peace of God, given to us by the fruit of the Spirit,

Starts in our spirit	Romans 5:1, John 14:27
Connects to our mind	Isaiah 26:3, Philippians 4:6–7
is Present in all our actions & reactions	Hebrews 12:14, James 3:17–18

Let us compare "Peace" to the structure of a house.

The Foundation

The foundation is the lowest part of a house. It is usually dug deep into the ground. The rest of the house is built on top of it. For the house to be strong enough to withstand different weather conditions, it must be firmly built on a good foundation. **Our spiritual house (our spirit Eph. 2:18–22 and body 1 Cor. 3:16), must also be built on a firm foundation (our faith Matthew 16:16–18, 1 Corinthians 3:10–11).**

When we accept Jesus Christ as our Lord and Savior, then our faith in Him changes our relationship with God. We become the children of God. We have **Peace with God** who is now our spiritual Father.

> **"Therefore being justified by faith, we have peace with God through our Lord Jesus Christ."**
> Romans 5:1

The Walls

The walls of a house must be firmly built on top of the foundation. They must also securely connect to the roof. When the walls are secure, they help keep harsh weather conditions out and the desired controlled conditions inside of the house. Spiritual walls of Peace are also needed in our spiritual house to connect the Peace a person receives from accepting Jesus as their Lord, to the everyday peace they need in their minds (spiritual roof).

The walls of Peace for our spiritual house will be secure as we talk to, learn about, and trust in God from praying and studying God's Word each day.

> **"Be careful for nothing; but in every thing by prayer and supplication with thanksgiving let your requests be made known unto God. And the peace of God, which passeth all understanding, shall keep your hearts and minds through Christ Jesus.**
> Philippians 4:6–7

The Roof

The roof of a house covers the top of it. It must be securely connected to the walls to protect homeowners from unwanted outside activity. If the roof has a problem, then harmful things such as rain and animals can enter inside the house.

The roof for our spiritual house is our mind. If we are not strong in spiritual knowledge and faith in God, then all kinds of unwanted thoughts can enter our minds to make us confused and unhappy.

> **"Thou wilt keep him in perfect peace, whose mind is stayed on thee: because he trusteth in thee.**
> Isaiah 26:3

The Rooms

Homeowners decorate each room in their house for comfortable living. In addition, homes are smartly designed to meet the homeowners' needs. Even if there are harsh weather conditions happening outside the house, there are inside rooms where everyone can gather for additional protection. In our spiritual house, when a person approaches us in different ways, we should do everything we can to respond to them in a peaceable manner.

Like different rooms in a house are decorated for pleasure and to meet a homeowner's needs, when people approach us in different ways, we should try to be peaceful and comfortable to talk to, even in unpleasant times.

> **"Follow peace with all men, and holiness, without which no man shall see the Lord."**
> Hebrews 12:14

Termites

Termites are tiny bugs that can destroy the structure of a house by eating through the wooden parts. It is possible for them to begin destroying your house while you are unaware. Sometimes they are not discovered until they have done a great deal of damage. Homeowners will spend a lot of money and time to get rid of termites to recover from the damage. Regular bug spray can not destroy termites because of their small size. It takes an Exterminator using a special chemical solution to get rid of them. If a house is built to protect against termites or if termites are detected early, then repair costs can be low.

Warning: "Spiritual termites" can damage our spiritual house.

Read 'BEWARE OF SPIRITUAL TERMITES' for a spiritual solution.

'BEWARE OF SPIRITUAL TERMITES'

'They can destroy your peace before you know what is happening!'

**Below are some Spiritual Termites
and the special spiritual solution to get rid of them.**

Some things that could be considered "spiritual termites" are listed below. "Exterminator Scriptures" are provided beneath each one. These scriptures are the "special spiritual solution" you need to destroy the spiritual termites.

Directions for using the Exterminator Scriptures: For <u>all the things</u> that disturb your peace, use the truth of God's Word to restore your peace. Do this by speaking God's Word out loud so your ears and heart can hear it. Repeat the scriptures and meditate on their meaning until your heart is reassured to have faith in God. (Isaiah 55:10–11 and Hebrews 10:17)

Spiritual Termite 1: Challenges to Your Foundational Christian Beliefs in God (2 Peter 2:1–3, 1 Timothy 4:1–3, 2 Peter 3:3–4)

> **Exterminator Scriptures**: Matthew 16:16–18, John 14:6, 1 John 5:1, 10–13

Spiritual Termite 2: Fear (1 John 4:18 [fear has torment]; 2 Timothy 1:7a [spirit of fear])

> **Exterminator Scriptures**: 1 John 4:18 [love casts out fear]; 2 Timothy 1:7b [power, love, sound mind]

Spiritual Termite 3: Evil Tidings/Bad News (Psalm 112:7, Job 1:1, 12–19)

> **Exterminator Scriptures**: Psalm 112:7–8, Job 1:21–22, 2:10, 13:15

Spiritual Termite 4: Worry (Luke 10:41, Psalm 73:2–16)

> **Exterminator Scriptures**: Matthew 6:25–34, Proverbs 3:5–6, Ephesians 3:20

Spiritual Termite 5: Confusion (James 3:16)

> **Exterminator Scriptures**: 1 Corinthians 14:33, Isaiah 54:11–17

Spiritual Termite 6: Fiery Darts (meaning attacks on your life) from Satan (Ephesians 6:11 – 12)

> **Exterminator Scriptures**: Ephesians 6:13 – 18, Ephesians 1:19 – 23

Spiritual Termite 7: Not Wanting to Wait (Impatience) (Hebrews 10:35)

> **Exterminator Scriptures:** Hebrews 10:35–39

Spiritual Termite 8: Doubt (James 1:6–8)

> **Exterminator Scriptures**: James 1:2 – 5, Proverbs 3:5–7, 1 John 5:13–15, Matthew 21:22

Make PEACE!

But the wisdom that is from
above is first pure,
then peaceable,
gentle, and easy to be intreated,
full of mercy and good fruits,
without partiality,
and without hypocrisy.

And the **fruit of righteousness
is sown in peace of them that
make peace.**

James 3:17–18

LONGSUFFERING, The Hard Part of the Fruit

This part of the fruit could be compared to a lemon.

A regular lemon tastes sour. Yet if you mix sugar and water with the juice of a lemon, then you produce the sweet, refreshing drink of lemonade.

Similarly, LONGSUFFERING is not a fun experience. It could "sour" your faith in God as you wait for deliverance or an answer to your prayer.

But,

If you suffer as a Christian (1 Peter 4:16, 19), and

You add the study of God's Word to your suffering experience, this could be thought of like adding water (Ephesians 5:26), and

You add the sweet presence of Jesus going through the hard times with you (John 16:33, Hebrews 13:5–6, Psalm 34:8), then

Your LONGSUFFERING will produce sweet, refreshing work in your life. (1 Peter 1:6–9; 5:6–10)

Longsuffering is the part of the fruit of the spirit that helps the Christian to accept bad times or bad experiences in their life patiently. For example, a person who is longsuffering is not quick to get angry. They show kindness in their reactions to being treated in a wrong or unfair way. The longsuffering Christian has a mind to wait on God to work in their life to turn their bad experiences into a good outcome.

The Bible explains that a Christian should expect to suffer persecution (2 Timothy 3:12). This applies when a Christian experiences the same kind of suffering that Jesus experienced or denies themself of things to follow in the ways of Christ (1 Peter 4:1–2, Matthew 16:24–26). Jesus wants His disciples to share in some of His sufferings so they can share in His glory (meaning the good rewards from God for enduring suffering - Romans 8:18). Below are some examples of the type of suffering a Christian can expect to experience:

Because you are a Christian, people may do these things to you:

- Speak evil things about you. 1 Peter 4:4, 13
- Do mean things to you. Matthew 5:11
- Hate you. John 15:18
- Give you all kinds of trouble. 2 Thessalonians 1:4
- Try to get you to do something wrong / sinful. James 1:13–16

When you suffer as a Christian, God will reward you with many things in this life and in the future world, which is to come!

When you suffer for the right reasons, some rewards to receive are:

- You will be exceedingly joyful when Jesus' glory is revealed to everyone. 1 Peter 4:13–14
- You will be glorified with Jesus and receive a royal inheritance. The glory you receive in this life and in the world to come is so great that it will make all your suffering seem insignificant. Romans 8:17–18
- The end of your patient waiting on God in faith will result in you gaining all you really want in life. James 1:4
- People who wait on God will receive renewed strength after their waiting period is over. Isaiah 40:28–31, Psalm 103:5
- You receive many blessings like homes, land, good family, good friends in this life and many blessings in the next world. Mark 10:29–30
- The Kingdom of Heaven and all its benefits belong to you. Matt. 5:10

There are scriptures explaining that there is a type of suffering a person can go through that is not the kind Christians should be experiencing.

"But let none of you suffer as a murderer, or as a thief, or as an evildoer, or a busybody in other men's matters." 1 Peter 4:15

BUT EVERYBODY MAKES MISTAKES!

Problem: Christians who are trying to live for God with all their heart, will sometimes do things that displease God.

Solution: A Christian who sins and suffers for the wrong reason, needs to do the following things to get back on the right path:

1) Confess your sin to God, repent for having done it, and stop sinning. 1 John 1:9, 2:1–2; Psalm 51:2–17, 2 Chronicles 7:13–14
2) Accept God's forgiveness for your sin, forgive yourself and let God help you to heal and become whole. Philippians 3:13–14, Psalm 86:5
3) Prayerfully and humbly seek God's direction on what to do daily. Proverbs 3:5, Psalm 51:17, Micah 6:8
4) Completely follow all of God's directions during this difficult time. Proverbs 3:6, Psalm 51:6
5) Then, God will turn your heavy, unnecessary pain into a miraculous gain. Romans 8:28, Psalm 51:12–13, Psalm 32

Read two Bible stories of people who suffered for their own bad decisions but experienced the blessings of God after they repented:

David in 2 Samuel Chapters 11 & 12; Jacob in Genesis Chapters 27–50.

LONGSUFFERING

**will produce sweet, refreshing work
in your life like how a lemon produces lemonade
when water and sugar are added to the lemon juice.**

LEMON SOUR TYPE EXPERIENCES	+ GOD'S WORD AND PRESENCE	= LEMONADE TYPE EXPERIENCES
Unfair treatment on the Job 1 Peter 2:18–23	Water of the Word of God that leads and guides you through every step of your way. Ephesians 5:25–27 and The sweet presence of the living God carrying you through your hard times safely and victoriously. Psalm 34:7–8 Isaiah 43:1–2 (Galatians 3:13–14)	1 Peter 3:14–18 1 Peter 4:1–2
Unfair treatment in the family Luke 21:16–19		Mark 10:29–30 Acts 16:31
Unfair treatment from friends and associates 1 Corinthians 4:10–13		Romans 8:17–18
Unfair treatment just because you are a Christian 1 Peter 4:12–15		1 Peter 1:6–9
Many are the afflictions (sufferings) of the righteous (Christian) Psalm 34:19		Romans 8:26–28 2 Corinthians 4:16–18

For I reckon that the
**sufferings of this present time
are not worthy to be compared
with the glory**
which shall be revealed in us.

Romans 8:18

And we know that
**all things work together
for good to them that love God,**
to them who are the called
according to his purpose.

Romans 8:28

FAITH, ANOTHER HARD PART OF THE FRUIT

For Better or For Worse,

For Richer or For Poorer,

In Sickness and In Health,

Until Death or the Rapture Bring You Closest Together

For As Long as You Both Shall Live...

FAITH from the fruit of the Spirit helps each Christian to be faithful in serving God until they meet Him after death or the rapture (2 Timothy 1:12, 1 Thessalonians 4:13–18, Jude 24, 25). This attitude of "faithfulness" really helps when your beliefs do not work out like you thought they would. For example:

God told 75-year-old Abraham he would have a son by his old wife, Sarah. Abraham had to wait 25 years before that promise came true. He kept believing God even when it took a long time to happen, and he and his wife were too old to have children (Romans 4:17–21, Hebrews 11:11–12).

Another example is when God told Abraham that many people would be born as offspring (children) of his son Isaac. Abraham never doubted that God would keep that promise even after God told him to sacrifice his son. (Hebrews 11:17–19) Abraham faithfully trusted in God no matter what!

Another example is when the three Hebrew boys decided not to bow down to a golden statue. They would rather be thrown in the fiery furnace than bow down. When the king of Babylon threatened to burn them alive, they told him that they believed their God was able to save them from being harmed, but that if God did not save them, they would still not bow down. They said this because of their faithfulness to the true and living God (Daniel 3:13–18).

Another example is when Job kept believing in God's goodness in spite of the sad events that took away his riches and children in one day. He continued to believe in God after he became very sick with a lot of painful body sores. Job kept his love and respect for God even when he did not understand why these terrible things were happening in his life (Job 1:1–2:10).

"Faith" (meaning "faithful") from the fruit of the Spirit enables the Christian to be committed to God, believing in, serving, and loving God in good and bad times. This commitment **is like the wedding vows made between a man and a woman who promise to love each other for as long as they both shall live.** The <u>Faith</u> part of the fruit of the Spirit helps Christians to be faithful to God when times are:

For Better

Christians have a better relationship with God based on better promises, than the one between the Israelite nation and God in the Old Testament, because of Jesus Christ's sacrifice. Hebrews 8:6

For Worse

God allows His children to experience many problems in their lives, but He will help them overcome each one. Psalm 34:19, 2 Corinthians 12:7–10

For Richer

Christians have a rich, glorious inheritance (meaning treasure) that is theirs now and forever. They also have exceeding great power from Jesus ready to help them all the time. Ephesians 1:3, 17–23; 3:16–21

For Poorer

Christians can enjoy God when they do not have lots of material blessings. Philippians 3:8; 4:12; Proverbs 15:16

In Sickness

God will care for, strengthen and heal the Christian who is sick and weak. Psalm 41:3, James 5:15–16

In Health

God's Word will heal and strengthen your body, bones, flesh and so on. Psalm 107:20, Prov. 3:7–8, Hebrews 4:12, Psalm 27:2

Until Death or the Rapture bring You Closest Together

God will never leave or forsake His children. (Hebrews 13:5) When your spirit leaves your body due to death, it goes to be with the Lord in heaven immediately. (2 Corinthians 5:1–8) At the time of the Rapture, Christians on earth will join Jesus immediately in the air. 1 Thessalonians 4:13–18

For As Long as You Both Shall Live (Forever)

God loved us so much He gave us eternal life through Jesus Christ. (John 3:16) The last enemy "death" will be destroyed, and Christians will live with the Lord forever. (1 Cor. 15:26, Rev. 21:4–7)

Faithful

You are to be Faithful to God, because God is Faithful to You!

Lamentations 3:22–25, John 10:29, 1 Corinthians 1:9, Ephesians 5:25–27, Jude 24, Revelation 19:11

I, _____ ,

(write your name on the line)

Do take the True and Living God,
To be the Only Wise God my Savior,

To Have and to Hold
From this day forward,
For Better or for Worse
For Richer or for Poorer
In Sickness and In Health,
Until Death or the Rapture
Brings us closest together,
For as long as we both shall live,
which is forever.

Amen!

Faith - fruit of the Spirit - = Trust in God!

Trust in the Lord,

and do good;

so shalt thou dwell in the land,

and verily thou shalt be fed.

Delight thyself also in the Lord;

and he shall give thee

the desires of thine heart.

Commit thy way unto the Lord;

trust also in him;

and he shall bring it to pass.

Psalm 37:3–5

TEMPERANCE, THE REALLY HARD PART OF THE FRUIT

Temperance can be thought of as practicing self-control in every area of your life.

Each of us needs to practice temperance or self-control to make the best choice on how we use our time within a day. God has given each person the ability and freedom to choose what they will do with their time. We can do anything we want at any time we want, but temperance helps us to exercise self-control in the choices we make.

For example, you have the ability and freedom to choose to watch movies for 24 hours. However, this is not practical because a healthy lifestyle includes time for work, study, exercise, relaxation and rest.

Overall, we need help to choose between participating in godly activities versus ungodly activities; and to choose between participating in activities that are healthy versus unhealthy for our body, our soul (meaning our thoughts and emotions), and our spirit.

The temperance part of the fruit of the Spirit will help you to practice temperance or self-control in your choices so you can choose a well-balanced life in the natural (physical) and spiritual areas of your life.

With the help of the temperance part of the fruit of the Spirit, you can control:

- **What You Say**
- **How You Act When You Are Alone or with Others**
- **Spiritual Actions**
- **Eating**
- **How You Spend Your Money**
- **How You Treat People Who Are in Charge**
- **How Much Time You Spend Working**
- **And so much more…**

With the Holy Spirit's help,
the Christian who practices Temperance
when making their everyday decisions
will live a well-balanced life!
They do not overdo things! They do not underdo things!

Christians need to let the Holy Spirit help them to have temperance in every area of their lives. As a Christian you should control:

Self-Control Area	Practice Temperance	Scripture References
What You Say	You need to control your tongue (meaning the words that come out of your mouth) so you do not hurt others by what you say	James 3:2–13, Proverbs 15:1–2, Ecclesiastes 5:1–7, Proverbs 18:20–21, 1 Peter 3:10, Matthew 12:36–37, Ecclesiastes 10:11 – 14
How You Act When You Are Alone and With Others	You should not do things to hurt your body or to hurt anyone else's body. This means not doing things to hurt yourself or others physically, mentally, or spiritually.	Colossians 3:17, Ephesians 5:18, 1 Corinthians 3:16–17, 6:9– 20; Deuteronomy 18:10–12, Proverbs 20:1, 23:31–32; Leviticus 19:26–31, 20:10–21
Spiritual Actions	God has order and timing for when you should or should not do something "in the name of the Lord". Your spiritual actions must also be balanced.	1 Corinthians 14:27–33, Romans 8:14, 1 John 4:1, Matthew 7:21–23, Proverbs 3:5–6
Eating, Drinking	You need discipline to determine the amount and types of food to eat; and who you will eat with.	Proverbs 23:1–3, 19–21, Romans 14:1–23, 1 Corinthians 10:27–31
How You Spend Your Money	God expects you to be wise in how you spend your money. Give God His tithe first. Then, spend some and save some of the rest. Some spending money should also be given back to God as an offering and to help those in need.	Ecclesiastes 11:1–6, Proverbs 3:9–10, Malachi 3:8–11, Luke 6:38, 2 Corinthians 9:6–11
How You Treat People Who Are in Charge	Respect and obey God's law, Parents' rules, and the laws of the government in which you live (school, work). You should be a good citizen.	Romans 13:1–7, Deuteronomy 28:1, 2, 9, 13–14; Ephesians 6:1–3; 1 Peter 2:13–17
How Much Time You Spend Working	You must work to provide for your needs, but you also need to take time to worship God, to relax and to get enough sleep	Proverbs 6:6–11, Ecclesiastes 12:12, Psalm 127:2, Proverbs 23:4
And so much more…	Read the Bible to learn how to have balance in EVERY area of your life!	Check out "**Know His Word Bible Study**" by this author. Go to => knowbiblestudies.com

THE SOFT PARTS OF THE FRUIT

GENTLENESS, GOODNESS, AND MEEKNESS
could be called the "soft" parts of the fruit of the Spirit.

This is because a Christian
who has these character traits from the Spirit
should be comfortable for all people
to approach and interact with.

It is not easy to walk in "gentleness," "goodness," and "meekness" all the time.

For example, it takes a lot of strength of character for a Christian to demonstrate these qualities during times when normal human nature wants to respond to a situation in a mean, rude and unkind manner.

From reviewing the scriptures on the following pages, we will discover,

To show Gentleness, Goodness, and Meekness
like Jesus Christ,

A Christian does things

That are kind and nice

To people they know,

To people they do not know,

To people who are nice and

To people who are not nice.

To get started,
let us first look at what the Bible means when it says a believer in
Jesus Christ should act with "Gentleness."

GENTLENESS: The Soft Part of the Fruit

♦ **God treats us with Gentleness.** He treats us with love and respect even when we do not love and respect Him.

> **"The Lord hath appeared of old unto me, saying,**
> **Yea, I have loved thee with an everlasting love:**
> **therefore with lovingkindness have I drawn thee."**
> Jeremiah 31:3

> **"It is God that girdeth me with strength,**
> **and maketh my way perfect...**
> **Thou hast also given me the shield of thy salvation:**
> **and thy right hand hath holden me up,**
> **and thy gentleness hath made me great."**
> Psalm 18:32, 35

♦ **We are to treat others with Gentleness,** meaning with godly love and respect, even when they do not love and respect us.

> **But love ye your enemies,**
> **and do good, and lend, hoping for nothing again;**
> **and your reward shall be great,**
> **and ye shall be the children of the Highest:**
> **for he is kind unto the unthankful and to the evil.**
> Luke 6:35

> **And be ye kind one to another,**
> **tenderhearted, forgiving one another,**
> **even as God for Christ's sake hath forgiven you.**
> Ephesians 4:32

> **But the wisdom that is from above is first pure,**
> **then peaceable, gentle, and easy to be intreated,**
> **full of mercy and good fruits,**
> **without partiality, and without hypocrisy.**
> James 3:17

> **Put them in mind to be subject to principalities and powers,**
> **to obey magistrates, to be ready to every good work,**
> **To speak evil of no man, to be no brawlers,**
> **but gentle, shewing all meekness unto all men.**
> Titus 3:1–2

♦ **We treat others with gentleness in the hope God can draw them to accept Christ** by our showing them His loving-kind nature.

GENTLENESS

Here are some expressions people may use to describe you when you show the Gentleness of Christ the right way!

When you are a Gentle Christian, people might say you are:

Kind

Nice

Smart

Friendly

Pleasant

Courteous

Considerate

A Gentleman

A Great Boss

A Peacemaker

Even-tempered

Quick to forgive

Good Company

The Nicest Worker

A Wonderful Teacher

Easy to get along with

Quick to say "I'm Sorry"

An All-Around Good Student

A person who smiles all the time

A Beautiful Young Lady inside and out

A person who gives good, helpful advice

A person who seems "Happy" all the time

Consider the following words of advice from Pastor Albert C. Macklin, Sr. of New Sweet Home Church, in East Palo Alto, California:

"It's Just Nice to Be Nice!"

GENTLENESS

Be Wise as a Serpent

But Harmless as a Dove

Being Gentle and Kind

Showing Everyone God's Love

**These twelve Jesus sent forth,
and commanded them, saying...**

**Behold, I send you forth as sheep
in the midst of wolves:
be ye therefore wise as serpents,
and harmless as doves.**

**But beware of men:
for they will deliver you up to the councils,
and they will scourge you in their synagogues;**

**And ye shall be brought before governors
and kings for my sake,
for a testimony against them and the Gentiles.**

**But when they deliver you up,
take no thought how or what ye shall speak:
for it shall be given you in that same hour what ye shall speak.**

**For it is not ye that speak,
but the Spirit of your Father which speaketh in you.**

Matthew 10:5, 16–20

GOODNESS: MEDIUM SOFT PART OF THE FRUIT

The "Goodness" part of the fruit of the Spirit is present to help Christians "do the right thing" meaning the "righteous thing" by God's standard.

A person can be "good" or righteous from God's viewpoint by:

a) Being born of the Spirit by accepting Jesus Christ as their Lord
b) Doing good works because they are born of the Spirit

Read Romans 3:9–18, Isaiah 64:6–7, Ezekiel 36:25–27, Hebrews 8:6, 10-12.

> Before a person is born of the Spirit (or born again) by accepting Jesus Christ as the Lord and Savior of their life, the Bible passages above reveal that they cannot be considered a "good" person according to God's definition of what it means to be good. No one is born with the right spirit to be or do "good" by God's standard.

Read Ephesians 2:1–10, 2 Corinthians 5:17, 21; Titus 3:4–6 and 1 John 3:7–10.

> A person can only become "good" or "right" or "righteous" in God's eyes after they repent of being a sinner and ask Jesus to become the new Lord (meaning leader) of their life. Through their faith in the risen Jesus Christ, a person's sinful nature is changed from being like God's adversary Satan, to being like their new heavenly Father God's nature.

After a person becomes a Christian (meaning a follower of Christ), the Bible says the Christian will be known because they do two things. They

Do Not Sin
(1 John 3:9)

and

Do Good Works
(Ephesians 2:10)

This is why the Holy Spirit places the "Goodness" part of His fruit inside the born-again Christian.

**Without the help of the Holy Spirit,
it is impossible for anyone to
be good and do good by God's standard.**

When the Holy Spirit is within us, He works to help us live sin free and to do good works that are pleasing to God. (Hebrews 13:20 – 21)

Doing the right thing all the time is not easy even with the Holy Spirit's help.

Here are four example reasons of why being a "good" person, who does the right thing all the time, is difficult:

1. Your friends, family and even strangers may make fun of you because you do not want to do some of the things they do.

2. Your willingness to do what is right will lead you down a lonely road at times because others around you want to do some wrong things.

3. Sometimes your ideas of what is right are different from what other people believe to be right. This could be because you know what the Bible says is right or because the Holy Spirit is leading you in the path of righteousness, so that you feel confident that you are right.

4. Sometimes you do not have enough knowledge of God's Word or have the confidence in following the leading of the Holy Spirit. This may result in temporarily doing something that is not right.

Here are encouraging words from the Bible on why you should:

Continue to do what is good and right even when it is not easy.

Pray and ask the Holy Spirit to help, lead, and guide you daily.

♦ You are the Salt of the Earth and the Light of the World!
Matthew 5:13–15

♦ Your good works will cause people to see the true nature of the only wise God our Savior.
Matthew 5:16, Jude 25

♦ Your good works will one day cause others around you to become Christians.
John 15:5, 8, 16

♦ In the long run, your good works will be rewarded here on earth and in the world to come.
Titus 3:8

Believe It or Not...

Believe It or Not: Sometimes being "good" means you need to stand up for what is right even if it makes people around you upset. (Daniel 3)

Believe It or Not: It was the goodness of God in Jesus that caused Him to get upset and turn the tables over in the temple. (Matthew 21:12–16)

Believe It or Not: It was the goodness of God in Jesus that caused Him to be direct in telling the Pharisees that they were hypocrites and unknowledgeable preachers. (Matthew 15:7–14; Matthew 22:29)

Believe It or Not: You may have to say or do things people do not agree with because the "goodness" of God within you makes you believe your actions are necessary. (Consider Proverbs 27:5 and Matthew 10:32–39)

Warning!

There is a way that seemeth right unto a man,
but the end thereof are the ways of death.
Proverbs 14:12

Enter ye in at the strait gate:

for wide is the gate,		**because strait is the gate,**
and broad is the way,		**and narrow is the way,**
that leadeth to	**Matthew 7:13–14**	**which leadeth unto**
destruction,		**life,**
and many there be		**and few there be**
which go in thereat		**that find it.**

The Bad Path is "WIDE" and Leads to Eternal Death	The Good Path is "NARROW" and Leads to Eternal Life

Ye are the light of the world.

A city that is set on an hill cannot be hid.

Matthew 5:14

Let your light so shine before men,

that they may see your good works,

and glorify your Father which is in heaven.

Matthew 5:16

MEEKNESS: VERY SOFT PART OF THE FRUIT

- Definition: What is "Meekness"?
- Purpose: Why does God want His children to be "Meek"?
- Results: What rewards do you get for being "Meek"?

- **Definition: What is Meekness?**

Christian meekness could be thought of as having four parts:

Part 1. New Attitude Towards God (Micah 6:8, James 3:13–18)
A person is meek when they accept the things that happen in their life, including bad experiences, as an opportunity for God to work out something special for them. They know that God loves and cares for them so much that He will allow nothing to occur in their life by accident. They patiently wait for God's amazing purpose to be accomplished in their every experience. They trust God.

Part 2. New Attitude Towards Others (Philippians 2:3–4, Titus 3:1–2)
A person is meek when they use kind, patient and gentle actions when dealing with others. They need the character of God.

Part 3. New Attitude About Life (1 Peter 5:5–7, James 1:21–25)
A person is meek when they understand that they do not know how to think correctly. They totally depend on God to show them the right way to think and act in every situation. They need to know God and His Word.

Part 4: New Attitude About Self (John 15:5, Matt. 22:37–40, Rom.12:3)
They know they can do NOTHING without God, God's love, God's faith.

> **The Meek Person has a New Attitude Towards God.**
> Micah 6:8, James 3:13–18

> **The Meek Person has a New Attitude Towards Others.**
> Philippians 2:3–4, Titus 3:1–2

> **The Meek Person has a New Attitude About Life.**
> 1 Peter 5:5–7, James 1:21–25

> **The Meek Person has a New Attitude About Self.**
> John 15:5, Matthew 22:37–40, Romans 12:3

- **Purpose: Why does God want His children to be Meek?**

  There are at least 3 reasons God wants His children to be meek:

  1. We cannot think in the way God wants us to think without God's help because our natural thoughts are not like God's. Isaiah 55:8 -9; Isaiah 64:6

  2. Our minds, with their thoughts, emotions, and desires, need to be transformed into thinking like God thinks. Romans 12:1–2, Ephesians 4:23–24

  3. God knows what we do not know. He knows the mind, heart, history and potential of everyone. Also, God loves everyone equally so that He is the only one who can be just and fair in reaching out to everyone and in judging situations. When we are meek enough to follow God's instructions, God can use us to accomplish His will in reaching out to others, even when we do not understand everything He is doing. 1 Corinthians 13:9, 12; 2 Peter 3:9, James 2:1–9; Acts 10:34–35

- **Results: What rewards do you get for being Meek?**

  God rewards His children for having a meek character.

  Here are 7 rewards God promises His children will receive:

  1. God will guide the meek in judgment and teach the meek His way. Psalm 25:9

  2. God will beautify the meek with salvation. Psalm 149:4

  3. The meek will inherit the earth (meaning to possess or receive as a gift from God). Psalm 37:11, Matthew 5:5

  4. The Lord will lift the meek up. Psalm 147:6, 1 Peter 5:6

  5. The meek shall increase their joy in the Lord. Isaiah 29:19

  6. The meek shall eat and be satisfied. Psalm 22:26

  7. The meek will be able to help people who are hard to reach (such as fallen Christians and tough sinners) come to God. Galatians 6:1, 2 Timothy 2:24–26

But the fruit of the Spirit is…

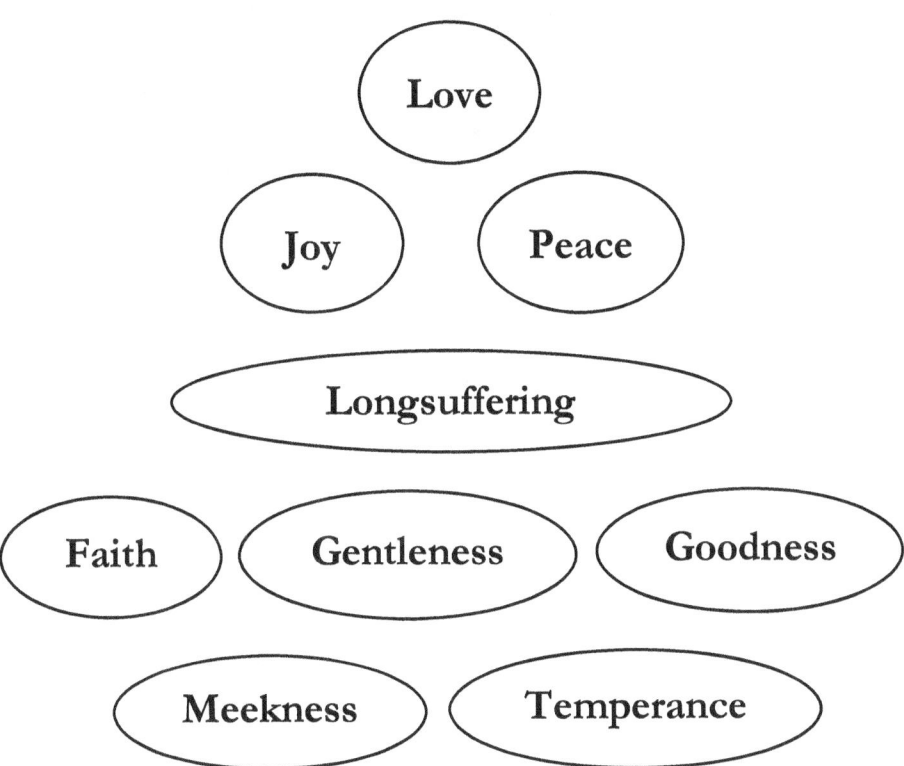

Love

Joy   Peace

Longsuffering

Faith   Gentleness   Goodness

Meekness   Temperance

against such there is no law.

A good tree cannot bring forth evil fruit,

Neither can a corrupt tree bring forth good fruit.

Wherefore by their fruits ye shall know them.

Matthew 7:18, 20

'If
the Fruit of the Spirit is not working in your lives,
then
the Gifts of the Spirit cannot work.'

Quote from Bishop Robert E. Woodard, Jr.

After a person has been born and filled with the Spirit, the person should first allow the Holy Spirit to transform his or her own life into the image of Christ. Once the Christian is a walking, talking, Christ-like child of God, then they can become a great witness for God. God will be able to work through the changed Christian to perform His mighty acts.

On the other hand, when a person confesses to be a Christian, but their lifestyle does not change from the way it was before they became a Christian, then their Christian walk seems phony. This type of Christian behavior turns people who do not know God away from desiring to follow Him.

This is why the first job of every Christian is to allow the fruit of the Spirit to make them more like Christ day by day. Then the gifts of the Spirit will flow through them to everyone's benefit.

Jesus said,

"Not every one that saith unto me, Lord, Lord, shall enter into the kingdom of heaven; but he that doeth the will of my Father which is in heaven.

Many will say to me in that day, Lord, Lord, have we not prophesied in thy name? and in thy name cast out devils? And in thy name done many wonderful works?

And then will I profess unto them, I never knew you: depart from me, ye that work iniquity."

Matthew 7:21–23

"But be ye doers of the word, and not hearers only, deceiving your own selves.

For if any be a hearer of the word, and not a doer, he is like unto a man beholding his natural face in a glass:

For he beholdeth himself, and goeth his way, and straightway forgetteth what manner of man he was.

But whoso looketh into the perfect law of liberty, and continueth therein, he being not a forgetful hearer, but a doer of the work, this man shall be blessed in his deed."

James 1:22–25

Chapter 8:

This Spirit's for You!

(That is, Nothing but the Holy Spirit)

Adult Bible Study Handouts

Chapter 8

Detailed Contents

Note:

This section contains handout material for Adult Bible Study sessions.

Some of the material is new from that presented in the Lesson sections.

Some of the material is repeated from the Prep and Lesson sections.

All the material in this section is organized to be a quick reference study guide and a review summary.

TABLE 8-1 JESUS AND THE HOLY SPIRIT

Table 8-1 Jesus and the Holy Spirit highlights what Jesus did and said as it relates to the Holy Spirit during His first coming to earth. Scripture references are primarily taken from the Bible book Gospel of John.

Scripture	Jesus and the Holy Spirit (HG/HS=Holy Ghost/Spirit)	Additional References/Comments
John 1:33	Jesus was baptized with water and filled with HG	Luke 3:21-22 Jesus prays, 4:1
John 1:33	Jesus baptizes believers with the Holy Ghost	Matthew 3:11, Mark 1:8; Acts 1:4-5
John 1:47-51; 2:1-11	Jesus manifests spiritual gifts and miracles only after being filled with the Holy Ghost	Word of Knowledge + First Miracle/ Luke 2:40,52; Isaiah 11:1-2, 50:4-5
John 3:3-8	Jesus explains being Born of the Spirit	John 1:12-13, 2 Corinthians 5:17,21
John 3:34-35	Once filled, God gave Jesus the full measure of HG, not just a portion of His Spirit	Not limited like: Moses and men in Numbers 11:17, 24-29 and double portion on Elisha in 2 Kings 2:9-10
John 4:24 (John 14:15-17; 16:7,13)	God is a Spirit; we must worship Him in Spirit and in truth	I Cor 2:9-14 we need HS to understand the things of God
John 5:19-20	Jesus did nothing of Himself but did what He saw God do, as led by the Holy Spirit	Acts 10:38, Matthew 12:28 (Matt 1:23b - Emmanuel)
John 6:63	Jesus says "It is the spirit that quickens"	Quicken: to impart spiritual life
John 7:38-39	Out of belly flow rivers of living water = HG	HG not yet given; Jesus not yet glorified
John 8:59 (7:46)	Jesus moves through the people unseen	(Jesus taught with authority and did miracles)

TABLE 8-1 JESUS AND THE HOLY SPIRIT CONTINUED

Scripture	Jesus and the Holy Spirit (HG/HS=Holy Ghost/Spirit)	Additional References/Comments
John 9	Jesus healed man who had been born blind	John 9:32-33 never done before
John 10:37-38; 14:12	Jesus did Father's good works by HG	Acts 10:38, Matthew 12:28
John 11:49-52	Spirit of prophecy on sinful High Priest Caiaphas, to make God's plan happen	Similar to how the Spirit came on backslidden Balaam in Num. 22-24
John 12:1-8	Jesus discerned people's spiritual actions	Mary was not wasting perfume
John 13:3-11	Spirit caused Jesus to be humble, to serve	Philippians 2:5-11, Jesus knew who He was
John Chapters 14, 15, 16	Jesus teaches on HS to disciples before his agony in the garden	Chapters 14, 15 and 16 have lots of info on the Holy Spirit
John 14:15-16; John 14:26; 16:7	Jesus sends the Comforter, which is the Holy Ghost, to walk alongside each believer to provide help and counsel forever	Greek word Parakletos: HS is our help on earth (Rom. 8:26-27), Jesus is help/advocate in heaven (1 John 2:1, Heb 7:25)
John 14:17	Spirit of truth, whom world cannot receive	All people do not have HS; Romans 8:9, 1 Corinthians 2:9-14
John 14:17	Jesus explained a greater relationship with HS was coming, from with you to in you	John 16:7,12-15, 23-24, Jesus had to go away
John 14:21-23	How HS is manifest to believers but not to world	God and Jesus abide in us by HS
John 14:26	HS will teach us all things, bring all things to our remembrance Jesus taught	Father sends HS in Jesus' name to teach us all things 1 John 2:20, 27

TABLE 8-1 JESUS AND THE HOLY SPIRIT CONTINUED

Scripture	Jesus and the Holy Spirit (HG/HS=Holy Ghost/Spirit)	Additional References/Comments
John 15:26	Comforter = Spirit of Truth, testifies of Jesus	(John 12:32)
John 16:7	HS will reprove the world of sin, of righteousness and of judgment	Reprove means to convict, convince, or call attention to with intent to assist you in changing
John 16:12-15	Spirit of truth will guide you into all truth, He shall not speak of Himself; but speak whatever He hears, show us things to come, and GLORIFY JESUS	Messages from God the Father to Jesus to Holy Spirit to You John 12:49; John 14:10
John 17: 20-23	Same glory, same oneness, same ability to hear from God what to do	Ephesians 2:17-22
John 18:15-27	Peter denied Jesus despite having some level of the Spirit and faith	Mark 6:7–13, John 13:37, 14:17
John 20:21-23	Jesus breathes HS on disciples=born of Spirit	Genesis 2:7 disciples became new living souls
Acts 1:2-8	Jesus told disciples to wait for the promise of the Holy Ghost before proceeding to spread the Gospel / witness	Luke 24:49, Mark 16:15-20, (Acts 2:32-33, 38-39)

Three big enemies of the Church are:
1. Ignorance (Hosea 4:6) and 2. Unbelief (Matthew 13:58)
and 3. Fear (1 John 4:18)

Study & Meditate on God's Word to be Blessed!
(Romans 10:17, 2 Timothy 2:15, Psalm 1)

YOU AND THE HOLY SPIRIT—JUST LIKE JESUS
(BORN, FILLED, FRUIT, GIFTS, PRAYING, FLOWING)

Purpose and History for the Coming of the Holy Spirit

God moved from a few having His Spirit on them to all being able to have His Spirit in them

> ➢ Ezekiel 36:26-27 – God foretold prophets He would put His Spirit in people & give them a new heart so they could keep His judgments. Galatians 3:13-29, Ephesians 2:17-22 (Acts 2:38-39, Heb 9:13-22)

> ➢ Joel 2:28-29 – God foretold that He would pour out His Spirit upon all flesh so all could prophesy

Old Testament Feasts of the Lord for Israel represented major New Testament spiritual events, including Holy Spirit coming to bring in last days soul harvest, 50 days after Jesus' resurrection.

> ➢ Feast of Firstfruits represented Jesus' resurrection Leviticus 23:9-14, 1 Corinthians 15:20,23

> ➢ Feast of Weeks = Harvest = Pentecost = 50 days after Firstfruits Leviticus 23:15-21, Exodus 23:16; Acts 2:1; Acts 1:3 => Acts 2:1 when the Day of Pentecost was fully come which represented the beginning of God's worldwide soul harvest

A. Born of the Spirit

Believing in Jesus, that God raised Him from the dead, and accepting the risen Jesus as your Lord and Savior is how you become Born of the Spirit of God. (Born of the Spirit = Born-again = becoming Saved)
John 1:12-13, John 3:3-6, 16-18, Romans 10:9-10, 2 Cor 5:17

B. Filled with the Spirit

Several scriptures make it clear that after believers believe on Christ, being filled with the Holy Spirit is a separate experience with the same Holy Spirit. Acts 2:1-4; Acts 8:5-17-24; Acts 19:1-6; Luke 11:9-13

C. Fruit of the Spirit

",,, love, joy, peace, longsuffering, gentleness, goodness, faith, meekness, temperance: against such there is no law. "If we live in the Spirit, let us also walk in the Spirit." Galatians 5:22-25; Romans 8:13

'If the Fruit of the Spirit is not working in your lives, then the Gifts of the Spirit cannot work.' (quote by Bishop R.E. Woodard, Jr., 1998)

D. Gifts of the Spirit

**"Now there are diversities of gifts, but the same Spirit...
differences of administrations, but the same Lord. And there are
diversities of operations, but it is the same God which works all in all."**
1 Corinthians 12: 4–6 [Role of the Triune God in the Church]

YOU AND THE HOLY SPIRIT—JUST LIKE JESUS CONTINUED
(BORN, FILLED, FRUIT, GIFTS, PRAYING, FLOWING)

➢ **Nine Spiritual Gifts** – I Corinthians 12:1-11 (separate handout has details)

1. Gifts of revelation – the mind gifts (supernatural thoughts from God)
   a) Word of Wisdom, b) Word of Knowledge, c) Discerning of spirits

2. Gifts of power – working gifts (supernatural power from God)
   a) Faith, b) Working of Miracles, c) Gifts of Healing

3. Gifts of inspiration – vocal gifts (supernatural speech from God)
   a) Prophecy, b) Divers kinds of tongues, c) Interpretation of tongues

➢ **Seven Gifts of Grace** – Romans 12:6-8
Prophecy, Ministering, Teaching, Exhortation, Giving, Ruling, Mercy

➢ **Five-fold Ministry Gifts** – Ephesians 4:7-16
Apostles, Prophets, Evangelists, Pastors, Teachers

➢ **Ministers** – 1 Timothy 3:1-13; Titus 1:5-9; Acts 6:1-6
Bishops, Elders & Deacons

➢ **Ministry of Helps** – 1 Corinthians 12:28
Example: Romans 16:1-6

➢ **Ministry of Governments** – 1 Corinthians 12:28
Example: Acts 15:1-31

➢ **Every Church Member's Gift is Important** – 1 Corinthians 12:13-31

E. Praying with the Spirit – *1 Corinthians 14:14-15*
*'Your language in the Spirit is of all languages, unique. It is many-sided in its effects, for when you speak in tongues, many things are accomplished.
You worship me, you magnify Me, you intercede for others, and you edify yourself, all inclusive.'* (Message to Intercessors from the Lord, circa 1998)

> John 7:38 – Out of your innermost being…
>
> I Corinthians 14:2 – Speak to God mysteries…
>
> John 4:23, 24 – Worship God…
>
> Acts 10:46 – Magnify God…
>
> Romans 8:26, 27 – Intercession…
>
> I Corinthians 14:4 & Jude 20 – Edify, build up

- ◆ The Spirit helps us pray according to God's will. Romans 8:26-27
- ◆ We do not always understand what the Spirit is saying when He prays through us. Ephesians 6:18, Romans 8:26, 1 Corinthians 14: 4, 13-16
- ◆ Praying with the Spirit without the Word of God is not enough to change you into a strong Christian. Matthew 22:29, John 7:38-39
- ◆ Praying in Spirit without the love of God filling your heart is not enough to develop you into a strong Christian. I Corinthians 13

F. False spiritual experiences

1 John 4:1-6

> "Beloved, believe not every spirit, but try the spirits whether they are of God: because many false prophets are gone out into the world."
> (1 John 4:1-2)

Deuteronomy 18:10-12, Leviticus 19:26-31

> Beware of counterfeits to God's Spiritual Gifts that lead to destruction such as: witchcraft, charmers, cults, astrologists, familiar spirits, palm readers, Ouija boards, séances, and other occult activities which have demonic influences behind them.

Colossians 2:8

> "Beware lest any man spoil you through philosophy and vain deceit, after the tradition of men…"

Acts 8:9-11

> Magic spells, mind readers, gurus, metaphysical groups, curses, and the like have demonic influences behind them.

G. Flowing with the Spirit of God

Born of the Spirit

=> Filled with the Spirit

=> Rooted and grounded in God's Word

=> Developing the Fruit of the Spirit

=> Rooted and grounded in God's Love

=> Operating in Gifts of the Spirit

=> Harvesting souls for Christ!

> Then saith he [Jesus] unto his disciples,
> The harvest truly is plenteous, but the labourers are few;
> Pray ye therefore the Lord of the harvest,
> that he will send forth labourers into his harvest.
> Matthew 9:37–38

SPEAKING IN TONGUES – WHAT THE BIBLE SAYS

Scriptures show that being filled (baptized) **with the Holy Spirit is:**
- for all believers in Jesus Christ who are born of the Spirit
- continues to be available for today's believers, including the evidence of speaking in tongues, which means speaking in foreign languages, foreign to and unlearned by the speaker

The below scriptures give support to speaking in tongues for all believers:

1. Mark 16:16-20 — One of the Signs that follows believers
2. Luke 11:9-13 — HS given to those who ask, seek and knock for it
3. Acts 2:38-39 — HS is promised to all believers, those who are afar off (far away such as Gentiles or future), and for children
4. Acts 8:14-24 — HS given to the Samaritans
5. Acts 10:44-48 — HS given to the Gentiles, too
6. Acts 19:2-7 — Paul said to some disciples, "Have ye received the HS since ye believed?"; then laid hands on them to receive
7. Ephesians 5:18 — Commandment: Be filled with the HS
8. Eph 1:19, 3:20 — Greatness of God's power extended to all who believe
9. Romans 8:32 — With Jesus, God freely gives us all things
10. 1 Cor. 14:5-28 — Apostle Paul gives instructions on speaking in tongues in the Church assembly and in private prayer time

Eight ways the King James Version refers to speaking in tongues:
(tongues refers to different languages that are foreign to the speaker)

1. Isaiah 28:11 — Stammering lips and another tongue
2. Mark 16:17 — Speak with new tongues
3. Romans 8:26 — Groanings which cannot be uttered
4. I Corinthians 12:10, 28 — Divers kinds / diversities of tongues
5. I Corinthians 13:1 — Tongues of men
6. I Corinthians 13:1 — Tongues of angels
7. I Corinthians 14:2 — Unknown tongue
8. I Corinthians 14:21 — Other tongues and other lips

Reasons for speaking in other tongues

(This list primarily describes tongues as a prayer language in private)

1. God wanted to use another way to communicate to His people – Isaiah 28:9-11, 1 Corinthians 14:21
2. Praying in tongues provides for spiritual refreshing – Isaiah 28:10-12
3. Sign that follows them that believe – Mark 16:17
4. Tongues, initial sign of baptism/filling with the Holy Ghost – Acts 1:5, 2:1–4
5. Praying in tongues/groanings aligns prayers with God's will – Rom. 8:26-27
6. Praying in tongues helps with praying for the unknown – Romans 8:26–27, 1 Corinthians 14:14–15
7. Speaks mysteries in the spirit unto God – 1 Corinthians 14:2
8. Tongues for personal spiritual edification – 1 Corinthians 14:4
9. When you pray in tongues your spirit is praying – 1 Corinthians 14:4
10. Tongues allows your spirit to pray and sing – 1 Corinthians 14:14-15
11. Tongues for giving thanks to God – 1 Corinthians 14:15-17
12. Sign for them that do not believe – 1 Corinthians 14:22
13. Benefits personal communication with God – 1 Corinthians 14:28
14. Praying in the Holy Ghost helps build faith – Jude 20

Speaking in other tongues in Public

1. Do not use speaking in tongues if actions are not motivated by God's charity (love) – 1 Corinthians 12:30–31 and 1 Corinthians chapter 13.
2. Do not behave unseemly; Do seek to benefit others – 1 Cor. 13:5, 14:23
3. Sign to the unbeliever – 1 Corinthians 14:22
4. Intercessory Prayer – Romans 8:26-27 (God's will), Ephesians 6:18 (Spirit-led); 1 Corinthians 14:14-19 (limit tongues in public)
5. Spiritual gift of divers kinds of tongues plus interpretation of tongues equal gift of prophecy – 1 Corinthians 14:5–13 (1 Corinthians 12:10)
6. Do not go forth in tongues (messages from the Lord in tongues) if there is no interpreter – 1 Corinthians 14:28
7. Limit tongues and interpretation of tongues (messages from the Lord in tongues) per instructions – 1 Corinthians 14:26-28
8. Do not use tongues to disrupt prophecy, preached word, God's truth – 1 Corinthians 14:6-13, 19, 23-25
9. Do not forbid to speak with tongues, but let all things be done decent and in order – 1 Corinthians 14:39-40

Explanation on why Jesus did not speak in tongues

- Jesus came to minister to the Israelites. (Matthew 15:21-28)

- When Jesus was filled with the Holy Spirit, His sign or evidence that He was filled with the Holy Spirit came in the shape of a dove resting upon Him and the voice of God from heaven. (Luke 3:21-22)

- Jesus gives speaking in tongues as a sign. (Mark 16:16-20)

There is a "decent and in order" use associated with speaking in tongues

1 Corinthians 14:26-33

If when you pray in tongues you are disruptive to the flow of what a spiritual leader or presenter is doing, but you feel a burden to pray, then either

    a.   pray under your breath

    b.   leave the room or

    c.   stop praying in the Spirit.

You always are in control of when you operate the spiritual gifts. This is because "the spirits of the prophets are subject to the prophets." (I Corinthians 14:32)

Finally

Do NOT seek after signs!

Do NOT seek after tongues!

DO seek to be filled with the Holy Spirit of God!

When you are filled with the Holy Spirit of God, the tongues will manifest themselves immediately, or in due time, or one of the other manifestations will appear in your life. (Acts 2:17-18)

All who are filled with the Holy Spirit do not speak in tongues, but the scripture indicates the ability to speak in tongues is available to all believers as a sign. (Mark 16:17)

Pray without ceasing by the Holy Spirit!

Being filled with the Holy Spirit
and speaking in tongues
help the believer to
"pray without ceasing"
as instructed in

1 Thessalonians 5:17–20

NINE SPIRITUAL GIFTS DEFINED

Introduction

Reference Books
- "Holy Bible" – King James Version (KJV)
- "The Gifts and Ministries of the Holy Spirit" by Dr. Lester Sumrall
- "Questions and Answers on Spiritual Gifts" by Howard Carter
- "Know His Spirit Bible Study" by Jennifer B. Price - Chapter 6: Spiritual Gifts

---

"Now concerning spiritual gifts, brethren, I would not have you ignorant."
1 Corinthians 12:1

**"Follow after charity, and desire spiritual gifts,
but rather that ye may prophesy."**
1 Corinthians 14:1

**The Nine Spiritual Gifts are Supernatural and of the Holy Spirit of God—
Not Carnal, Not Natural, Not "Soulical"—
meaning they are not a result of the human mind's work.**

- Holy Spirit is omnipotent – He has unlimited authority or influence
  Zechariah 4:6, Luke 1:35–37, Ephesians 3:20

- Holy Spirit is omnipresent – He is present in all places, at all times
  Revelation 5:6, Proverbs 15:3, Psalm 139:7–10

- Holy Spirit is omniscient – Unlimited awareness, understanding and insight
  Job 34:21, Psalm 147:5, Hebrews 4:13

**Two Foundation stones that are prerequisite to Spiritual Gifts
operating properly within the Church—
1) Unity and 2) Love**

1 Corinthians Chapters 12 through 14 should be read as one contextual
passage of instruction on how the Spiritual Gifts should operate in the Church.

"Nine Spiritual Gifts Defined" Study Approach

For the purposes of this study, the nine spiritual gifts have been classified in
three categories:

- **Gifts of revelation** – mind gifts (supernatural thoughts from God)
  1) word of wisdom, 2) word of knowledge, 3) discerning of spirits

- **Gifts of power** – working gifts (supernatural power from God)
  4) faith, 5) working of miracles, 6) gifts of healing

- **Gifts of inspiration** – vocal gifts (supernatural speech from God)
  7) prophecy, 8) divers kinds of tongues, 9) interpretation of tongues

NINE SPIRITUAL GIFTS DEFINED

CATEGORY I. REVELATION GIFTS
— Word of Wisdom, Word of Knowledge, and Discerning of Spirits

In this prime category – the revelation gifts – the infinite God, Creator of the universe, is revealing His truth to humankind. There is a revelation from heaven of certain facts which a person could not know by way of their physical senses.

1) **Word of Wisdom** – not the gift of wisdom, but the "word" of wisdom

God gives a small portion of information from His vast storehouse of wisdom. Wisdom has to do with that which is unborn, or of the future. When God gives a word of His wisdom, He is revealing something that has not yet come to pass. The word of wisdom is a part or portion of the great omniscience of God.

➢ Examples:
  o God revealed to Noah the coming of the flood (Genesis 6:12, 13)
  o Jesus foretold signs that would accompany His return to Earth (Matthew 24, Luke 21:5-36, and Mark 13)
➢ Examples of How Manifested:
  o Joseph and Daniel through dreams, visions (Gen. 37-45, Daniel)

2) **Word of Knowledge** – a word of God's knowledge, not man's knowledge

This gift is related to fact. The gift of the word of knowledge deals with that which exists, whether it be in the past or in the present.

➢ Examples:
  o The Lord revealed Elisha's servant Gehazi's sin when he took money from Naaman (2 Kings 5:20-27)
  o Jesus knew Nathaniel sitting under tree (John 1:47-51)
  o Jesus knew Samaritan woman had been married 7 times and currently not married to man she's living with (John 4:5–42)

3) **Discerning of Spirits** – not a metaphysical or human mind operation

This gift is not thought reading, not psychoanalysis or projection of extrasensory perception, as it has nothing to do with the realm of the human mind or human spirit. It is not a discernment of things and not the gift of suspicion. It IS the discerning of spirits. Through this gift we can discern divine spirits, demonic spirits and the intention of the human or natural spirit. Through this gift, God reveals the spirit that motivates a human being's action, whether good or evil. This revelation comes from the Holy Spirit.
➢ Examples:
  o Peter discerned Simon, the soothsayer, wanted to lay hands on people to receive HS for profit and personal gain (Acts 8:9-24)
  o Peter discerned that Ananias & Sapphira lied to HG (Acts 5:1-11)

CATEGORY II. POWER GIFTS

— Gift of Faith, Working of Miracles, Gifts of Healing

In this second category – the power gifts – God imparts from omnipotent power to humankind. These power gifts involve a supernatural ability and energy which people do not naturally possess. Overall, the operation of spiritual gifts is like a chain. Often linked together with others in such a way that sometimes it is difficult to divide the links and distinguish between them. This is because they are so interrelated. We see this especially in the gifts of power as both the gift of faith and working of miracles operate together in the supernatural.

4) Faith – gift of faith, not the saving or measure of faith common to all

This is not the faith that everyone has according to each person having a measure of faith described in Romans 12:3. The "Gift of Faith" is in operation when God, through the power of HS, performs supernatural exploits that cannot be humanly explained. The gift of faith can operate in the areas of divine protection and divine provision for the person God uses to pronounce this faith.

➤ Examples:
- o Hebrew boys in fiery furnace, Daniel in lion's den (Daniel 3, 6)
- o Jesus sleeps in boat during violent storm (Mark 4:37–41)

5) Working of Miracles –

The Holy Spirit gives a person the ability to perform things, which are normally undoable or impossible by natural earthly laws.

➤ Examples:
- o Moses (Exodus 7-14)
- o Jesus feeds the 5000 (John 6:5-14)

6) Gifts of Healing –

This is the only gift of the nine that begins with "gifts". HS gives a supernatural power to heal all manner of sickness and diseases without scientific human aid or medicine, but no one has all aspects at one time.

➤ Examples:
- o Naaman healed in Jordan (2 Kings 5:1-14)
- o Jesus heals everywhere (Matthew 15:30-31)

➤ Examples of How Manifested:
- o by laying hands on people and praying for them
- o by speaking the Word of God to them
- o This is the only gift where only Jesus had the ability to heal EVERY type of disease and sickness. For example, believers may just have the gifts of healing for certain types of infirmities

CATEGORY III. INSPIRATION GIFTS
— Gift of Prophecy, Gift of Tongues, and Interpretation of Tongues.

In this third category – gifts of inspiration – God brings His anointing and His blessing to the Church when in corporate assembly together and upon individual members of the Church body in private.

7) Prophecy

HS gives a special message from God that is spoken in a familiar language to the hearers. The message includes words that lift the human spirit (edify), encourage the soul (exhort), and soothe the heart (comfort) of the hearer(s). 1 Corinthians 14:3-4

➢ Examples:

- o David's comforting good shepherd-reflecting Psalm (Psalm 23)

- o Jesus comforted people who were poor and sad (Matthew 5:1-12)

8) Divers Kinds of Tongues

HS gives a person special words or utterances that are spoken in different languages, all of which are foreign / unknown to the speaker.

➢ Examples:

- o Prophesied to come in the Old Testament (Isaiah 28:11)

- o Jesus foretold would come in the New Testament (Mark 16:17)

- o Instructions on use in Church assemblies (1 Corinthians 14:26-28)

9) Interpretation of Tongues

HS gives a person the ability to share the interpretation of a foreign language spoken by the spiritual gift of divers kinds of tongues where the foreign language is unknown by the speaker and by the person giving the interpretation. The message is a prophetic word that edifies, encourages, or comforts the individual, group, or the entire church.

➢ Scriptural explanation and instruction

- o Isaiah 28:9-12

- o Matthew 15:24

- o 1 Corinthians 14:5, 6, 12, 21-33

1. The Nine Spiritual **Gifts** of 1 Corinthians 12:8-10 (also called "Gifts of the Spirit" and "Sign Gifts") **ARE** supernatural manifestations from the Spirit of God. They **ARE NOT** an increase in or higher level of man's natural abilities or talents in the subject areas.

    For example:

    a. A person can receive wisdom from God (James 1:5-8, Proverbs 1:1-7) and a person can increase in the amount of wisdom they receive from seeking God's wisdom (Luke 2:52, Colossians 1:9-10), but this is different than the spiritual gift of the "word of wisdom." "Word of wisdom" is a supernatural thought from God transferred to a person specifically to reveal insight from God on His future plans or purpose. With this gift a "word" of wisdom is revealed not all of God's wisdom.

    b. Similarly, a person can have knowledge of spiritual things from studying God's word and can increase in this knowledge (1 Corinthians 2:9-16, 2 Peter 3:18), but this is different from the spiritual gift of the "word of knowledge." Through this gift a "word" from God's omniscient knowledge is revealed to an individual without their having any way to know the information themselves, whether it is from the present or in the past.

    c. Similarly, every believer has a measure of faith (Romans 12:3); and can obtain healings, miracles and many wonderful things through exercising a small amount of general faith in God and through increasing in this general faith (Matthew 17:20, Luke 17:5-6). However, saving and general faith is different than the spiritual gift of "Faith." This spiritual gift is supernaturally imparted to the believer for a specified event and does not depend on the believer's faith effort for that event.

        i. And so on and so forth it is with all the Gifts of the Spirit as compared with a human being's natural abilities that are spiritually blessed by God.

    d. **A person's natural abilities and talents that are blessed by God AND the manifestations of the nine spiritual gifts in and through a believer's life are equally important. One should not be favored over the other. It is very important that believers desire to flow in the spiritual gifts... without neglecting "working out their own salvation with fear and trembling."** (Philippians 2:12-13)

2. Spiritual Gifts have to do with "Dunamis" (Acts 1:8) and "Energes" (James 5:16) power (Greek words), which picture a transfer of God's power to believers in an explosive, dynamite manner with great effective, working energy resulting in fulfillment of God's powerful, positive purpose. They operate as "signs and wonders" or as God's calling cards drawing unbelievers to Christ as believers manifest the Spirit of God, and bear witness, therefore, to the Lord. The manifestation of the Spirit is given to every believer to profit their lives and the lives of others. (1 Corinthians 12:7, 11; 1 Peter 4:10)

3. The working of Satan includes power and signs and lying wonders (2 Thessalonians 2:1-10), such that it will take the power of the True and Living God, through the Spirit of Truth, to war against and expose Satan's lying wonders. (2 Thessalonians 1:11-12)

4. These Bible Study lessons provide an "introduction" on the Gifts of the Spirit and are by no means an in-depth study. The purpose of these lessons is to "whet your whistle" so to speak on the topic and hopefully get you to desire spiritual gifts, by providing you with a balanced foundational understanding of what they are and how you can get them. Although the Holy Spirit is the one that determines which gifts and how many gifts of the Spirit the believer receives (1 Corinthians 12:8-11), believers are instructed to do several things to prepare to obtain these gifts. You receive the gifts of the Spirit by...

   a. First - Born of the Spirit (John 3:3; 14:17); then - Filled with the Spirit (Acts 1:8); then - Follow after charity and Desire spiritual gifts (1 Corinthians 14:1); and Covet earnestly the best gifts (1 Corinthians 12:31)

   b. You keep the Gifts of the Spirit flowing through your life by

      i. Understanding how they operate (Hosea 4:6; Proverbs 4:7)

      ii. Walking in Faith, Love, and Unity (Galatians 5:6, 1 Corinthians Chapters 12 through 14)

      iii. Keeping un-confessed sin and weights out of your life (Hebrews Chapter 12)

5. The first work of being filled with the Spirit is to help you, the believer, to clean up and strengthen your own walk with God (Romans Chapter 8), making you more like Christ. Then the Gifts of the Spirit will be ready to flow properly in your life. (Galatians 5:16-26)

6. It is very important to believe on Jesus **as the scriptures has said**, then the believer will receive the abundant flow of the Holy Spirit in their lives. (John 7:38-39; Matthew 22:29; 2 Peter 1:1-11)

7. The passage of scripture in 1 Corinthians 12:4, 7-11, 13 is clear that there are diversities of gifts, but the same Spirit distributes them to believers as He wills. Ephesians 4:3-4 is clear that there is only one Spirit of God. Yet, Revelations 5:6 refers to the seven Spirits of God.

> **"And I beheld, and, lo, in the midst of the throne**
> **and of the four beasts, and in the midst of the elders,**
> **stood a Lamb as it had been slain,**
> **having seven horns and seven eyes,**
> **which are the seven Spirits of God**
> **sent forth into all the earth."**
> Revelation 5:6

To understand the explanation for this seeming discrepancy in God's Word, you must understand how God teaches us knowledge of His word, and how He makes us to understand doctrine. Specifically, the Word of the Lord is revealed to us as "precept upon precept, line upon line, here a little, and there a little" (Isaiah 28:9, 10, 13). This means you must read many scriptures on a topic to get the proper big picture understanding of doctrine/knowledge. Therefore, the explanation on how Revelation 5:6 describes the Holy Spirit can be best understood when you also read Isaiah 11:1-2, Isaiah 61:1, John 1:33; and Luke 3:22, 4:14, 18-21.

> "And the
> **1) spirit of the Lord** shall rest upon him, the
> **2) spirit of wisdom** and
> **3) understanding**, the
> **4) spirit of counsel** and
> **5) might**, the
> **6) spirit of knowledge** and of the
> 7) **fear of the Lord**"
> (Isaiah 11:2 with *bold & numbers by the author*)

The fullness and power of the Holy Spirit of God covers these seven areas when manifested unquenched in the body of Christ! These do not represent titles, because the Holy Spirit has many more titles, but rather the perfect work abilities of the Spirit.

Read the following to have assistance in reading and understanding the entire Bible, from Genesis to Revelation, **Know His Word Bible Study – 1st, 2nd, 3rd and 4th Quarter** books, **by Jennifer B. Price**. Website: **knowbiblestudies.com**

SPIRITUAL GIFTS ARE GIVEN TO EVERY MAN TO PROFIT WITHAL

"But the manifestation of the Spirit is given to every man to profit withal."
1 Corinthians 12:7

**"As every man hath received the gift,
even so minister the same one to another,
as good stewards of the manifold grace of God"**
1 Peter 4:10

Bible Old Testament

A few Israelites were filled with the Spirit before the Day of Pentecost

Below are 7 examples of the Holy Spirit said to be IN, INTO and WITHIN men, before the experience of New Testament Acts Chapter 2 took place.

1. Joseph – Genesis 41:38
2. Moses – Isaiah 63:11
3. Joshua – Numbers 27:18
4. David – Psalm 51:10
5. Ezekiel – Ezekiel 2:2; 3:24
6. Daniel – Daniel 4:8, 18; 5:11-14; 6:3
7. John the Baptist & his parents – Luke 1:13-17, 41, 67 (New Testament passage but John was the last of the Old Testament type Prophets)

Old Testament saints had many HS experiences and blessings, as follows:

Filled with Spirit Exodus 28:3; 31:3; 35:31; Deuteronomy 34:9; Micah 3:8

Had the Spirit IN Genesis 41:38; Numbers 27:18; Daniel 4:8, 18; 5:11-14; 6:3

Within Psalm 51:10-11; Isaiah 63:10-14

Into Ezekiel 2:2; 3:24

Upon Numbers 11:17-29; Judges 3:10; 6:34; 11:29; 14:6, 19; 15:14

"Moved" many Judges 13:24, 2 Peter 1:21

Bible New Testament

Jesus sent the experience of Him baptizing believers with the Holy Spirit after His Ascension

Matthew 3:11-12; Mark 1:8; Luke 24:49; John 1:33; Acts 1:4-14, Acts Chapter 2

Today! YOUR TURN! Read On!

See the handout:
"How to Receive Being Filled with the Holy Spirit"

HOW TO RECEIVE BEING FILLED WITH THE HOLY SPIRIT

Definition: The expression "filled with the Holy Ghost (same as Holy Spirit)**" describes the experience in which a person receives from God, in their spirit, extra power and boldness to live and witness for God.** (John 7:38-39, John Chapters 14, 15, 16; Acts 1:8, 2:1-40)

> The expressions "received the Holy Ghost" (Acts 19:2), "filled with the Holy Ghost" (Acts 2:4), and "baptized with the Holy Ghost" (Acts 1:5) all refer to the same experience.

A. Jesus has already sent the Holy Spirit to us.

> ➤ Before Jesus passion and death, He promised He would send the Holy Spirit – John 14:16, 26; John 16:7, Luke 11:13, 24:49, Acts 1:2-8

> ➤ After Jesus' resurrection and ascension, He sent the Holy Spirit just like He said He would – Acts 2:1-4

> ➤ After the Holy Spirit was sent, the apostles confirmed that the Holy Spirit was now available for everyone to receive – Acts 2:17-18, 38-39; Galatians 3:13-14

B. The cleansing power in Jesus' blood makes believers eligible to receive being filled with the Holy Spirit in the instance of their New Birth into the Kingdom of God (New Birth = born again = born of the Spirit = Saved)

> ➤ **First: Before you can be filled with the Holy Spirit, you must be born of the Spirit** – Colossians 1:12-14; John 1:12-13, 3:3-8, 16-18, Romans 10:9-10, 2 Corinthians 5:17, John 14:17, Acts 19:1-6

> ➤ **Second: When you are born of the Spirit, the blood of Jesus washes you clean from all sin. You become the righteousness of God by the powerful work of God's grace and your faith.**
> Being clean enough or good enough before you are filled with the Holy Spirit can never be accomplished by any human effort. – 2 Corinthians 5:17, 21; Romans 5:1-9; Ephesians 2:4-9; Hebrews 9:13-15; Hebrews 10:10, 19-23

> ➤ **Hunger and thirst after righteousness:**

> > ○ You can be filled with the Holy Spirit immediately following your New Birth experience – Acts 19:1-7

> > ○ **To hunger and thirst after righteousness is instructed and rewarded by God.** – Matthew 5:6; Luke 11:9-13, Hebrews 11:6

> **Hunger and thirst after righteousness continued:**

  o When we hunger and thirst after righteousness, then the Holy Spirit helps us identify and mortify the deeds of our sinful flesh. Romans 8:13, 26; Colossians 3:1-17. We need the Spirit in us to help us to live pure, holy lives – Romans 7:15-25; 8:1-14

  o There can be hindrances to you receiving the Holy Spirit immediately after you are born again, and for that reason you should continue to seek God through yielding your mind, body and soul to draw closer to God. (hunger and thirst for Him)

C. YOU just RECEIVE the Holy Spirit

1) The Holy Ghost is a gift; 2) God has already given Him; 3) It is up to us to receive Him. It is not a matter of God giving us the Holy Spirit. It is a matter of our receiving being filled with the Holy Spirit. – Acts 2:38; 8:15, 19; 19:2

> When the Holy Spirit moves upon you, He will bring a supernaturally inspired utterance, but YOU must speak it out in faith. The Holy Spirit will not force you. YOU must speak, as the Spirit gives YOU utterance Acts 2:4

> If you do not receive the Holy Spirit immediately with the sign of the evidence of speaking in tongues, then work on your faith and "yielded-ness" and/or pray the **blood of Jesus to remove/destroy the work of demonic spirits that could hinder you from having an assurance that you have received being filled with the Holy Spirit.**

Note:

- Like human blood imparts life in the physical body, Jesus' Blood imparts Spiritual life to us. Genesis 2:7, Leviticus 17:11, Hebrews 10:5-23, Ephesians 1:5-7, Rom. 3:24-25, 1 John 5:8

- The blood of Jesus purges your conscience. You spiritually sprinkle His blood on the heavenly altar when you pray. Then Jesus' Blood and Word will obtain a sure victory for you to receive all of God's promises and gifts for your life. – Hebrews 9:11–28, Hebrews 12:24, Revelation 12:9-11

Exercise:

Complete "**Table 5-1: Methods of Receiving the Holy Spirit**" on the next page that reviews New Testament experiences.

HOW TO RECEIVE BEING FILLED WITH THE HOLY SPIRIT

Table 5-1: Methods of Receiving the Holy Spirit *

Directions: Read the Reference Scriptures and then fill in the blanks.
For some answers feel free to use words like "many" for the
"# of People" column and "in the city" for the "Where Filled" column.

How Filled	Reference Scriptures	# of People	Where Filled	What Evidence
A believer, who has the gift from God, can lay their hands on your head and pray that you are filled with the Holy Spirit, and you're immediately filled	Acts 8:5–6, 12, 14–17	_____	_____	See Acts 8:18
	Acts 9:17	_____	_____	See 1 Cor. 14:18
	Acts 19:1–7	_____	_____	
You can be with a group of people who all have the desire to be filled. As you ask God to fill you, then you all receive Him.	Acts 1:13–15, Acts 2:1–4	_____	_____	_____
	Acts 4:31–33	_____	_____	_____
You can be filled with the Holy Spirit following being born again.	Acts 19:1–7	_____	_____	
You become filled at some unknown amount of time after you are born of the Spirit.	Acts 8:12 - 17			See Acts 8:18
You can just hear the wonderful Gospel message and become filled.	Acts 10:1–8, 19–48			
You can be alone seeking God to be filled & it happens.	Mark 16:17	_____	_____	
	Luke 11:9–13	_____	_____	
You can be filled while praising and worshipping God, deep in your heart.	Ephesians 5:18 –21	_____	_____	

* Table 5-1 is from Chapter 5 in "Know His Spirit Bible Study" by Jennifer B. Price

PRAYER: FOR YOU TO RECEIVE THE HOLY SPIRIT

Pray this Prayer to Receive the Holy Spirit

In the Name of my Lord and Savior Jesus Christ, I accept God's gift of the Holy Spirit. I bind the spirit of unbelief. I loose the dynamic, effective working power of the Holy Spirit to confirm God's Word to me with God's signs following, according to the truth of God's Word that I have heard, studied and meditated upon. I pray for the precious Blood of Jesus to bind any work of the enemy that would keep me from being baptized by Jesus with the Holy Ghost. By the access I have to God's gift, through the wonder-working power in Jesus' Blood, and the mighty power in Jesus' Name, I receive the Holy Spirit right now.

Instructions on what to do after the prayer:

1. **Confess** — To God that you love Him and want to live for Him daily. You repent of all your sins, and you accept His Son Jesus Christ to be the Lord and Savior of your life. You acknowledge that you need to be filled with His Holy Spirit to help you live for Him daily.

2. **Praise God** — For giving you the gift of His Holy Spirit to bless you, help you and empower you to live for Him and to be a bold witness for Jesus.

3. **Thank Jesus** — For His precious Blood which is alive and cleanses your heart from sin and purges your evil conscience, thereby making you worthy to be filled with God's Holy Spirit.

4. **By Faith Profess** — You Receive God's gift of the Holy Spirit right now!

5. **Joyfully Express** — Praise to the Lord, while your body is relaxed and your tongue is yielded. Relax and receive the utterance of speaking in other tongues from the gentle Holy Spirit. If the utterances you speak do not sound like a distinguishable language, keep praising God in your mind and heart. The Holy Spirit WILL be there!

References used to develop this Bible Study material:
- **For Overall works of the Holy Spirit**
    - The Holy Bible – King James Version
    - "Know His Spirit Bible Study" by Jennifer B. Price
- **Gifts and Ministries of the Holy Spirit**
    - "Questions and Answers on Spiritual Gifts" by Howard Carter
    - "The Gifts & Ministries of the Holy Spirit" by Dr. Lester Sumrall
- **The Power of Jesus' Blood as it relates to receiving the Holy Spirit**
    - "April 2, 1999 Good Friday Message at Williams Temple COGIC" by Bishop R.E. Woodard, Jr.

This Spirit's for You!
(That is, Nothing but the Holy Spirit!)

Have
you
received
the Holy Ghost
since
you
believed?

(Act 19:2)

Appendices

Look Inside
To Find Answers

Appendices

Detailed Contents

Appendix

CHAPTER 1: WHO HE IS!

Lesson 1. Holy Ghost = Holy Spirit = the Spirit = the Spirit of God

1) Holy Ghost, 2) Spirit, 3) Spirit of God, 4) Holy Spirit, 5) Comforter,
6) Because He comforts you, 7) Spirit of truth, 8) He always tells the truth

Lesson 2. The Holy Ghost is Not Really a Ghost!

1) He = male, 2) He gives spiritual gifts to everyone as He wills or decides,
3) intelligent, 4) grieve, 5) yes, 6) mind, 7) talks, 8) wind, 9) He dwells with
us and shall be in us, 10) Jesus Christ is come in the flesh, 11) Jesus Christ
is come in the flesh (This means they will not confess that Jesus came in
the flesh.), 12) spirit of antichrist, 13) Jesus, 14) Guide you into all truth, Not
speak of Himself, Speak what He hears, Show you things to come, Glorify
Jesus, and Receive of Jesus and show it to us

Lesson 3. A Promise and A Gift

1) Comforter, 2) teach the disciples all things and bring all things to their
remembrance that Jesus had told them (and us from John 17:20), 3) the
promise of the Father, 4) Holy Ghost, 5) I am usually excited when my friend
keeps a promise, I feel like I can trust them. 6) I am usually very happy
when I receive gifts, and I hurry to open them to see what I received. 7) I
feel confident in God's love for me when I know He kept His promise to send
His Holy Spirit to be my helper. 8) When I receive a gift from a friend, I am
excited because I expect it to be good. I expect this gift from God to be
amazing because I believe God is my best friend. This makes me excited.

Lesson 4. Before you can be filled with the Spirit, you must be born of the Spirit.

Part 1. Born of the Spirit

1) Any man or person in Christ becomes a new creature, 2) being in Christ
is what makes the person a new creature, 3) old things are passed away,
4) God, 5) the kingdom of the Son of the Father, meaning the kingdom of
Jesus Christ, 6) the spirit of the prince of the power of air, meaning the devil,
7) the new man has been put on, 8) The man became new when he was
renewed in knowledge after Him that created him. This means that a
person changes when they learn how to live like God, who is their creator,
wants them to live., 9) I put off the old man with his deeds. This means that
as I learn how to live like God wants me to live, I stop doing those things
which are against God's ways.

Part 2. Filled with the Spirit

10) receive, 11) see, 12) know, 13) know, 14) with, 15) in

Lesson 5. Speaking in Other Tongues
Part 1. Its first appearance

1) about 120 people including women, Mary the Mother of Jesus, Jesus' brothers, and His disciples, 2) The Spirit gave them the utterances, meaning the Holy Spirit gave them the words to say., 3) The men, who were visiting Jerusalem from other countries, heard the disciples speak the native languages they speak from their home countries. 4) the wonderful works of God

Part 2. Before its first appearance!

5) Verse 17, 6) those who believe the gospel of Jesus Christ that is preached to them, 7) confirm God's Word to everyone

Part 3. More Bible first times!

8) for they heard them speak with tongues and magnify God, 9) they spoke with tongues and prophesied, 10) Simon had to have seen people instantly speaking in unknown foreign languages. Notice that He had already seen miracles and other signs of God's power done by Philip as stated in verse 13, but he did not want to buy the ability to perform these miracles. So, the only thing Simon had not seen before was people speaking in foreign languages after Peter and John laid hands on them. 11) Saul (Paul) received his sight back, then he became filled with the Holy Ghost, and he was baptized.
12) When Ananias laid hands on him in Acts 9:17–20 where it says he was filled with the Holy Ghost.

Part 4. The Purpose for Speaking in Tongues

13) Rest and is the refreshing, 14) believe, 15) God, 16) believe not, 17) stammering lips and another tongue, 18) new tongues, 19) groanings that can not be uttered, 20) tongues of men and tongues of angels

CHAPTER 2: PURPOSE

Lesson 6. The Law of the Spirit Makes Us Free
Part 1. Adam Gave Us Sin and Death

1)   To dress and keep the garden of Eden, 2) of every tree of the garden he could freely eat except, 3) do not eat of the tree of the knowledge of good and evil, 4) in the day Adam ate from the tree of the knowledge of good and evil, he would surely die, 5) yes, 6) from v.17-18: the ground was cursed for Adam so that now he would have to work very hard to produce his own food from the ground. Food would no longer be easily provided for him to get; from v.19: he would have to work hard until he returned to the ground from which he came from. This meant that Adam would now die. 7) God kicked

Adam and Eve out of the garden of Eden, 8) Death was passed on to all people born of a man because they are born as sinners spiritually

Lesson 6. Part 1. Answers continued...
A. Old Testament forgiveness of sins came by the blood of animals
9) the blood, 10) the life of the flesh, 11) once every year, 12) No
B. New Testament forgiveness of sins comes by the blood of Jesus
13) None, 14) Death and Hell, 15) Eternal life, 16) lamb, 17) believe in Jesus, 18) We must confess with our mouth the Lord Jesus. This means we must confess that Jesus is the Lord of our lives.

Part 2. Sin Wants to Boss You Around
19) Sin is the transgression of the law, which is the act of disobeying or violating God's instructions. 20) All have sinned. 21) Sin causes everyone to come short of the glory of God. This means they stop some of God's perfect goodness from happening in their lives by their sin. 22) A hard life, 23) The wages or payment of sin is death. 24) After death every person must face the judgment of God. 25) God will send sinners that die to Hell. 26) Hell is a place where there is fire that will never stop burning. Also, the worm (or sorrowful, dead sinner) will never stop existing and feeling the tormenting fire forever. 27) I did not know what was wrong to do until I was given instructions from God on what is right and what is wrong. 28) When we know the law, then a longing to sin or to break the law is present in us. In other words, people naturally want to do things they are not supposed to do. 29) When I know something is wrong to do, and the desire to sin makes me do it, then I sin. After I sin, I cut off my blessings from the life-giving God. If I do not repent of my sin, I will die and be punished by being separated from God forever.

Part 3. Did you know you were a slave to sin?
30) law of sin, 31) in my members, 32) law of my mind, law of my members, 33) in my members really means inside of me – the real war is between my flesh and my spirit, 34) Yes, through the help of Jesus Christ our Lord

Part 4. Law of the Spirit makes us FREE from the Law of Sin & Death
35) the law of the Spirit makes me free from the law of sin and death, 36) by having life in Christ Jesus, 37) be in Christ Jesus, do not walk in the flesh, walk after the Spirit, 38) Walking after the Spirit causes the righteousness of the law to be fulfilled in us (causes us to be right with God), 39) it has to dwell or live in you all the time, 40) from v. 13: mortify (meaning to kill) the deeds of the body; 41) from v. 14: be led by the Spirit of God; 42) from v. 15: receive the Spirit of adoption so that you call God your Father, 43) The Law of the Spirit makes me free from sin controlling me to make me do wrong.

The Spirit gives me the power to do the right things despite my sinful desires. The Spirit gives me true life and peace instead of fear and death.

Table 2-1. More Names for the Holy Spirit

Scripture(s)	Holy Spirit's Name	Lesson Learned
John 14:17 John 16:12–15	Spirit of <u>Truth</u>	He guides us into all truth, He speaks what He hears from God & Jesus, He shows us things to come, He glorifies Jesus
John 16:8	<u>He</u> (This is a two-letter word that tells the Holy Spirit's gender, whether male or female.)	He reproves the world of sin, righteousness and of judgment. This means He lets people know what sin is in God's eyes; he lets people know that God will punish for sin, reward for right actions.
Matthew 3:16 Matthew 12:28 (Acts 10:38)	Spirit of <u>God</u> (These scriptures explain how the Holy Spirit helped Jesus)	The Spirit descended on Jesus like a dove. Then, He gave Jesus power to cast out devils, and to heal the sick and oppressed.
Luke 4:18 2 Corinthians 3:17, 18	Spirit of the <u>Lord</u>	Anointed Jesus to preach, heal, & to set people free. Changes us into the image & glory of God.
Romans 8:11	Spirit of Him that raised <u>Jesus from the dead.</u>	He quickens our mortal bodies; meaning to help us be lively people; and He will cause us to raise up from the dead after we die
Romans 8:15–17 (Galatians 4:4–7)	Spirit of <u>Adoption</u>	Through the Spirit, we are now called the <u>children</u> of God. What does it mean to be an heir? To receive an inheritance.
1 John 2:20	<u>Unction</u> from the Holy One	How are you able to know all the necessary things concerning salvation? By having the unction, meaning you hear the spirit speak to you from inside of you.
1 John 2:27	The <u>Anointing</u>	Where does the teacher abide? <u>In Us</u> What does He teach? <u>All things</u>

Table 2-2. Holy Spirit Jobs

Scripture(s)	Holy Spirit's Jobs or Personal Character	Lesson Learned / What does this mean to You?
John 14:18–23 Ephesians 2:11–13 Ephesians 2:14–22 (re-read verse 22)	He brings Jesus and God the Father to us and in us (Jews and Gentiles who believe in Christ)	Spiritually speaking we have God on the inside of us
Ephesians 2:18 John 4:24	Jesus gives us access to God the Father by means of the Holy Spirit	Like flesh talks to flesh, spirit talks to spirit. If God is a Spirit, how can we communicate with Him? Since God is a Spirit, we need the Holy Spirit to help our human spirit talk to God.
John 16:7–11	Reproves the world of sin, righteousness and judgment	What does reprove mean? To convince people about sin, right living, and the coming judgment.
Romans 5:5 (also read verses Romans 5:1–4)	Sheds or pours out the love of God in our hearts, giving us hope that good things can happen from God, even when bad things are happening to us	How does knowing that almighty God loves us, help us during the bad times in our lives? It helps us not to be scared or to feel like giving up. We feel like good things are always possible.

Scripture(s)	Holy Spirit's Jobs or Personal Character	Lesson Learned / What does this mean to You?
Jude verse 20 Ephesians 3:16–17 1 Corinthians 14:2, 4, 14	When we pray in the Holy Spirit our holy faith increased. Also, our spiritual self becomes stronger, even if our minds cannot understand everything completely.	What part of us do we want our spiritual self to be stronger than? Remember what you learned in Lesson 7 from Romans 7:22–23. We want our spiritual self to be stronger than our flesh.
1 John 2:20–21 Romans 8:14 (Look at how the Holy Spirit led Jesus after His baptism in Mark 1:9–12. Look at how Paul received direction in Acts 16:6–7.)	Gives us direction from within our hearts.	The Holy Spirit will tell us what to do and what not to do. He will lead us in specific ways in our everyday lives.
2 Corinthians 3:18 2 Corinthians 5:17 Colossians 3:10	We are changed more into the image of God, day by day, by the work of the Holy Spirit in our hearts and our lives.	Notes: Humankind was originally created in the image of God. Then God's adversary the Devil deceived the first man Adam to disobey God which caused all of humankind to lose our Godly nature. Now people are born with the nature of satan. But, when we accept Jesus as our Lord and Savior, then the Holy Spirit gives us a new Godly spiritual nature. Then the Holy Spirit begins to work in us to make us more and more like God. This occurs as we read our Bibles, pray and act upon God's words as shown to us by the Holy Spirit.

Scripture(s)	Holy Spirit's Jobs or Personal Character	Lesson Learned / What does this mean to You?
Acts 10:38 Acts 6:5, 8 Acts 8:39 1 Corinthians 12:8–10	The Holy Spirit is the one who causes miracles to work through us	When you read John 1:29–34 and John 2:1–11, you find out that Jesus did not perform any miracles until after He was filled with the Holy Spirit. Just like Jesus we need to be filled with the Holy Spirit before miracles can flow through us.
Romans 8:13–14 Galatians 5:16–18 Galatians 5:19–25	The Holy Spirit helps you to mortify or kill or get rid of those wrong thoughts and habits in your life that are against God's nature.	After we are saved, there is a daily process of cleaning up our lives, which happens as the Holy Spirit works with us. He shows us how to change our habits and actions day by day.
1 Corinthians 2:9–12 John 14:26 John 16:12–14	Helps us to understand spiritual things	The Holy Spirit teaches us the spiritual things of God. We can not learn them without His help.
1 John 4:1–6 1 John 2:18–28	Helps us to know the difference between the Words from Christ and the words from the devil or anti-christ	He teaches us how to identify wrong spirits in people and wrong teaching from people.
1 Corinthians 14:15 Romans 8:26–27	Helps us to Pray and Praise God. He helps us to pray for ourselves and for others	The Holy Spirit is our unseen prayer partner who prays through us for us and others
Acts 10:38 1 John 2:27 2 Corinthians 1:21–22 Luke 4:18	Anoints the saints of God, meaning He gives special power to God's people to do God's work	The Holy Spirit gives me something special from God which I did not have before – this is called the anointing.
1 Corinthians 2:9–10	The Spirit searches our hearts and searches the deep things of God. He then gives us new ideas from God.	He gives us ideas from God which no person could think of on his or her own.

Scripture(s)	Holy Spirit's Jobs or Personal Character	Lesson Learned / What does this mean to You?
Acts 8:29 1 Timothy 4:1 Revelation 2:7	The Holy Spirit can talk to us.	The Holy Spirit is a person that gives us information.
John 16:13 John 15:26 John 14:26	The Holy Spirit will only talk about things that come from God the Father and God the Son (Jesus) and Word of God (Bible)	The Holy Spirit will not say anything that is not right by God.
Acts 4:31 Acts 4:8, 13	The Holy Spirit helps us to have the boldness to tell people about Jesus. He also helps us to know what is the right thing to say to people.	The Holy Spirit can give us messages to share that cause us to seem wiser than expected.
Galatians 4:6	The Holy Spirit will cause us to call out and think of God as our Daddy! (A good Daddy, the best ever Father!)	Definition: "Abba" was used by the Jews to represent a loving, trusting name given to a Father by a baby. The Holy Spirit will help us to know that we are the real children of God. We will think of God as our Daddy.
2 Peter 1:21 1 Peter 1:10–12 1 Timothy 3:14–15	The Holy Spirit is the one that instructed men on what to write in the Bible.	The Holy Spirit not only inspires our speech and our actions, but He also inspires our writings.
Acts 5:3–11	The Holy Spirit can be (but should not be) lied to. Ananias and Sapphira were born of the Spirit and members of the Church. They probably were filled with the Spirit, too. But they decided to lie to the Church leaders about what they had done in private.	Note: You can even be filled with the Holy Spirit and yet make an active decision to lie and deceive other Christians. But the Holy Spirit always understands what you are doing, and the price you pay for your sin may be very high.

Scripture(s)	Holy Spirit's Jobs or Personal Character	Lesson Learned / What does this mean to You?
Acts 5:9	The Holy Spirit can tell you the secrets of people's hearts. He is very willing to do this if people are trying to deceive or hurt you, or if they are trying to hurt the work of the Church.	Ananias and his wife Sapphira tried to lie to the apostles about the amount of money they were giving for use by the Church. The Holy Spirit revealed to Peter that the couple was lying. Trying to tempt (or test) the Holy Spirit cost them their lives. We should not lie to the Holy Spirit either or it may cost us our life.
Acts 7:51	You can choose not to do what the Holy Spirit wants you to do.	The Holy Spirit is never forceful. He shows us right from wrong. But, we still have the freedom to choose what our actions will be.
Ephesians 4:30 (read verses 17–30 to understand completely)	The Holy Spirit is hurt or grieved when we do not follow His leading.	We are never forced by the Holy Spirit to do anything. He gives us instructions, but the choice is ours to follow those instructions or not.
Matthew 12:31	You can say bad things about the Holy Spirit. But God does not want us to say bad things about Him because He sent the Holy Spirit to help us.	God considers blaspheming the Holy Spirit a sin that He will not forgive.
Acts 19:2	From the time the Holy Spirit was first given until now, some people do not know Him. Also, some people do not believe in the complete works of the Holy Spirit. The Holy Spirit is not forced on anyone.	Although the Holy Spirit is on earth, it is possible to not have Him in your life. It is also possible to not know the right information about how He works.

Lesson 9. Holy Spirit's Power

Part 1. The Bible describes the Holy Spirit's Power
1) the power of the Highest, 2) God is everywhere, 3) God knows everything, 4) God is all powerful.

Part 2. The Holy Spirit gives of its Power to People
1) The Holy Spirit helps us to pray the right way.

2) God is brought to live inside of us by the Holy Spirit. Then God talks to us through the Holy Spirit in us talking to our human spirit.

3) The Holy Spirit makes us have true feelings of love for others.

4) Letting the Holy Spirit pray through me helps my faith in God to get stronger.

5) The Holy Spirit gives us power to be real, good Christians.

6) The Holy Spirit helps us not to be scared to tell others about Jesus.

7) The Holy Spirit shows us things that will happen in the future, before they happen, as needed.

8) The Holy Spirit anoints a person to do signs and wonders in the name of the Lord.

In the author's own words, the 8 types of powers show that God is omniscient, omnipotent, and omnipresent:

- #1 shows that God is omniscient in that He knows the deep thoughts and needs of all people.
- #2 shows God is omnipresent in that He can be on the inside of everybody at the same time He is in heaven and everywhere else on the earth and in the universe.
- #3 shows God is omnipotent in that He has the power to make people love others the right way, even if they are our enemies
- #4 shows God is omnipotent in that He can use His own Spirit to help our faith in Him grow.
- #5 shows God is omnipotent in that He can change anyone from being a sinner to being a good Christian.
- #6 shows God is omniscient and omnipotent in that He can give us the wisdom and boldness to tell others about Him.
- #7 shows God is omnipotent in that He knows the future and can tell it to us before it happens.
- #8 shows God is omnipotent in that He can give us power to do miracles.

9) Dove

Lesson 10. He's Coming! (meaning the Holy Spirit
When Fulfilled:
1) After Jesus came and rose up from the dead and sent the Holy Spirit back in Acts 2:1–4. The time of fulfillment is now for all those who believe on Jesus and receive the Holy Spirit.
2) Acts 2:1–4 and Now for all those who believe on Jesus as the scriptures hath said.
3) Acts 2:1–4 and Now for all those who receive the Holy Spirit. [This means Acts 2:38–39 applies to all 3 answers also.

Lesson 11. Day of Pentecost Fully Comes
Part 1. The Feast of Pentecost was One of the Original 7 Yearly Feasts
1) Passover, 2) Unleavened Bread, 3) Sheaf of the Firstfruits of the harvest, 4) a) Old Testament Name is Feast of Weeks, b) New Testament Name is Feast of Pentecost, 5) Trumpets, 6) Atonement, 7) Tabernacles, 8) Sunday

Part 2. Passover and Pentecost Feasts are Important to Christians Today
9) Passover, 10) lamb, the Lamb of God, 11) which taketh away the sin of the world, 12) Celebration of the Resurrection of Christ (Easter), 13) 40 days, 14) Jesus was the first resurrected child of God to go live with God in heaven after His resurrection. Everyone who believes in Jesus will also become resurrected children of God, who will receive new bodies when Jesus comes again. All the resurrected children of God will be a part of the spiritual harvest or fruit who will live with God in the new heaven and new earth forever. 15) 10 days.

Lesson 12. Different Ways People in the Bible were Filled with the Holy Spirit
Part 1. Jewish Believers were the first to be filled with the Holy Spirit
1) one accord, in one place, 2) a tornado or hurricane, 3) cloven tongues like as of fire, 4) all the 120 people were filled with the Holy Spirit, 5) all the 120 people spoke with other tongues as the Spirit gave them utterance, 6) the Holy Ghost, 7) the place was shaken, they were all filled with the Holy Ghost, they spoke the Word of God with boldness, 8) No, 9) The people gave heed to the things Philip spoke. This means they listened and believed his words concerning Christ. Then, the people were saved and healed and were filled with the joy of the Lord. 10) Peter and John laid hands on the people, and they received the Holy Ghost. 11) Simon saw the people speak in other tongues or foreign languages. 12) the disciple Ananias, 13) Ananias laid his hands on Paul

Lesson 12. Continued...
Part 2. The Holy Spirit is for Gentiles, too!
14) While Peter was preaching, the Holy Ghost fell on all of them that heard him (meaning all the Gentile believers in Cornelius' household). 15) for they heard them speak with tongues and magnify God, 16) after they were filled with the Holy Spirit, 17) They had not even heard about the Holy Ghost, 18) They had been baptized in water by John the Baptist, when he was in the wilderness. Their baptism was based on them repenting of their sins. It was not based on their faith in Jesus Christ. 19) First, Paul led them to believe on Jesus Christ, then Paul baptized them in the Name of Jesus. Then, Paul laid hands on them and the Holy Ghost came on them. They immediately began speaking in other tongues and prophesying.

Lesson 13. Jesus was filled with the Holy Spirit Without Measure
1) No, 2) the Spirit came down from heaven in the shape of a dove and sat on Jesus. 3) God the Father spoke and said, This is my beloved Son, in whom I am well pleased. Listen to Him. 4) to the lost sheep (meaning the lost people) of the house of Israel, 5) the language of the Israelite people, 6) No, 7) from John 7:38: out of the bellies of believers shall flow rivers of living water; from Mark 16:17: cast out devils and speak with new tongues.

Lesson 14. The Church is filled with the Holy Spirit Without Measure
Part 1. The Holy Spirit still fills Christ today Without measure.
There are no exercises needing answers.

Part 2. Individual members of the Church body are filled with a measure of Faith and Grace from the Holy Spirit.
1) There are many parts of the body that are connected together to make one complete body. Each part has an important job or function. Each part is needed to make the body complete. In the body of Christ there are many different people or Church members that make up the Christian Church. There are people of different cultures, and different abilities. But each person is important and is very much needed to make the body of Christ complete.
2) Each part of the body works for the benefit of the whole body. For example, the ear hears for the whole body. The feet walk for the whole body. The arms do work for the whole body. The ear cannot do anything without the help or participation of the whole body. It cannot function by itself. Have you ever seen a body that only consisted of a leg? So, if the leg wants to be successful in running, then it must have the cooperation of the entire body to do that job.

Lesson 14. Part 2 Continued…

3) Just like the members of the natural body must work together to accomplish anything that the brain thinks of them to do, so the members of the Christian Church need to work together to accomplish anything that Christ wants done. Every member of the Church is important and needed to do a work for God. The scripture in verse 26 lets us know that if a member of the Church is hurting, then the pain or loss of the one member affects the whole Church. 4) God has established the Church to be just like a family. He wants each of the members of His family to love, respect and use each other's different talents and abilities. This way everyone benefits.

CHAPTER 4. YOU IN THE SPIRIT

Lesson 15. Led by the Spirit – There are no exercises needing answers.

Lesson 16. Living in the Spirit - There are no exercises needing answers.

Lesson 17. Walking in the Spirit
Part 1. Introduction to Walking in the Spirit
1) Spirit, Flesh

Part 2. The FLESH Must Lose
2) Below are the 17 actions of the flesh from Galatians 5:9-21 definitions

1. Adultery– Having intimate relation with another person's husband or wife
2. Fornication – Having intimate relations when you are not married
3. Uncleanness– Unclean lifestyle in a person's habits, speech or thoughts
4. Lasciviousness – Not able to restrain oneself from shameful conduct
5. Idolatry – The worship or wrong praise of people or things over God. The use of human or animal sacrifices in worship of a god. The sin of having a mind that is against God.
6. Witchcraft – the use of drugs and special drinks, along with ungodly chanting to try and get cult like powers to accomplish anything
7. Hatred – malicious and unjustifiable feelings toward others
8. Variance – To have strife or to be argumentative with people, tending to cause division and confusion among people
9. Emulations – to over concentrate on being just like another person to the point of trying even to outdo that person.
10. Wrath – Filled with the desire to get revenge or to do violence to others
11. Strife – Argumentative and wanting to fight all the time.
12. Seditions – rebellious attitude against the government or laws of the land.
13. Heresies – A religious belief that is against the accepted doctrine of the Christian Church

14. Envying's – The wrong desire to have what someone has to the point that it affects your ability to treat them with Christian love and respect.
15. Murders – the unlawful killing of a person
16. Drunkenness – To be drunk with alcoholic beverage; to be intoxicated
17. Revellings – to be riotous and rowdy such as how a person would act after being drunken

3) Below are 5 actions of the flesh from Colossians 3:5-7 with definitions
1. Fornication – same as in previous answer
2. Uncleanness – same as in previous answer
3. Inordinate affection – Having a love or lust for things that are against the laws of God.
4. Evil concupiscence – evil desires or evil, lustful passions of the mind
5. Covetousness – Greediness to possess money, things or people that are not rightfully yours

4) Below are the 6 actions of the flesh from Colossians 3:8-9 with definitions

1. Anger – a strong negative passion against another person or thing
2. Wrath – a more intense and destructive form of anger
3. Malice – a wicked, vicious attitude that actively seeks to hurt others
4. Blasphemy – words spoken in hateful contempt against God or sacred things
5. Filthy Communication – filthy speech such as cursing and blasphemies
6. Lying – To deliberately and purposefully not tell the truth

Part 3. … and The SPIRIT RULE!!!
5) crucify the flesh with its affections and lusts, 6) mortify my members which are on the earth, 7) put off the old man with his deeds, 8) mortify (meaning to stop or kill) the deeds of the body, 9) They are telling us that we must actively work to stop doing things that are not approved by God, as revealed to us in God's Word and by the Spirit of God. 10) from Galatians 5:22-23 – love, joy, peace, longsuffering, gentleness, goodness, faith, meekness, temperance, 11) from Colossians 3:12-14 – bowels of mercies, kindness, humbleness of mind, meekness, longsuffering, forbearing one another (meaning to accept one another's shortcomings but not sin), forgiving one another, and charity which means showing Godly loving actions.

Lesson 18. Praying in the Spirit–There are no exercises needing answers.

CHAPTER 5. THE SPIRIT IN YOU

Lesson 19. Why I Need to be Filled

1) Be not drunk with wine in excess (meaning do not get drunk),

2) Be filled with the Spirit,

3) unto the uttermost part of the earth,

4) me, my children, and to all afar off, as many as the Lord shall call,

5) for the Gentiles through faith in Jesus Christ,

6) whoever believes on Jesus as the scripture has said,

7) the divine power of God,

8) through the knowledge of Him that has called us to glory and virtue,

9) d)

10) first by repenting of sins and accepting Jesus Christ as your Lord, then by being filled with the Holy Spirit,

11) exceeding abundantly above all that we ask or think,

12) in spirit and in truth,

13) Spirit of truth,

14) He will help you to worship God in spirit and in truth because He is the Spirit of Truth

Lesson 20. How I Can be Filled

Part 1. Step 5. B. Signs are Evidence that You Have Received the Holy Spirit

1) Prophesy: sons and daughters will prophesy,

2) Dreams: old men will dream dreams,

3) Visions: young men will see visions,

4) Cast out devils,

5) Speak with new tongues,

6) take up serpents,

7) if drink any deadly thing it shall not hurt them,

8) lay hands on the sick and they shall recover

Part 1. Step 5. C. Table 5-1. Methods of Receiving the Holy Spirit

Table 5-1 Methods of Receiving the Holy Spirit

How Filled	Reference Scriptures	# of People	Where Filled	What Evidence
A believer, who has the gift from God, can lay their hands on your head and pray that you are filled with the Holy Spirit, and you're immediately filled	Acts 8:5–6, 12, 14–17 Acts 9:17 Acts 19:1–7	All or most of the people of Samaria 1 person (Saul) ~12 men	Samaria In a house Maybe on a road, or house,	See Acts 8:18 See 1 Cor. 14:18
You can be with a group of people who all have the desire to be filled. As you ask God to fill you, then you all receive Him.	Acts 1:13–15, Acts 2:1–4 Acts 4:31–33	~ 120 people A multitude	Upper room in Jerusalem A place where they were assembled	See Acts 2:4 See Acts 4:31
You can be filled with the Holy Spirit following being born again.	Acts 19:1–7	~ 120 people	~ 12 men	
You become filled at some unknown amount of time after you are born of the Spirit.	Acts 8:12 - 17	Possibly a whole city	Unknown, maybe outdoor or a place that could hold most of the city	See Acts 8:18
You can just hear the wonderful Gospel message and become filled.	Acts 10:1–8, 19–48	A whole household of people	In Cornelius house	
You can be alone seeking God to be filled & it happens.	Mark 16:17 Luke 11:9–13	1, some, or many Individual seeker	Anywhere Anywhere	
You can be filled while praising and worshipping God, deep in your heart.	Ephesians 5:18 –21	1, some, or many	Anywhere there is a gathering of 1 or more Christians who are seeking and praising God.	

Lesson 20. Part 1. Step 6. Fill Up

Comparison exercise:

9) Talks to themselves, usually babbling. Will say things without considering how another person feels about what they are saying. 10) Sing songs maybe to themselves or to others. 11) Sometimes thankful to people or resentful to people. 12) May give themselves to others in regretful ways, when it is not planned.

Contrast exercise:

13) Their speaking and singing is mainly non-Christian songs, and not for the purpose of worshiping God. 14) likely non-worship songs of varying types. 15) Sometimes they may give themselves to others in ways they will later regret. They will do things they wished they had not done.

Lesson 21. What to do after I am Filled – No exercises needing answers.

Lesson 22. Conduct: Decent and in Order

Guideline #1. Let all things be done decently and in order. This means there is an order to using God's gifts and a disorderly way to use them. There is a decent way to do things and a non-decent way. Decent and in order are God's way.

Guideline #2. God is not the author of confusion but of peace. This means God does not allow His gifts to work through us to cause chaos, trouble, fights, and confusion.

Guideline #3. Having and sharing the love of God with people is the more excellent way. Doing works and sharing gifts in the name of the Lord with no love of God behind the sharing, does not please God.

CHAPTER 6. SPIRITUAL GIFTS

Lesson 23. Operations, Administrations and Gifts – No answers needed.

Lesson 24. Nine Spiritual Gifts – No answers needed.

Lesson 25. Phony spirit experiences – No answers needed.

Lesson 26. Seven Gifts of Grace

1) Prophesying
2) Ministering
3) Teaching
4) Exhorting
5) Giving
6) Ruling
7) Showing Mercy

Lesson 27. Five-fold Ministry Gifts

Part 1. Introducing the Five-fold Ministry Gifts

1) Apostles, 2) Prophets, 3) Evangelists, 4) Pastors, 5) Teachers,
6) perfecting of the saints, 7) work of the ministry, 8) edifying of the body of Christ (This means to spiritually build up or strengthen the Church members in the ways of God.), 9) till we all come in the unity of the faith, 10) and of the knowledge of the Son of God, 11) unto a perfect man, 12) unto a measure of the stature of the fullness of Christ; this means they help us to become what God wants us to become 13) children, 14) to, 15) fro,
16) every wind of doctrine, 17) sleight of men, 18) cunning craftiness of men, 19) deceive,
20) speak the truth in love, 21) grow up into Christ in all things

Part 2. Each Five-fold Ministry Gift Defined

A. Apostles

22) The 12 Apostles selected by Christ: Simon Peter, Andrew, James, John, Philip, Bartholomew, Thomas, Matthew, James, Lebbaeus, Simon, and Judas Iscariot who betrayed Jesus

The other 12 Apostles mentioned in the Bible are:
13. Matthias, 14. Barnabas, 15. Paul, 16. Andronicus, 17. Junia, 18. Apollos, 19. James, 20. Silvanus, 21. Timotheus, 22. Titus, 23. Epaphroditus, 24. Christ Jesus

B. Prophets

23) New Testament Prophets: Jesus, Agabus, Barnabus, Simeon, Lucius, Manaen, Saul (Paul), 24) New Testament Prophetesses; Anna, the four daughters of Philip

C. Evangelists
25) Philip, Timothy, Jesus

D. Pastors
26) Jesus, 27) Elders

E. Teachers
28) Barnabus, Simeon, Lucius, Manaen, Saul (Paul), Jesus, Paul

Part 3. False Ministries – No answers needed.

Lesson 27. Part 4. B. Ministries

29) Phebe,

30) She was a succourer of many. She cares for the needs of strangers. Definition: "succourer" means to "take in and care of the needs of strangers."

31) Priscilla and Aquilla

32) Put aside their own needs to save the life of Paul

33) Mary

34) Bestowed much labor on Paul and his companions

35) The house of Stephanas

36) the ministry of the saints

37) the Church of Corinth with all the saints in Achaia

38) praying for Paul and Timothy and their companions

Lesson 28. Filled, Then Flowing with Gifts – No answers needed.

APPENDIX B
ANSWERS TO COMMON QUESTIONS ABOUT THE HOLY SPIRIT

While writing this book, I, the author, decided to include a section providing answers to common questions about the Holy Spirit. I knew all your questions would not be answered satisfactorily by reading the material in this Bible Study. The Lord blessed me to find some excellent handbooks that contain the answers to all the questions I had planned to include, and more. This section lists the four handbooks I found.

1. **Book Name:**   **A Handbook on Holy Spirit Baptism**

    Author: **Don Basham**

    Publisher: **Whitaker House**

    Description: It is written in an easy-to-follow question and answer format, with each Chapter answering one question.

    Examples of questions that are answered in this handbook:
    -   Is every Christian meant to have the baptism in the Holy Spirit?
    -   My minister claims the age of miracles is past and that the charismatic gifts, including speaking in tongues and healing, are not meant for today. How can I answer him?
    -   Can one receive the baptism in the Holy Spirit and not be aware that he has received it?
    -   Why is it that people baptized in the Holy Spirit are not in agreement on all points of doctrine?
    -   Is the desire to speak in tongues uncontrollable?

2. **Book Name:**   **Questions and Answers on Spiritual Gifts**

    Author: **Howard Carter**

    Publisher: **Harrison House**

    Description: This book is authored by the man who is considered the father of explaining how the spiritual gifts operate for the present-day Pentecostal Church. During the first World War, Carter began a 30-year study on the gifts of the Spirit. The late Rev. Howard Carter was also considered an authority on the gifts of the Spirit. This book is written in an easy-to-follow question and answer format.

    Types of questions that are answered in this handbook:
    -   Rev. Howard Carter defines and provides explicit examples of the gifts of the Spirit.

3. **Book Name:**   **Tongues, Interpretation & Prophecy**

    Author: **Don Basham**

    Publisher: **Whitaker House**

    Description: **Each Chapter answers one question.**

    Examples of questions that are answered in this handbook:
    - What is the difference between the gifts of the Holy Spirit which Paul lists in 1 Corinthians 12:8-10 and the list in 1 Corinthians 12:28-30?
    - What is the difference between spiritual gifts and man's talents?
    - Can a person have spiritual gifts without being baptized in the Spirit?
    - How do you know when you are going to interpret tongues?
    - What inner indication do you receive?
    - If the gift of prophecy is from God, why must it be judged?

4. **Book Name:**   **The Gifts & Ministries of the Holy Spirit**

    Author: **Dr. Lester Sumrall**

    Publisher: **Whitaker House**

    Description: The author of this book was a long-time close spiritual friend and companion to Rev. Howard Carter of London England. God first used Rev. Howard Carter to help explain more fully to the modern church the glorious truths of how the gifts and ministries of the Holy Spirit should be operating in the Church.

    The late Dr. Lester Sumrall and Rev. Carter were both considered the world's leading authorities on the gifts and ministries of the Holy Spirit.

    Although this book is not written in question-and-answer format like the other handbooks, it is easy to read and understand.

    This book explains clearly how the gifts and ministries of the Holy Spirit are "the weapons of our (meaning Believers) warfare" that can destroy any force the devil might use against us.

Youth Lessons 1 – 28 Study Handouts
with Youth-Friendly Presentation Tips

APPENDIX C
YOUTH LESSONS 1 – 28 STUDY HANDOUTS

The purpose of this section is to provide presentation tip handouts for teachers who plan to use this Bible Study curriculum in their Youth Church School or Bible Study sessions.

The tips explain how to present the material with a little extra "oomph" and "zest." The Disney movie character Mary Poppins explained that a spoon full of sugar can help medicine go down in a most delightful way. In other words, even though Youth Bible Study sessions are good for the youth, the lessons need to be presented in a lively manner, or the students may not receive the Word in their hearts and instead tune you out.

With any group of youth, you will always have some students who comprehend information faster, some whose vocabulary is not as large as others, and some who have short attention spans for study sessions that require reading text and looking up answers. The teaching techniques that seem to work best for today's youth, who are accustomed to "fast-pace", "lots of bright colors" and who are quick to say, "I'm bored", are techniques that include:

a. Group participation where youth are helping youth, so that the students feel like they are "mini teachers"

b. Interactive learning styles where the students learn by doing skits, plays, learning games, and hands-on activities

c. Using lots of visual aids like object lessons, videos, and models or examples that vividly describe or show the lesson content.

The recommendations in this section are from ideas the author used in working with the youth in her Church, and from ideas the Holy Spirit laid on her heart. Even if you do not use these ideas, maybe they can help you think of others best suited for presenting to your youth or even adults.

For your information, the author tries to spend little or no money to implement her ideas. It turns out that some of the most fun activities are those that use items from around your home, or collected from a garage sale, or items no longer in use.

My prayer is that God give you as much joy teaching these lessons as He gave me in writing them.

Sincerely Yours in Christ,

Jennifer B. Price

Lesson 1.   Holy Ghost = Holy Spirit = The Spirit = The Spirit of God

- **Activity Objective**
  - To make sure youth know that they are made up of three different smart operating parts – the body, soul and spirit. (three realms)

- **Activity Materials**
  - Draw a balloon shaped person on the chalkboard or on paper to use in explaining the three operating parts. Use the example picture in the pamphlet that follows this page. Although the figure is comical looking, children are very comfortable with learning from pictures of stick drawings as well as other crude drawings.

- **Activity**
  - After students complete the Lesson 1 exercise, use the scriptures in the lesson and the image on the following page to discuss with them the concepts of the three realms that make up a person.
  - In 1 Thessalonians 5:23 these three realms are identified as the body, soul and spirit — body (1 Corinthians 6:19-20, 1 Corinthians 12:12-27), soul (Philippians 1:27, Hebrews 4:12) and spirit (John 4:24, 1 Corinthians 2:11-12).
  - Then, play a review game to reinforce what they should have learned from the lesson and the image. In this game four youth will be able to win a prize by describing the information from the pamphlet. Give the students time to look at the image on the next page. Ask students to volunteer to explain to the group one of the four topics from the page. Specifically, the students should:
    - Describe what the soul, spirit and body are.
    - Describe what the "spirit of the world" is and how it relates to our human spirit.
    - Describe what happens to a person's human spirit when they are born again in Christ Jesus by the Holy Spirit.
    - Describe what happens to a person's human spirit when they become filled with the Holy Spirit.
  - Continue the game until four students explain the four topics correctly.
  - Give each of the four students a special prize.
  - Finally, give everyone a participation reward because everyone who attends Church school / Bible Study is a winner!

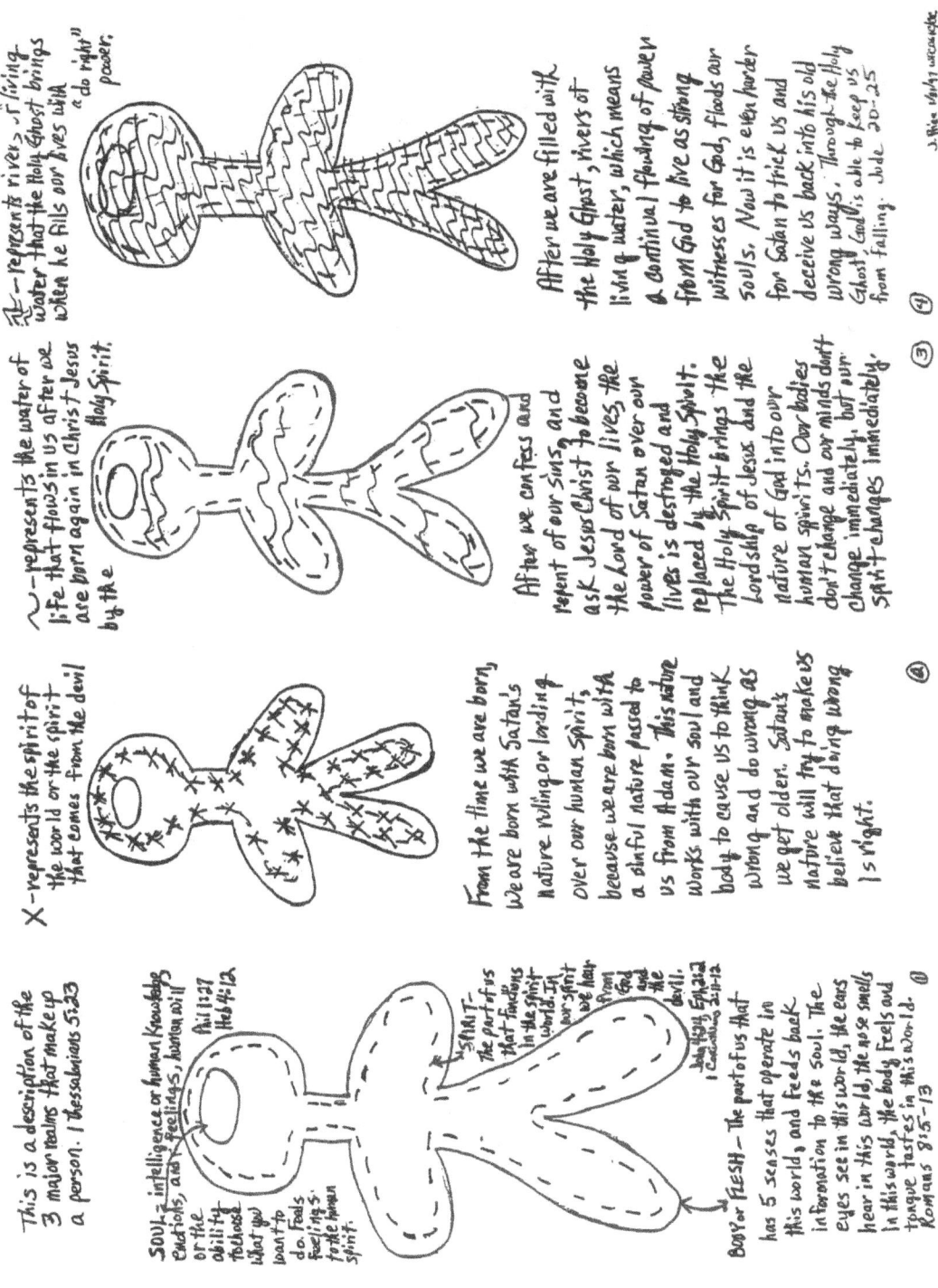

≈ - represents rivers of living water that the Holy Ghost brings when he fills our lives with "do right" power.

~ - represents the water of life that flows in us after we are born again in Christ Jesus by the Holy Spirit.

X - represents the spirit of the world or the spirit that comes from the devil

This is a description of the 3 major realms that make up a person. 1 Thessalonians 5:23

SOUL - intelligence or human knowledge, emotions, and feelings, human will or the ability to choose what you want to do. Feels feelings to the human spirit. Phil 1:27 Heb 4:12

SPIRIT - the part of us that functions in the spirit world. In our spirit we hear from God and the devil. John 4:23-24 1 Corinthians 2:11-12

BODY or FLESH - The part of us that has 5 senses that operate in this world, and feeds back information to the soul. The eyes see in this world, the ears hear in this world, the nose smells in this world, the body feels and tongue tastes in this world. Romans 8:5-13

From the time we are born, we are born with Satan's nature ruling or lording over our human spirit, because we are born with a sinful nature passed to us from Adam. This nature works with our soul and body to cause us to think wrong and do wrong as we get older. Satan's nature will try to make us believe that doing wrong is right.

After we confess and repent of our sins, and ask Jesus Christ to become the Lord of our lives, the power of Satan over our lives is destroyed and replaced by the Holy Spirit. The Holy Spirit brings the Lordship of Jesus and the nature of God into our human spirits. Our bodies don't change and our minds don't change immediately, but our spirit changes immediately.

After we are filled with the Holy Ghost, rivers of living water, which means a continual flowing of power from God to live as strong witnesses for God, floods our souls. Now it is even harder for Satan to trick us and deceive us back into his old wrong ways. Through the Holy Ghost God is able to keep us from falling. Jude 20-25

① ② ③ ④

J. Rose 12/11/97 incomplete

Lesson 2.   The Holy Ghost is Not Really a Ghost

- **Activity Objective**

  - To explain what it means to have the Holy Spirit "intercede" for you.

- **Activity Players**

  - Perform a skit using four characters. One adult plays God. One adult plays Jesus. One adult plays the Holy Spirit. One praying youth.

- **Activity**

  - **God and Jesus**; Stand together on one side of the room.

  - **Youth and Holy Spirit:** Seat the praying youth on the other side of the room with the Holy Spirit near them while he or she prays.

  - **Youth Prays:** "Lord, thank you for blessing me and my family. Please forgive me for my sins. And Lord, please bless me with a new bike. In Jesus name I pray, Amen."

  - **After the Prayer**: The Holy Spirit leaves the child and goes over to God and Jesus. The Holy Spirit begins to talk to them about the child, and the child's prayer request.

  - **The Holy Spirit Intercedes**: "Father, did you hear your child's prayer. You know he (or she) gave himself to you on one Christmas holiday. Ever since that day he has tried to do what is right. I think you should bless him with that bike."

  - **Jesus Intercedes**: "Yes, Father, he accepted me on December 25, 1996, and my blood washed away his sins. You should convince his parents to get him that bike."

  - **Discussion:** After this short skit, ask the children if they can explain what "interceding" means. Let them know that the Holy Spirit and Jesus both interceded for the praying youth.

Lesson 3.   A Promise and A Gift

- **Activity Objective**

  - To assure youth that Jesus did not abandon the disciples or us when He went back to heaven. Explain that Jesus sent the Holy Spirit to take His place on earth and to bring Jesus back to us in a better way.

- **Activity Materials**

  - Two sheets of drawing paper and something to use for drawing on the paper sheets

- **Activity**

  1. Hang the drawing paper on the wall or on a board so the children can draw on them. In the center of each sheet draw a circle and tell the children that it represents earth. At the top of each paper, draw a shape to represent heaven. Draw another shape to represent God in heaven. Then, draw small circles on the earth to represent disciples and Christians.

  2. Have a student read John 16:7 from the King James Version of the Bible. Ask a volunteer to draw where they think Jesus is and where the Holy Spirit is based on what this scripture says up to the last semi-colon. They should show Jesus on earth. They could show the Holy Spirit in heaven with God the Father, or inside of Jesus. The best drawing would show the Holy Spirit inside of Jesus (John 3:34). However, either answer could be correct since the three divine persons in the Trinity make up One God that is in complete unity or oneness with each other.

  3. Now, have a student to re-read the words after the last semi-colon in the KJV version of the John 16:7. On the second sheet of paper, have a student draw where the Holy Spirit is and where Jesus is, after Jesus rose from the dead. In this drawing the student should show Jesus in heaven and the Holy Spirit inside each of the small circles. This represents that the Holy Spirit is inside the disciples / Christians.

  4. Finally, have a student read John 14:23, 26. Help students understand that the Holy Spirit's purpose is to bring Jesus to live inside each of us. This puts Jesus in a better relationship with us than He could have ever been in if He had remained on earth.

Lesson 4.   Part 1. Born of the Spirit

- **Activity Objective**
  - To compare how being born again spiritually is like being born into a good family, with a father who is seen as being a good Father.
  - A second objective is to learn if students have negative feelings about their family life, so you can ask God to help and heal them.

- **Activity Materials**
  - Round table discussion session with the youth

- **Activity**
  - Background: Youth who have negative thoughts about their fathers or their family life will have a more difficult time thinking of God as their good heavenly Father. They will have a hard time trusting God with their lives. They may want to believe in God, but their negative thoughts about family will hinder their ability to trust Him completely.
  - Before, During, and After the Church School / Bible Study session
    1. Prior to class, pray and ask God to lead you in helping youth discuss whether they have positive or negative thoughts about their family life.
    2. Before setting up the session, inform the parents or guardians of the youth about the plan to talk about family life, with the objective of helping them understand the concept of spiritual family life. It is wise to obtain permission from the parents for their youth to participate in the session, perhaps in writing.
    3. Arrange the seating in a manner that will best help students to talk freely and comfortably. For example, you may want to place the chairs in a circle or in an open classroom layout. Every adult should also sit and not stand as in a position of authority.
    4. Use the Lesson Exercise to begin the family life discussion by explaining how the born-again Christian is born into a new spiritual family. Allow the youth to describe examples of family life. Use their examples to further explain the Christian family concept. During the discussion, listen carefully for any signs that a youth may not be happy about their family situation.
    5. Do not do anything to make any child feel embarrassed or uncomfortable. If you sense that a youth may have concerns about their family life, let the Holy Spirit lead you in how to help them. Their healing will help them learn to love and trust in God.

Lesson 4. **Part 2. Filled with the Spirit**

- **Activity Objective**
  - To use the example of Peter's life to demonstrate the difference between being born of the Spirit and being filled with the Spirit.

- **Activity Materials**
  - Review the Drama in Appendix D entitled "Peter – Before and After Being Filled." The drama covers Peter's life from when he was a "hothead" inner circle disciple of Jesus, to becoming afraid, and then timid, to finally becoming a bold Apostle.

- **Activity**
  - Let the youth act out the Drama in Appendix D. Use as many dress-up clothes and props as you can. There is no need to have youth memorize lines. You can just let the youth read the lines. Or, you can use an adult to be the Narrator and "drama conductor," who talks the children through what they should do and say.

Lesson 5.   Speaking in Other Tongues

- **Activity Objective**
  - To encourage youth to really learn what is in this lesson by doing a post lesson review game, which includes using money change.

- **Activity Materials**
  - Select questions from the Lesson 5 Exercises.
  - Have a lot of quarters available (i.e. 25 cent coins)

- **Activity**
  - To liven up the willingness of the students to get into doing the exercises in all of Lesson 5, prior to teaching, tell the students there will be a review game after the lesson. The review game will include having two teams that will be in a contest between each other so that one team can become the winner. The team that wins will receive a team reward, such as eating snacks first at the end of the game. Also explain that individual rewards of money can be won.
  - Here is how the game works:
    - Each team takes turns answering the questions selected from the Lesson Exercises by the adult coordinator. If one team does not answer a question correctly, then the other team has an opportunity to answer it.
    - From within each team, the first student that raises their hand gets the first opportunity to answer the question. Every time a student gets a correct answer, they earn 25 cents for their personal reward.
    - Monetary personal rewards can be given to the youth as soon as they answer the question, or a total amount given to them after the game. For example, if a student answered 4 questions correctly, he or she receives 4 quarters.
    - At the end of the game, the winning team is rewarded with eating their snacks first.

- **Warning:** Use impartial, unbiased people to determine which students raised their hands first and to keep score. Youth are very sensitive to whether a game is being implemented fairly or not.

Lesson 6. **Part 1. Adam Gave Us Sin and Death**
Part 2. Sin Wants To Boss You Around

- **Activity Objective**
  - To make sure youth fully appreciate the great thing Jesus did by sacrificing Himself for our sins. Do this by acting out the Old Testament sacrifice rituals and comparing them to what is required to approach God today. This activity will probably take more than one meeting session to complete.

- **Activity Materials**
  - You will need an easy description of the Tabernacle design from the time of Moses and the children of Israel in the wilderness. There is an easy-to-understand write-up in the Children's Ministry Resource Bible developed by Child Evangelism Fellowship (CEF).
  - You will also need a description of the High Priest's outfit, which can be found in that same Bible.
  - Then you will need to find materials to use in building a life-size model of the Tabernacle and to use in outfitting a student as the Priest.
  - Use Leviticus Chapter 9 and Hebrews Chapter 9 as procedure guides for conducting the makeshift sacrifice offering.
  - No real animals are to be used in this exercise; a stuffed animal or a drawing on paper can be used.

- **Build a life-size model of the tent-like Tabernacle in the Old Testament.**
  - Here is a description of how the author, J. B. Price, built one for a Children's Church presentation without spending any money at all.
  - Folding chairs were used to represent the front entrance to the outer court. White sheets were placed over the chairs, except for the 2 chairs that represented the gate.
  - A small table was used for the altar of burnt offering and a Tupperware bowl for the bronze laver.
  - The Holy Place and Most Holy Place were separated out by using chalkboards.
  - Refrigerator-sized cardboard boxes were used to create the two rooms.
    - o At the time of this exercise, the refrigerator boxes could be obtained for free from any store that sells refrigerators.
  - In the Holy Place, a small jar of incense was placed on top of a small table to represent the altar of incense. Twelve candles were used to represent the golden lampstand. Two separate food storage bags containing 6 slices of bread were placed on a small stand for the Table of Showbread.

- In the Most Holy Place a medium-sized box was used to represent the Ark of the Covenant with two doll-like angels on top of it for the two Cherubim.

- Inside the Ark of the Covenant box: The top and bottom of one small cardboard box was used to represent the Ten Commandments inside the Ark. A shortened version of 5 commandments was written on each box half. A ruler was used for the rod of Aaron with a flower taped on it for the bud and a small sandwich bag of corn kernels to represent the manna. All these items were placed inside the medium-sized box that represented the Ark.

- Sheets and colored blankets were used to cover the tops of the boxes / chalkboard and chairs that were as close to the colors described in the write-up as we could get.

- Optional: Materials for dressing up a student to be the Priest can also be supplied from materials in the home.

- **Activity**

  - Give each student a copy of the write-up on the Tabernacle based on the write-up in the Children's Ministry Resource Bible.

  - Have the students help build some of the Tabernacle (if some parts are already pre-staged) or all of it based on the write-up description.

  - Once the Tabernacle replica is built, use the write-up to explain to the youth the significance of each item in the Tabernacle.

  - Use a student volunteer to be the Priest. Optional: Dress up the student to look as much like the description of the Priest as possible.

  - Walk through a sacrifice offering ceremony as described in Leviticus Chapter 9. Use stuffed animals or a drawing of the sacrifice animals. Optional: use red food coloring and pour it into a cup instead of sprinkling it on any objects.

  - Following this activity, which may take one or two meeting sessions to complete, conduct a review game to see what the children can remember about the different parts of the Tabernacle design.

  - **Very Important Ending:** The end of this activity should conclude with discussing Hebrews Chapter 9 with the students.

    o The passage in Hebrews compares Jesus' sacrificial experience to that of Moses and the Priests in the wilderness.

    o **It also explains why Jesus' sacrifice makes people access to God so much easier for us today.**

Lesson 6. **Part 3. Did you know you were a slave to sin?**
Part 4. The Law of the Spirit makes us FREE...

- **Activity Objective**

  - To help youth understand what it means to be oppressed or denied the opportunity to do what you really want to do by reviewing what it means physically to understand what it means spiritually.

- **Activity Materials**

  - Round table discussion session with the youth

- **Activity**

  - Have youth review and discuss the experiences of people who have been oppressed so they can better understand the oppression that can occur within one's soul.

  - Here are four examples of topics for discussion:
    - The Hebrews (Israelites) experience in Old Testament Egypt during the time of Moses and evil Pharaoh (approximately 1400 years before the birth of Christ)
    - The African American experience during Slavery days (began in 1619)
    - The African American experience with "Jim Crow" laws. (discussion could begin in 1828 or focus on 1954 era)
    - The Jewish Holocaust experiences under Hitler in Germany (1933–1945)
    - War experiences occurring in the Middle East today.
    - The struggle with fasting or giving up a boyfriend or girlfriend because of parental intervention.

- Discussion Points:
  - Slavery and War are horrible, and all free countries should not take this lightly.
  - When there is no physical oppression, there can still be "Slavery" and "War" occurring within a person's soul.
  - The sinful desires of the flesh, that crave for what it should not have or do, becomes a real struggle between the desire to sin and the desire to do what is right.

Lesson 7.   Holy Spirit's Names

- **Activity Objective**
  - To talk about the meaning of names. Also, to divide and conquer the task of completing the Exercise Table among the youth.

- **Activity Materials**
  - What's in a name? Bring a book of names to discuss the meaning of each child's name.
  - Bring in a handout with, or be prepared to briefly discuss, the many names for God, such as Jehovah-Jireh, El Shaddai, and Jehovah-Rapha.
  - Also be prepared to discuss the meaning of the names that Jesus called Himself.

- **Activity**
  - Prepare the youth to learn the names of the Holy Spirit by first talking to them about the meaning of names.
  - Use a book of names to discuss the meaning of their own names. Tell them that in some cases their parents selected their names because they just like the sound of the name. In some cases, their parents focused on the meaning that went along with their name of choice.
  - Next discuss the importance of why the Israelites called God by certain names at different times. Explain how these names really described a characteristic about God that the Israelites needed to know or use at the time.
  - Likewise, discuss the meaning of some of the names Jesus called Himself.
  - Finally, to complete Table 2-1 in the Lesson Exercise, divide the task of filling in the sections among teams of students. Then let each team share their answers with everyone.
    - For example, let each team have the number of students in their group as the number of scriptures in the block from the table. In this way, each student only needs to look up one scripture and write down what they learn.
  - After the teams complete their assigned blocks, let each team report their answers to everyone.

Lesson 8.   **Holy Spirit's Job's**

- **Activity Objective**

  - Like Lesson 7, divide and conquer the task of completing Table 2-2.

- **Activity Materials**

  - Use the team concept to complete the Lesson Exercise.

- **Activity**

  - Once again you could use as many students as you have scriptures in a block.

  - Note that some of the blocks already have all three columns filled in.

  - During reporting time, when the students are providing their answers to the class, the teacher should discuss the contents of the blocks that have already been completed.

Lesson 9.   Part 1. The Bible describes the Holy Spirit's Power

- **Activity Objective**
  - Discuss cartoon superheroes and their weaknesses. Compare them to the all-powerful Holy Spirit of God.

- **Activity Materials**
  - Bring in comic strip / graphic novel examples of as many superheroes as you can.
  - Be prepared to discuss the weaknesses of each one.

- **Activity**
  - Show the children how when people create superheroes, they still have weaknesses. For example, Batman cannot fly. Superman is weakened by Kryptonite, Ninja Turtles and Power Rangers can be hurt, and so on.
  - Let the youth read the lesson text and discuss each concept of Omnipresent, Omniscient, and Omnipotent.
  - Some youth might ask the age-old question of "if God is so powerful, then why is there so much evil in the world?" You need to be prepared to explain that God blessed Adam and Eve to be fruitful and multiply before they sinned. He did not just end their earthly experience after they sinned. Instead, God gave humans and satan a certain amount of time to continue to live and exist until He completely produces a new family of faithful children. Then, after satan and this earth's time are up, God will create a new heaven and a new earth for His new family, where no sin or destruction will ever occur again for the rest of eternity.

Lesson 9.   Part 2. The Holy Spirit gives of its Power to People

- **Activity Objective**
  - To use a skit to show how the Holy Spirit and the Devil both work to influence a child's prayer life and faith.

- **Activity Materials**
  - Need 6 characters for the skit –
    1. The Holy Spirit, **2.** Christian youth named Christian or Christine,
    3. A friend of the youth, **4.** Devil dressed in an orange or black cape,
    5. God the Father dressed in a white cape or sheet, and **6.** Jesus dressed in purple or red cape.
  - If possible, use the cape or sheet colors as follows:
    God in white, Jesus in red, Holy Spirit in blue, Devil in orange

- **Activity**
  - Write a skit based on the idea below. Prior to class, prepare 6 youth to perform the skit.
  - Perform the skit before reviewing the Lesson material, as an Intro.
  - Here is the basic idea of the skit

    Show a youth praying to be filled with the Holy Spirit. While they are praying, the Holy Spirit comes and joins His life, meaning walks along side the youth everywhere they go. Then, show the Holy Spirit call God the Father and Jesus to come live inside the youth also. Show the youth walk around with the actors playing the three Divine Persons of the Godhead going with them everywhere they go. Next, show the youth see a friend and go over to talk to him or her. The youth tells their friend that they have been filled with the Holy Spirit, and they feel like a new person. The friend responds that the youth does not look any different to them. But the Christian youth keeps telling him that something special has happened to them. Then, show the friend burst out laughing at the Christian. The friend walks away laughing harder and harder.

    Now have the Devil come up to the Christian youth and tell him that nothing special has happened to him. The Devil continues by saying they are just the same, and that all the stuff they heard in Church is phony.

    Next, show the Trinity on the boy's right side telling them that something special happened. Show the Devil on the left side of the youth telling them that nothing special happened.

    Have the youth pray and ask God to help them know what to believe. Then, have the boy say, "I know I have been filled with the Holy Spirit." End the skit by having the three Divine persons in the Godhead surround the boy and say, "You sure have been filled." All four of them walk away together.

Lesson 10.   HE'S COMING! (meaning the Holy Spirit)

- **Activity Objective**
  - To help youth understand what prophecies are, that "foretell" events.
  - To demonstrate how God used "foretelling" prophecies all through the Bible, and He still uses foretelling today.
  - To make sure youth do not confuse God's foretelling with the Devil's evil attempts at foretelling.

- **Activity Materials**
  - Chalkboard and chalk (or whiteboard). Write some Bible prophecies on note paper where:
    - Side A has a Prophet's name, a scripture with one of his prophecies and the approximate year the prophecy was given; for example, 700 years before the birth of Christ.
    - Side B contains the scripture reference for when the prophecy was fulfilled, and the approximate year of fulfillment; for example, 29 years after the birth of Christ.
    - Note: See examples on the next page.

- **Activity**
  - **1. Before starting Lesson 10: Let** the students build a timeline on the chalkboard using the prophecies you prepared. Draw a straight line across the board. This will be your timeline. In the middle of the timeline draw a baby above the timeline and draw a short hash mark extending below the line under the baby. Label this mark 4 B.C. and put "birth of Jesus." Add additional hash marks to represent other years on the left and right side of the timeline.
  - See an example on the next page. (Same as on Chapter 3 cover)
  - Explain that B.C. stands for "before Christ" and A.D. stands for Anno Domini which really means "after Christ" or "in the year of the Lord."
  - Next let the youth mark the prophecies from side A on the timeline from your notes.
    - Let one group mark the prophecies from side A on the timeline using a picture or a short description.
    - Let another group write the fulfillment of the prophecies from side B in a similar manner.
  - Use this timeline to explain the concepts of prophecies and fulfillment of prophecies.

- **2. After Lesson 10 and the Lesson Exercise is complete**: talk to the youth about any prophecies and fulfillment of prophecies in your own life, or in the lives of people you know.

- **3. Finally, end this discussion by talking about the Devil's counterfeit experiences for God's real thing:** Devil (also known as Satan) counterfeit or phony prophecy attempts include psychics, fortunetellers, palm readers, astrology who make predictions about events in people's future. Review God's warning against engaging with such persons in Deuteronomy 18:10-12 and Leviticus 19:26-31.

Example Prophecies for your note paper:

Side A	Prophet's Name	Scripture	Approx. Year Spoken
	Micah	Micah 5:2	700 B.C.
Side B	**Scripture for Prophecy Fulfillment**		**Approx. Year Fulfilled**
	Matthew 2:1		4 B.C.
Side A	**Prophet's Name**	**Scripture**	
	David	Psalm 22:1, Psalm 22:6-18	1000 B.C.
Side B	**Scripture for Prophecy Fulfillment**		A.D. 29
	Matthew 27:46, Matthew 27:27-43		A.D. 29

~ 4000 YEAR SPAN TIMELINE

B.C. (Time: Before Christ) | (Time: After Christ = Anno Domini) A.D.

| 2000 | 1000 | 800 | 400 | 4 | 0 | 29 | 100 | 400 | 800 | 1000 | 2000 |

Abraham & Israel Begins — Moses — Isaiah — Malachi — Birth of Jesus — Death of Jesus — ◆ Holy Spirit descends & Church Begins — * You Are Here

Old Testament = Old Covenant between God and Humankind

New Testament = New Covenant between God and Humankind

Lesson 11.   Part 1. The Feast of Pentecost was one of the Original 7

- **Activity Objective**
  - To understand the two-fold purpose of the Old Testament feasts.
  - One purpose was to bless the Jews back then to have fun and fellowship with God, their own families and with their whole nation.
  - The second purpose was to represent activities to occur in the future

- **Activity Materials**
  - Prepare Feast materials of hot bread, cooked lamb (or sausage), herbs and punch to feed the entire youth group.
  - Make place mats out of Table 3-1 "Yearly Feasts of the Lord." Placemats can be made by making copies of the Table for all youth and having each copy laminated. Or place the copies in clear "sheet protectors" that can be purchased from an office supply store.

- **Activity**
  - **Mimic the Passover feast celebration as closely as you can** by eating bread, lamb and punch. The pattern for this feast should be based on the Passover celebration described in Exodus Chapter 12.
  - **During this time of fellowship with the youth, use Table 3-1 placemats to review the meaning of all the feasts.**
    With notes from the table, help youth understand how the real reason for four of the feasts has already come to pass. Then, discuss how the purposes for the other three feasts will be fulfilled surrounding events for the Second Coming of Jesus Christ.
  - **Here are two more lessons you could teach the youth:**
    1. Explain how Jesus spent 3 days and 3 nights in the grave (Matthew 12:40). Additional explanation can be found in the book *Born to Die* by Robert Boyd.[1] Notes: Bible times Jewish culture determined a day from "sunset to sunset" (SS to SS). When Jesus was crucified, His death and burial happened on days like this:
    - Jewish Thu. to Thu. SS – Jesus was crucified & buried.
    - Jewish ThuSS-Fri. to Fri SS – Jesus spent 1st night & day in grave. This was also a high sabbath (Passover) & not regular sabbath (John 19:42).
    - Jewish FriSS-Sat to Sat SS – Jesus spent 2nd night & day in grave. (Matthew 27:62)
    - Jewish SatSS-Sun to Sunday SunRise (SR) – Jesus spent 3rd night & part of the day in the grave. (Matthew 28:1)
    - Jewish Sunday Sunrise – Jesus rose early from the dead sometime before dawn on that Sunday morning. (Mark 16:1-7)
  - **2. Explain Christians adopted Sunday as the main Day of Worship service in honor of Jesus' resurrection on Sunday morning**

Lesson 11. Part 2. Passover & Pentecost Feasts are Important Today

- **Activity Objective**
  - To explain where the spirits of dead people went before Jesus rose from the dead.
  - To discuss where Jesus went and what He did after He died on the cross.
  - To discuss what happens to the righteous dead today.

- **Activity Materials**

  Background scriptures and discussion notes
  - Luke 16:19-31 & Luke 23:43 describe where the soul-spirits of the wicked dead and the godly dead went before Jesus rose from the dead. All souls either went to Sheol in the Hebrew or Hades in the Greek (also referred to as Hell) after death, but they went to different compartments. The wicked dead went to the torment compartment. The godly dead went to Paradise or "Abraham's bosom" compartment. All the dead souls were held captive there until Christ conquered Death, the Grave, and Hell.
  - Ephesians 4:9 and Psalm 16:10 (also reference Acts 2:27) explain what happened to Jesus' soul and body after He dies on the cross. These passages explain that Jesus' soul-spirit went to Hell, but His body did not decay while it stayed in the grave.
  - 1 Peter 3:18-20 explains Jesus preached to the spirits while in Hell.
  - Matthew 27:52-53 and Ephesians 4:8-10 explain Jesus took the saints out of Hell and took them with Him up to heaven.
  - Hebrews 2:14-15 and Revelation 1:18 explain that through Jesus' death and resurrection, He obtained the keys of Hell and Death.

- **Activity**
  - Review the background scriptures and discussion notes above with the students. Explain to them how Jesus was the first one to go to heaven with His new "glorified" body. This is why Mary and the two men on the road to Emmaus had trouble recognizing Jesus. Jesus' new body took on a different form than it had before, but He was still able to help His family and friends recognize Him. Reference John 20:11-17 and Luke 24:13-32.
  - After His resurrection, Jesus emptied Hell of the spirits of the saints. Now when the saints of God die, their spirits go to be with the Lord (2 Corinthians 5:8). But their bodies stay and decay in the grave (or wherever located) until the resurrection of their bodies at the Second Coming of Christ (1 Thessalonians 4:13-18). Then the saints will all have new bodies joined with their souls and spirits (1 John 3:2, 1 Thessalonians 4:13-18)

Lesson 12. Part 1. Jewish Believers were the first to be filled with HS

- **Activity Objective**
  - Explain how the Samaritan people thought of themselves as a part of God's chosen people, but the Jewish people did not accept them as part of their race.
  - Discuss how the Jews and Samaritans became enemies.
  - Give the youth a new appreciation for the parable story of the "Good Samaritan"

- **Activity Materials**
  - Review how the Jews and Samaritans became enemies in Old Testament times and were enemies at the time of Jesus Christ. Read 1 Kings 16:21-24 and Nehemiah 4:1-9.
  - Review how Jesus did not approve of this enemy relationship. See scriptures under the Activity section.

- **Activity**
  - Explain to the youth that Samaria was a part of the Promised Land area that God gave to the Jewish nation. *(Note: God gave the Jews the Promised Land area because of the iniquity of the original people who lived there causing God to remove and replace them with the Israelites, meaning the Jewish nation.)*
  - In the Old Testament, when the Jewish nation's sin led them to becoming a divided nation, they were divided into two kingdoms. The Northern Kingdom became known as Israel, and the Southern Kingdom became known as Judah. Samaria was the capital city of the Northern Kingdom, while Jerusalem was the capital city of the Southern Kingdom.
  - Eventually the sin of both kingdoms brought God's wrath on their nations. As a result, the Northern Kingdom was conquered first by the Assyrian nation. The land was destroyed and the Jewish people living in that area were forced to intermarry with the other races of people. God had commanded the Jewish people not to intermarry. God allowed the Babylonian nation to conquer the Southern Kingdom, destroying the land and the Temple. But many of the Jewish people of the area were taken captive to live in Babylon. In Babylon, they were able to live in their own community. So they did not intermarry with the Babylonians.
  - After the Israelites' punishment was complete, God used King Cyrus to allow the Jews in Babylon to return to their homeland, and used prophets, priest, and Nehemiah to help with rebuilding the people, the Temple and the city.

- During the time of Nehemiah, he rallied his countrymen to rebuild the wall around Jerusalem, which was the capital city of Judah. A clear distinction and clash between the Jews who had returned and the Samaritans occurred which continued into the New Testament times.

- Because of their part Jewish heritage, the Samaritans felt they had every right to be a part of God's chosen people as the Jews who had not intermarried with people of other races. There was a rivalry of race and religion between the two cities of Samaria and Jerusalem, between the Samaritan people and the Jewish people.

- But Jesus did not uphold this prejudicial thinking when He walked the earth. Review the following three stories about Jesus and Samaritans:

    o Luke 17:11-19 – Jesus healed Samaritan and Jewish lepers but only one Samaritan returned to say "Thank You"

    o John 4:1-42 – Jesus caused many Samaritans to believe in Him

    o Luke 10:30-37 – Review the story of the Good Samaritan. The Samaritan chose to have compassion on the Jewish victim, who he should have considered an enemy, while the hurt man's Jewish countrymen would not stop to render him aid.

Lesson 12. Part 2. The Holy Spirit is for Gentiles, too

- **Activity Objective**
    - Explain how Christian Gentiles are considered spiritual Jews in God's eyes, because all Christians are God's special people.
    - Explain how all the Jewish people by heritage are also still special in God's eyes.

- **Activity Materials**
    - Background Scriptures: Matthew 3:7-12, Romans Chapter 11, and Galatians 3:13-14, 26-29

- **Activity**
    - Matthew 3: 7-12, Galatians 3: 13-14, 26-29—
    Discuss with the youth how all Christians are God's special people. In other words, spiritual speaking, there is no such thing as Jews and Gentiles among the children of God, which means all individuals who have accepted Jesus Christ as the Lord and Savior of their lives, regardless to their earthly bloodline heritage.

    - Romans Chapter 11—
    Discuss with the youth how naturally speaking, God still has some promises to keep with the Jewish people who are the biological descendants of Abraham, Isaac, and Jacob.

Lesson 13.   **Jesus was filled with HS Without Measure**

Lesson 14.   **Part 1. The Church is filled with HS Without Measure**

- **Activity Objective**
  - Use a picture to clarify the concept that Jesus was, and still is today, filled with the Holy Spirit without measure.

- **Activity Materials**
  - Chalkboard and colored chalk (or whiteboard)

- **Activity**
  - **Draw a line down the middle of the chalkboard.** On both sides of the line draw a blue/brown earth in the center (could just be a circle), and a shape at the top of both sides to represent heaven.

  - **On the left side,** draw Jesus on earth and shade the inside of Him to represent Him being filled with the Holy Spirit. Ask the children if they remember when and how Jesus became filled when He was on earth (from Lesson 13). Now ask the children how much power they believe Jesus had after He was filled with the Holy Spirit. (John 3:34)

  - **On the right side,** draw Jesus in heaven and small circles on the earth to represent disciples meaning Christians. Now fill in each circle with the same color you used to shade Jesus with on the left side. Explain that the same Holy Spirit is in Christians today that was in Jesus. In fact, Jesus said that we who were on the earth after Him would do greater works than He did when He walked the earth. (John 14:12, Hebrews 13:8)

  - **Now explain that every person has a different level of faith to use in believing God for certain things.** On the right side, under different circles, write examples of different faith abilities that Jesus had, which He has now given to His followers. For example:
    - Under one circle write "faith to believe for healing from blindness"
    - Under another circle write "faith to be a missionary in China."

  - **In this way explain that the collective Church together still has all the power against the Devil by the faith of the individuals that make up the Church. (Hebrews 13:8)**

Lesson 14. **Part 2. Individual members of the Church body are filled with a measure of faith and grace from the Holy Spirit**

- **Activity Objective**
  - Demonstrate the concept of how a job can get done more effectively with a team of people, when each person on the team is allowed to use their best talent, skill or ability.

- **Activity Materials**
  - Basketball and Basketball Court for 3 sets of competition games. Or use some other game that accomplishes the objectives of the activity described below.
  - Alternate: Show video(s) on "basketball" to demonstrate the activity

- **Activity**
  - Play a basketball competition game three times to gain insight on how to perform an activity effectively using a team of people
    - o 1. Use individuals to play the game in a one-on-one competition. Have the students observe the performance of the individuals.
    - o 2. Use teams of people to play competitive games. This time the teacher randomly selects people to fill the positions on each team with no regard for their skill set to play the game. Have the students observe the performance of the teams.
    - o 3. Play competition games again. This time allow the youth within the teams to identify which positions they should play based on their own knowledge of their skill set or they could choose to be a support member of the game event by keeping score or being the timekeeper. For this occurrence, every student must participate in some form. Have the students observe the performance of the new teams.
  - After performing the game three times as described above, bring everyone together to discuss their general observations about how everyone felt about their participation in either playing or watching the games. The lesson that should be learned is that the best experience for everyone involved happened in the last game when everyone did a role that was best suited for their skill set, talent, and ability.
  - Finally, relate this activity example to how the Church organization will function best when all the people are using their talents, skill and abilities in the right place in ministry.

Lesson 15.   Led by the Spirit

- **Activity Objective**

  - Use a short story or video to give an example of a youth who was led away from danger because they listened to the leading of the Holy Spirit.

- **Activity Materials**

  - Example of Good Stories on Video: Videos from the Gospel Bill Ministry which can be located on YouTube @thegospelbillshow. Note: The Gospel Bill show videos use adult actors, but the videos were designed to be presented to children. The setting for the show is an old western town with a sheriff, his sidekick and the prayerful general store owner who work to keep the town safe from outlaws.

- **Activity**

  - First ask the youth if they have ever felt an uncomfortable feeling about a situation they were in or about to get into. Give them a chance to share some of their experiences of how they were led away from danger by listening to this uncomfortable feeling.

  - Ask them what influence in their lives do they think caused God to help them in their everyday lives in those uncomfortable situations. For example, was it because of:

    - o   Their prayers at the start of the day

    - o   Being filled with the Holy Spirit

    - o   Their parents or grandparents praying for and teaching them

    - o   All of the above

    - o   Something else

  - Next tell the good story or video you found of a youth or person that was saved from danger by following the leading of the Holy Spirit.

  - Discuss the concept of the Holy Spirit giving a warning on the inside of your spirit about danger, through giving you an uncomfortable feeling and a sense of what to do to avoid harm.

Lesson 16. Living in the Spirit

- **Activity Objective**

  - To use the object of "water" in 3 different ways to visually demonstrate the difference between being born of the Spirit, being filled with the Spirit, and being cleansed daily or sanctified by the Spirit.

- **Activity Materials**

  - Object Lesson #1 – Use materials identified in the Lesson Exercise

  - Object Lesson #2 – You will need two posters and markers

  - Object Lesson #3 – Use the scriptures identified below

- **Activity**

  - **First:** Do the Object Lesson as described in the Lesson Exercise

  - **Second:** Put up two posters that have water drawings on them based on the scriptures John 4:14 and John 7:39. In John 4:14, Jesus uses the concept of a well of water to describe the experience of being Born of the Spirit. In John 7:39, Jesus uses the concept of rivers of living water flowing to describe the experience of being Filled with the Spirit. Use the posters and scriptures to show youth that Jesus described two different "water = spiritual experiences" that would happen to believers.

    o On one poster, draw a picture based on John 4:14. Draw a well that sits on top of the ground. The ground underneath the well should show a stream of water that flows into the well from another source. Show the source of the stream is Salvation from God through Jesus Christ (Isaiah 12:3). Discuss how Jesus described being Born of the Spirit as being when a person has a well of water inside of them springing up into everlasting life.

    o On the other poster, draw a picture based on John 7:38-39. Here Jesus describes an experience where there are rivers of living water flowing out of a person. So, draw a picture of many rivers of water flowing down from several mountains. Explain how Jesus described this experience as happening after the Holy Ghost would be given on the Day of Pentecost to all who believe in Jesus.

  - **Third:** Discuss how Jesus used water to describe the cleansing experience the Holy Spirit would take believers through using the Word of God. Review with the youth what the scriptures reveal about this in John 15:3, Ephesians 5:26, Hebrews 4:12-13, John 6:63.

Lesson 17.   **Part 1. Introduction to Walking in the Spirit**
         Part 2. The Flesh Must Lose…

- **Activity Objective**
  - To explain more clearly how our flesh is a strong acting, separate-operating part from the spiritual part of us.

- **Activity Materials**
  - Have youth read 1 John 2:15-17, then re-read verse 16.
  - Use a chalkboard (whiteboard) presentation to discuss 1 John 2:16.

- **Activity**
  - Write the below three phrases from 1 John 2:16 on the chalkboard. Show the youth how Satan uses the same techniques to trick people today that he used on Eve in the Garden of Eden.
  - Let youth review the story from Genesis and tell you which scriptures show the concepts in 1 John 2:16

from 1 John 2:16	Matching Concepts from Genesis 3:1-6
Lust of the flesh	Genesis 3:6 (the woman saw tree was good for food)
Lust of the eyes	Genesis 3:6 (the tree was pleasant to the woman's eyes)
Pride of Life	Genesis 3:5 (she thought the tree would make her wise like a god based on what the serpent told her)

  - Help youth see how Satan operates, by looking at the before and after scenes from the Garden of Eden story.
  - 1) Satan twisted God's commandment in Eve's mind to make her believe that God was unnecessarily restrictive. The truth is Adam and Eve could eat from every tree in the Garden except one. There could have been a million other trees. And since it was a garden, many trees had good-looking food on them to eat. But Satan took Adam and Eve's one restriction and made them believe God was denying them something special.
  - 2) Next explain how after Satan was successful in getting Adam and Eve to sin, the loss they experienced was unimaginably worse than they could ever have thought of. Similarly, today, when we choose to commit sin, we lose big time. The blessings that we gain from being obedient to God's Word are super wonderful. On the other hand, the price we pay for being disobedient is worse than we could ever imagine.
  - The moral of the story is: "Do things God's way, even when you do not understand His way fully." God's blessings will be worth your sacrifice of obedience. And when you are obedient, God can help you to understand His wisdom.

Lesson 17.   Part 3. ... and the Spirit Rule!

- **Activity Objective**
  - Use a skit with "2-endings" to show a youth's struggle with trying to do the right thing instead of the wrong thing.

- **Activity Materials**
  - 3 Main Characters – Flesh Gordan, Holy Spirit Man, Christian Youth (either Christian or Christine).
  - Add other youth as desired to play parts in this skit such as the Father and friends or Narrator.

- **Activity**
  - **Skit Theme**: Christian's struggle with coming home at the exact time his father instructed him to do, because his friends try to convince him to stop at the store to purchase a game.
    - o Christian's friends twist his father's words in his mind to convince him that he would not really be disobeying his father. What Christian does not know is that his father gave him a specific time because he had a special treat in store for his son.
    - o If Christian comes home on time, he will get to go to a Basketball game with his father to see his favorite team.
    - o If Christian does not go home on time, then he misses the special game experience with his father, and he also gets punished for two weeks which lead to him missing some other fun things he wanted to do.
  - **Two Endings:** Perform the skit with two different endings so youth can see the benefits of Christian's obedience in the 1st ending, and the sad consequences of Christian's disobedience in the 2nd ending.
  - **Flesh Gordan and Holy Spirit Man:** During the skit, use 2 or 3 friends to try to convince Christian to sin. However, let Flesh Gordan and the Holy Spirit Man represent the invisible forces who also speak to Christian in both versions of the skit.
    - o **1st version of the skit:** Show how the Holy Spirit Man repeats the father's instructions so Christian knows that if he goes along with his friends, he will definitely be disobeying. In this ending Christian obeys his father and receives surprise blessings.
    - o **2nd version of the skit**: Show how Flesh Gordan manipulates the father's instructions in Christian's mind so that Christian begins to believe he is not really doing anything wrong. In this ending, Christian disobeys his father and receives punishment that causes him to lose multiple blessings and hurts his Father.

Lesson 18. **Part 1. The Spirit helps us to pray correctly**
Part 2. You may or may not understand the Spirit

- **Activity Objective**
  - To act out an example of a youth praying for one thing that is not exactly what they should be praying for. The Holy Spirit adds to their prayer so that by the time the prayer gets to God it is correct.

- **Activity Materials**
  - 5 characters – God the Father, Jesus, Holy Spirit, Christina & Mom

- **Activity**
  - **Let the youth know this "skit" is not a perfect representation of God's conversation, BUT it gives a view to the general idea.**
  - **Locations:** Begin with the youth Christina on her knees praying. The Holy Spirit is partially hidden beside her. God and Jesus are across the room in heaven.
  - **Christina prays**: "God, thank you for blessing my family. And God, please forgive me for all my sins, Finally, God, please bless me with that special gaming system. Everyone I know has one, and I want one so I can be like my friends. I want to be able to talk with them about the game and well, you know. Please help me to have it, Lord. Thank you so much, In Jesus name I pray, Amen."
  - **Next show the child fall asleep.** The Holy Spirit rises from beside Christina to take her prayer to God the Father.
  - **Holy Spirit speaks to God the Father**: "Father, your child Christina was praying tonight. She wants a gaming system like her friends, but first she needs to learn to be more obedient to her mom. She also needs to stop speaking rudely to her teachers, and she needs to stop being a bully to the people she does not like. She first asked in her prayer for forgiveness for her sins. Please forgive her for all her wrongdoing and help her to be a good girl."
  - **Jesus speaks to God the Father**: "Father, Christina is my little sister because she believes I am alive, and she calls me her Lord and Savior. I already know that as she reads her Bible more, she will change from being a mean girl to becoming a good Christian."
  - **Holy Spirit speaks again:** "Another thing, Father, Christina wants the gaming system so she can have what all her other friends have. If she gets it, she is not even going to play with it that much."

- **God the Father says to the Holy Spirit:** "Spirit, go help Christina to begin praying about being more obedient, to stop being rude to her teachers, and to stop being a bully."

- **Jesus says to the Holy Spirit:** "Spirit, when she goes to Sunday School, when she reads her Bible, when she hears the messages from my ministers, then help her to hear inside of her spirit that she needs to be a nicer person."

- **Next show the Holy Spirit go back over to Christina in her bed. The Holy Spirit speaks to the sleeping Christina.**

- **Holy Spirit:** "When you wake up, I want you to pray about being a better Christian. Ask God to help you be obedient and kind."

- **Christina wakes up, gets on her knees, and says the following prayer:** "Lord, thank you for waking me up this morning. Please help me to have a good day. And Lord, I have been thinking about how I have been acting. I have not been acting like a nice Christian. Dear God, in the Name of Jesus, please help me to be more obedient and to be a nicer person to my mom, teachers and everyone. In Jesus Name I pray, Amen!"

- **Narrator:** Tells the audience that several weeks have gone by. Christina comes home from school and shows her progress report to her mom.

- **Mom looks at the report and says:** "Wow, Christina, what an improvement! Good grades! And look at those glowing words about your good conduct, too!"

- **Christina responds:** "Mom I have been trying to do better at listening and obeying my teachers. And to be nicer to you, too!"

- **Then Mom says:** "You know Christina, I have truly noticed your good attitude towards me also. I am very proud of you. Since you have been working so hard to change for the better, I am going to give you a special reward. How about this weekend we go get that gaming system you have been wanting."

- **Christina's eyes light up and she says:** "Thanks Mom! I would love that very much. You are the greatest!"

- **Christina walks away from her Mom and looks up to heaven and says: "And God, You Are the GREATEST OF ALL!!!"**

The End!

Lesson 18.   Part 3. Praying in the Spirit without learning the Word of God is not enough to change you into a strong Christian

- **Activity Objective**
  - To reassure youth that there is no failure in God to meet our needs. If there are any shortcomings, they are always in us. God is faithful to accomplish His Word and His Word alone. (He is not committed to being faithful to our feelings or opinions.)

- **Activity Materials**
  - Round table discussion session.

- Ask the youth if they have ever felt like their praying or living for Christ is just not working. Give them a chance to tell of any experiences they have had where they felt like God failed them.

- If no one has had such an experience, then use this time to talk about some of the sufferings of God's special people (the Jews). Review the blessings in Deuteronomy 28:1-14 and the curses in verses 15-68.

- Explain how God warned the Jewish nation to always follow His Word. If they decided to forsake His instructions (His Word, wisdom, commandments), then the curses of Deuteronomy 28:15-68 would happen in their lives. Explain that although the consequences for their disobedience were not immediate, the Jewish people did eventually experience the curses. However, this only occurred after they were given many warnings through God's messengers, and they refused to keep God's laws. So, then the curses came.

- The Bible also warns Christians today, that if we decide to stop serving the Lord, then we will invite trouble into our lives. But just like the Jews the trouble will not come into our lives immediately. God will send many warnings and messengers to try and help us to change before sending trouble our way.

- You can also explain that the reason famine, poverty, and other such injustices are present in the world, is because of all the people who do not believe and obey God's Word.

- God has already provided everything for anyone and everyone to have His salvation, help, deliverance, and blessing. He did this when He sent Jesus, and Jesus paid the price for our sins. Then we must exercise our faith in God to change things in our lives. And add patience and trust in Him along with our faith.

- Meditate on the truth of Hebrews 11:6 to begin turning things around.

Lesson 18. **Part 4. Praying in the Spirit without the love of God filling your heart is not enough to develop you into a strong Christian.**

- **Activity Objective**

    - To explain how having "unforgiveness" in your heart will cause God to not answer your prayers.

- **Activity Materials**

    - Discuss the following Background scriptures in a round table discussion session.

        o Matthew 6:12, 14-15; Matthew 18:21-35

        o Mark 11:25-26 (Also read Mark 11:22-24)

        o Philippians 3:13

- **Activity**

    - The Holy Spirit can help the youth to forgive, heal, and be protected from hurt, harm and danger physically and emotionally going forward.

    - Let the scriptures and the Holy Spirit be your guide in conducting this round table discussion.

Lesson 19.   Why I Need to Be Filled

- **Activity Objective**

    - To make sure youth know they need to have salvation and a strong knowledge of God's word for themselves.

    - To convince them that their parent's salvation can not save them, their grandparent's salvation can not save them, their Pastor's salvation can not save them, but each person has to get salvation for him or herself.

- **Activity Materials**

    - Background Scriptures:

        o Matthew 24:40-42; 25:1-13; Luke 17:34-36

    - Scenery and props to go with acting out the Parable of the five wise and five foolish virgins

- **Activity**

    - First discuss the background scriptures with the youth.

    - In these scriptures, Jesus lets us know that each of us must have our own faith.

    - Then let the youth act out the Parable of the five foolish and the five wise virgins. Help the youth understand that by the Bible calling the ladies virgins, it was informing us that they were all considered precious daughters.

    - The skit scenario could look like this:

        o All of them were in Church. They were all waiting around to go to heaven when they die. But the five foolish virgins represent the people who never took the time to get closer to the Lord for themselves. They did not allow the Holy Spirit to work to strengthen their daily walk with God. Therefore, when Jesus came, they were not ready to go with Him because they were not in tune to spiritual things.

Lesson 20:   How I Can Be Filled Steps 1 – 5 A.

- **Activity Objective**
  - To demonstrate the different ways a person can "receive" something.
- **Activity Materials**
  - Short story below "The Birthday Party"
- **Activity**
  - Have youth read the short story and discuss what they learn from it about the different ways to receive gifts.

The Birthday Party

Christine's 4 girlfriends are hiding behind chairs.

Mom is looking out the window.

Mom: "Hush girls. I see Christine. She's about to come in the door."

Christine walks in through the door.

Mom: "Hi sweetheart, how was your day?"

Before Christine could speak…

4 girlfriends jump up and say: "SURPRISE!"

Christine is really surprised and happy. Mom brings her birthday cake out and the 4 girlfriends sing the Happy Birthday song. Everyone sits down. Mom brings out the birthday presents. Christine opens her gifts and shrieks with joy after opening each one. She receives a dress, a stuffed animal, a game, and a purse. Then, Mom gives Christine a gift in a special envelope. Before Christine could open it, her friends tell her they want to go to the Mall to see the last matinee showing of a movie.

Christine: "Okay, just let me go change into my new dress and purse."

In her rush, Christine drops the envelope gift underneath a chair.

After being out for hours, the girls return to Christine's house from their Mall excursion. Shortly after that, Christine's friends depart to go to their homes.

Mom: "Christine, it's time to put your gifts away and get ready for bed."

Christine found the stuffed animal and game but not the gift envelope.

Christine: "Mom, have you seen my gift envelope that you gave me?"

Mom: "No, dear, and that envelop has a lot of money in it for you. Well, you will just have to look for it tomorrow. Go on to bed sweetheart."

Discuss the concepts of "receiving" by asking the students the following questions based on the skit, "The Birthday Party"

   a. What gifts did Christine receive?
       Answer: dress, purse, stuffed animal, game and gift envelope

   b. What gifts did Christine enjoy the benefits of immediately after receiving them
       Answer: dress and purse which she wore and carried to the movies

   c. What gifts did Christine put aside to enjoy later?
       Answer: stuffed animal and game

   d. Which gift was initially received by Christine but could not be enjoyed because it was misplaced?
       Answer: gift envelope filled with money

   e. When would Christine really be able to enjoy the gift that was lost?
       Answer: Once she finds and uses/spends the money in the gift.

   f. If Christine never finds the money, do you believe she really received the gift?
       Answer: Yes and No. She received it, but she did not benefit from receiving it because she never got to spend it before it was lost.

   -   Now relate this discussion on the concept of "receiving the birthday gifts" to the concept of receiving being "filled with the Holy Spirit."

   -   Explain to the youth that to fully receive something means that you not only get it but that you use it to the fullest. Discuss how being filled with the Holy Spirit is kind of like the money in the gift envelope. God has already given us the Holy Spirit to fill our lives. But people will not be able to enjoy this gift of the Holy Spirit and His benefits until they

         o   Acknowledge receiving Him and

         o   Utilize His benefits in their everyday lives.

Lesson 20: Step 5 B. Signs are Evidence that You Have Received HS

- **Activity Objective**
  - To understand how signs help to verify that someone has received something.

- **Activity Materials**
  - Use the skit "The Birthday Party" from the previous Lesson

- **Activity**

  Discussion Notes:
  - Signs given to us by God, as a result of receiving the Holy Spirit, are very much like the birthday girl wearing the dress and purse that she received from friends.
  - In the skit "The Birthday Party", family and friends gave Christine a birthday party. But to those who did not attend the party, Christine probably did not look any different to them after the party than she did before the party. In other words, no one could really tell by looking at her that she had been given a party.
  - But she had proof or evidence of her party. The evidence was her new dress, her new purse, the stuffed animal, and the special treatment she received. Similarly, when a person is filled with the Holy Spirit, God gives them signs to a) let them know something special has occurred in their lives and b) to benefit them.
  - Let the youth discuss how others who did not attend the party, might be able to tell that Christine had a birthday party.
  - Then, discuss how the signs of the Holy Spirit work in the same way. They confirm to the person receiving the Holy Spirit, and to those observing the person who has received the Holy Spirit, that something special has taken place in their life.
  - Now explain that if Christine never wore the dress, never used the purse, and never spent the birthday money, that she would have missed out on the full joy associated with receiving her birthday gifts.
  - Similarly, when God gives us the Holy Spirit, He gives us a sign, and the signs are a gift. The purpose of the sign that comes with being filled with the Holy Spirit is to confirm to us, and to others, that this wonderful experience has taken place.
  - Once a person confesses that he or she has received the Holy Spirit, the evidence of their being filled will show up again and again in their lives.

Lesson 20: Step 5 C. Methods of Receiving the Holy Spirit

- **Activity Objective**

  - Most youth do not enjoy looking up lots of scriptures. So divide the task of completing each block in Table 5-1 among teams of youth. Then, allow each team to share their answers with everyone else.

- **Activity Materials**

  - Allow the youth to select their team members. There should be at least as many youth on a team as there are number of scriptures in a block.

- **Activity**

  - Allow the youth to divide into 7 teams. Assign each team one block to complete. Let the youth work together to fill in the blanks. Once the teams are finished, allow each team to report their answers to the group. Everyone should write down the answers in their own personal note pads or books.

Lesson 20: Step 6. Fill Up

- **Activity Objective**

  - This is a good time to do an anti-alcohol campaign. Most youth and adults will agree that illegal drugs are wrong. But there are many that think drinking for social fun is not harmful. Use this time to show the harmful effects that can occur even when drinking alcoholic beverage just for the fun of it.

- **Activity Materials**

  - An anti-alcohol / drug video.

  - A testimony by a local person on how God delivered them from alcohol or drug abuse

- **Activity**

  - **Confirm the "Danger" in getting high on alcohol and drugs:**

    o There are many anti-substance abuse videos available. Research to find one that is a good fit to show your youth

  - **Confirm the "Good" in getting high on the Holy Spirit:**

    o Use a local person in your church or community who can speak to how God took away the desire for substance abuse bringing great change into their life, through the work of the Holy Spirit.

Lesson 20: Step 7. Refresh

- **Activity Objective**

  - To teach youth to expect to live a balanced Christian life.

  - To let them know that even strong, Spirit-filled Christians have stressful and sad experiences.

- **Activity Materials**

  - Round table discussion session

- **Activity**

  - Talk to the youth about the realities of living day by day as a Christian.

  - Help them to understand everything is not "black or white," "high or low," "feast or famine."

  - Discuss how a person who lives a Christian life (meaning a person who tries to please God daily with their actions), will have some good days, bad days, boring days, mediocre days, happy times, trying times, sad times and some days where there seems like nothing spectacular is going on.

  - Explain that even when things are not working out like they had dreamed or planned, that they should never forsake following hard after God, living for Him, and loving Him.

  - Instead, the Christian should "hang in there," trusting God through every experience. The Christian life is one that proves itself in the "long run,"

  - God will prove His greatness and blessings in the life of the individual Christian who consistently lives for God each day.

  - Overall, the Christian walk is one that gets "sweeter as the days go by."

Lesson 21: Part 1. Privately

- **Activity Objective**

  - Write a catchy Praise Song for the youth to remember, based on this lesson and a popular song, like one from a commercial.

- **Activity Materials**

  - One or more catchy songs from a commercial or some other tune that is popular among the youth.

- **Activity**

  - Background: Many years ago, there was a commercial featuring the then popular basketball star "Michael Jordan." The song from that commercial was very catchy with simple lyrics and a catchy melody. The lyrics were simply, "Like Mike, I wanna be like Mike." For a Vacation Bible School skit, the author, Jennifer B. Price, used that tune to create a Praise song. To do this I changed the word "Mike" to "Christ."

  - Pray and ask the Lord to give you, and/or your youth group a catchy spiritual song that builds on the concepts the youth have been taught in this Lesson's Part 1.

    o "Be like Christ, Read your Bible and Pray every day.

    o Seek God for your purpose, and Desire spiritual gifts."

  - God can give you a new song in your heart, or you or the youth can try your hand at modifying a catchy song that the youth like to hear or sing.

Lesson 21: Part 2. Publicly, Share the Message of God's Love

- **Activity Objective**

  - To convince youth to fight against showing the unpleasant characteristics that are too often seen in teenagers: rudeness, meanness, short tempered, petty, disrespectful, insensitive, mocking, and bullying.

- **Activity Materials**

  - Round table discussion session

- **Activity**

  - Let the youth share their view of the world, meaning their view of teachers, other youth, and any adults they do not like.

  - First and foremost, LISTEN to what they have to say with the goal to really hear their side of the concerns. Listen empathetically. Do not be quick to judge and LET THEM TALK!

  - Then after they know that you have HEARD them, then discuss how Christians should act towards people they do not like.

  - Find scriptures that are applicable scriptures for them to meditate on.

  - Finally, try to help the youth to understand that sometimes you only know one side of another person's story. If they knew everything about the other person's life they may not be so harsh in their reaction to them.

  - Then, after the youth get to do a lot of the talking, pray with them and for them to grow in being "like Christ."

Lesson 22:   Conduct: Decent and in Order

- **Activity Objective**

  - To understand the meaning of 1 Corinthians Chapter 13.

  - Also to help youth memorize this important passage of scripture.

- **Activity Materials**

  - 1 Corinthians Chapter 13, King James Version

  - Arts and crafts activity to create symbols to represent the different segments in the passage.

- **Activity**

  - Read through and explain the meaning of 1 Corinthians Chapter 13.

  - Explain to the children that the word "Charity" in the King James Version is translated to the word "Love" in other modern Bible versions Also explain that ultimately 1 Corinthians Chapter 13 is one way of describing what True Love really looks like from God's viewpoint.

  - Create symbols to help the youth learn the different segments of the passage. The goal is that they would endeavor to memorize it over time.

  - Here are a few examples of symbols they could make to depict the different segments of the passage:

    - For the first part, cut out cloven tongues on yellow paper to represent speaking in tongues and draw or cut out paper angels

    - For the cymbal, draw that image on a paper

    - For knowledge, draw a book.

  - So on and so forth. Let the kids think of how to depict the different segments in this passage.

Lesson 23:   Operations, Administrations and Gifts

- **Activity Objective**

  - To use the familiar setting of a school's organizational setup to help youth understand the way the Church's organizational set up is designed by God.

- **Activity Materials**

  - Chapter 6, Figure 1 and Figure 2

- **Activity**

  - Discuss the two figures from the Lesson.

  - Tell the youth that this is a simplified comparison that just helps to understand the general concept of how God intended the Church to run. This comparison is just representative. However, it is possible that a Church may not seem to be implementing God's design as He intended. Explain that Christians do not always perfectly implement God's plans. And yet, God is still able to perform many great works despite our human imperfections

Lesson 24:   Part 1. Paul – Our Main Human Teacher

- **Activity Objective**
    - Allow the children to do a book report type activity on the different phases of Paul's life.

- **Activity Materials**
    - Get a book report form from a student or teacher who has used them or make up a form yourself to use for this activity. For example, the form could have lines for the student to write down:
        - Setting or Location
        - Characters involved
        - Mood of the Characters
        - Theme or Main idea of the passage
        - Story Climax or Ending
        - Also lines to place the students name and the date.

- **Activity**
    - Assign teams of youth to do the eight reading exercises from Lesson 24, Part 1. Let each team research one set of scriptures. Each team should use the book report form to write down what they learn about Paul from their set of scriptures. Encourage them not to leave any part of the form blank. For example, they may have to read a few more scriptures than identified to understand the location or setting for when the activity took place. After each team completes their Book Report form, let them choose a speaker to give the report to the general assembly. Make sure the team members all sign their names and put the date on the report they participated in creating.
    - After all teams have presented their scriptures using the Book Report form, then put them all together in a booklet style, with some sort of cover that you the teacher or youth assistant created. Use a three-hole punch to punch holes in the combined report booklet and place it in a finished folder.
    - Or, if your Church permits, you could make copies of the finished package and give a copy to each of the students to take home.

Lesson 24:   Part 2. Nine Spiritual Gifts Defined

- **Activity Objective**

    - Allow the children to divide up the task of studying the examples of the spiritual gifts in Table 6-1.

- **Activity Materials**

    - Assign individuals to research each block in the table. Provide the students with extra paper so they can write notes about what they read.

    - If you have any other literature or testimonies with examples of how spiritual gifts work, you should use those resources also.

- **Activity**

    - The teacher should begin by briefly reviewing with the youth the definitions of spiritual gifts as defined in the first column in Table 6-1. However, the real understanding for the youth will come as they look at the examples. Assign one block from the examples to one youth. Let that youth review / study the scriptures. The youth should then prepare themselves to explain to everyone what their example is. They should explain how their example clarifies the definition of what the spiritual gift is and describe how it is used.

    - As the youth complete their presentations on each spiritual gift, the teacher should add any other examples or testimonies they have of current people operating with the gift.

Lesson 25:   **Table 6-2. Phony spirit experiences**

- **Activity Objective**

  - To help youth identify Satan's counterfeit spirit experiences so they can avoid being tricked by people or organizations who represent false religion.

- **Activity Materials**

  - Find as many examples of the elements of witchcraft and sorcery as you can to bring to the youth for discussion.

  - Alternate: Review the table with the youth.

- **Activity**

  - Let the Holy Spirit guide you on if you should bring "show and tell" whether in print or from online resources, or if you should just use the information provided in the Table 6-2 to facilitate the discussion.

Lesson 26:   Seven Gifts of Grace

- **Activity Objective**
  - To use as many examples of the Gifts of Grace as possible to help the youth understand what they are and how they are used.

- **Activity Materials**
  - Prepare your own examples or bring in guest speakers that are gifted in these areas.

- **Activity**
  - Ask God to help you identify current examples of people with each Gift of Grace. God's gifts are in use everywhere, it is just that people do not normally analyze what gift is working in them on a day-by-day basis. Prayerfully ask God to help you come up with examples using people that the youth may know.
  - In fact, after you review the Table with the youth, the youth may be able to help you identify people who they can see for themselves are operating in these gifts.
  - If possible, invite guest speakers with these gifts so the youth can hear their testimonies firsthand and ask questions.

Lesson 27:   Part 1. Introducing the Five-Fold Ministry Gifts
Part 2. Each Five-fold Ministry Gift Defined

- **Activity Objective**
  - Help the youth do the exercises in the Lesson.

Lesson 27:   Part 3. False Ministries

- **Activity Objective**
  - To discuss how to identify Cults, False Religions, and people who are just "missing the mark" spiritually.

- **Activity Materials**
  - Round table discussion session

- **Activity**
  - Ask the Holy Spirit to guide you on how to present this topic.
  - Overall, explain to the youth how wrong thinking and a wrong understanding of the Truth in God's Word has caused people to make very bad or hurtful decisions that affects many people.

Lesson 28. Filled, Then Flowing With Gifts

For this lesson, prayerfully the youth will be ready to make an informed decision to Receive the Holy Spirit that God has freely given them.

So, I the author, Jennfier B. Price simply leave you with this short poem to share with the youth.

My Faithful Servant, Well Done!

Like a rushing, mighty wind
God the Spirit did descend
To bring God the Father and Son
To live in men, women, and children

The Holy Spirit is God
Third part of the Trinity
Father-Son-Spirit, three-in-one
One God in Perfect Unity

All who believe in Christ
Make Jesus Lord of their life
Are born of the Spirit, new creature
In God's Kingdom of Light

Believers have access
To God's Holy Spirit power
He will help you Know God
And bless you every hour

Be filled with the Spirit
Receive Him by faith
Walk in Dunamis Power!
Continue Jesus' works, miraculous and great!

Then when the end comes
And you stand before God
Rest assured you will hear God say
My Faithful Servant, Well Done!

CHARACTERS:

- Narrator, Jesus, Peter, Guard, 11 Disciples display on a poster, Judas, Girl 1, Girl 2, Foreigner and Prop Person
- Use actors playing Judas, Girl 1, Girl 2 and Prop person to play Extras

PROP IDEAS:

- Last Supper: Use poster display with Disciples set up behind a table.
- Garden: Use plastic plants to create outdoor garden scenery,
- Fishing: Use fishing pole or net and a boat made from a cardboard box.
- Upper Room: Cut shapes of cloven tongues out of yellow paper for HS.

COSTUMES:

- Peter, Jesus, Girl 1 and 2: use neutral-colored sheets or cloth such as white, beige or brown to wrap around the actors' bodies and bandanas or scarves to wrap around their heads.
- Foreigner: use a bright colored cloth to wrap around his body and head
- Guard: Use a sword that could be made from cardboard

SCENES: THERE ARE FOUR SCENES IN THIS DRAMA

- **Scene 1. Peter Before: Hothead**
  This scene highlights Peter's "strong but wrong" attitude before he was born or filled with the Spirit.

- **Scene 2. Peter Before – Now Afraid, Denies Knowing Jesus**
  This scene shows how before Peter was born or filled with the Holy Spirit, he easily became ashamed of confessing Christ when challenged.

- **Scene 3. Peter Before – Born of the Spirit but a Timid Disciple**
  This scene shows when Peter became born of the Spirit and how it affected him.

- **Scene 4. Peter After – Filled with the Spirit, Now Unafraid**
  This scene highlights how Peter became a bold representative of Christ after he became filled with the Holy Spirit.

SCENE PERFORMANCE NOTES:

Location descriptions in this drama are based on the original performance in a Church Chapel building.

The pulpit was on a raised platform in the center of the building with a piano on the left of the center and an organ on the right of the center.

The floor beneath the pulpit was where most of the scenes took place.

OPTIONAL: **Display a chalkboard or poster with each Scene Title.**
Play music that fits the mood of each scene.

APPENDIX D
DRAMA: PETER BEFORE AND AFTER BEING FILLED

Scene 1. Peter Before: Hothead

Setting: At the Last Supper, when Peter and the other 11 disciples are sitting around the table with Jesus. Peter brags that he would never desert Jesus, even if everyone else did. Then, scene switches to outside when Peter sees the guards arrest Jesus, and Peter cuts off one of the guard's ears.

Scenery: Setup a table with Peter, Jesus and the picture of the 11 disciples right of center. Place plants on the left side for an outside garden scene.

Narrator: Let's take a journey back in time to 33 years after Jesus was born. For the last 3 years of Jesus' life, He has spent a lot of time teaching His close friends, who were the 12 disciples, about spiritual things. You are now at an upper room in Jerusalem where Jesus, Peter and the other 11 disciples have just eaten the Last Supper they will have together on earth, before Jesus is crucified. They have already eaten the bread, which represents Jesus' body, which is about to be beaten, scarred and nailed to the cross. They have already drunken the wine, which represents Jesus' blood, which is about to be shed on the cross. They have already sung their last song together. Now they are headed on their way outside to go to the Garden of Gethsemane.

Look! Here comes Jesus and Peter.

Jesus: *(Jesus and Peter walk from the table scene to the garden scene.)* You are all going to desert me and leave me to face everything alone tonight. The scriptures explain why you will do this. It says that after God hurts the Shepherd, then His sheep will run away and be scattered.

Peter: Not me, Lord. I am Peter. Even if all the others leave you, I will not.

Jesus: Peter, the truth is, that before the cock crows at dawn tomorrow morning, you are going to deny knowing me, three times.

Peter: No, Jesus. I would die first before denying you.

Narrator: In the Garden of Gethsemane, Jesus began to pray because He needed extra strength from God to go through everything He was about to experience. He asked Peter, James and John to pray with Him, but they just fell asleep. Soon after this time of prayer, Judas Iscariot brought a host of guards to arrest Jesus. Let's see what Peter does after they arrive.

Judas: Hi Jesus!
(He kisses Jesus on the cheek, then walks away)

Guard: You are under arrest!
(raises the sword, grabs Jesus)

Peter: *(takes the sword from the Guard and pretends to cut off guard's ear)*

Jesus: *(puts his hand up to heal the guard's ear and says to Peter)*
> Peter, put away your sword. People who use swords will get killed.
> I could pray and a thousand angels could protect me. But I must be
> arrested so I can fulfill all the scriptures written about me.

Peter: *(Looks afraid and then runs away from Jesus.)*

Scene 2. Peter Before – Now Afraid, He Denies Knowing Jesus

Setting: Peter follows Jesus as He is carried from courtroom to courtroom from a distance. He denies knowing Jesus three times, then a rooster crows two times. After the rooster crows Jesus looks at Peter and Peter runs away crying. He is afraid and ashamed.

Scenery: Remove the disciples' display from the table. Leave the table and other things for Peter to hide behind. Show Jesus walking in the pulpit area, stopping 3 times – once at the left (by piano), once in the center (by pulpit) and once at the right side (by organ) – to represent different courtrooms. Let 2 people walk with Him to each spot and pretend to question Him. Jesus and the 2 people will be in the pulpit area. Peter, Girl 1 and Girl 2 will be on the floor area looking up at Jesus.

Actors' location at the start of the scene:
> *(Jesus and the 2 people walk to the left of the pulpit area.*
> *The 2 people pretend to question Jesus.)*
> *(Peter is on the floor on the left side beneath Jesus, Girl 1's nearby.)*

Girl 1: *(walks over to Peter on the floor where he is trying to see Jesus.)*
> You were with Jesus in Galilee. You are one of His disciples.

Peter: *(says loud & angrily)*
> Get away from me girl! I don't know what you're talking about!

> *(Jesus and the 2 people walk to center of the pulpit area.*
> *The 2 people pretend to question Jesus.)*
> *(Peter moves to the center of the floor near where Girl 2 is located.)*

Girl 2: *(points at Peter & says to audience)*
> This man was with that Jesus of Nazareth!

Peter: You are mad, Girl. I do not even know that man!

> *(Jesus and the 2 people walk to right of the pulpit area.*
> *The 2 people pretend to question Jesus.)*
> *(Peter hides near table to watch Jesus, but a Man sees him.)*

Man: I recognize you! And when I heard your voice you sounded like someone from Galilee. You are one of Jesus' disciples.

Peter: "Not so!" I do not even know that man.
(He points to Jesus.) (Prop person crows like a rooster)

Jesus: *(turns and looks at Peter)*

Narrator: After the cock crowed, Jesus turned and looked at Peter who had just denied knowing Him for the third time. When Peter saw Jesus look at him, he remembered how Jesus had told him that even he would be afraid to let anyone know that he knew Jesus. Peter ran away crying.

Peter: *(Runs away crying and ashamed; goes off stage on the right.)*

Scene 3. Peter Before – Born of the Spirit but a Timid Disciple

Setting: First the setting is on Resurrection Day, when Jesus appears to the disciples in a room. Then the scene takes place on the shore where Peter and the other disciples have returned to fishing.

Scenery: On right of the center stage, have a table with the picture of the disciples again. Have an "X" marked over one of the disciples to represent Judas Iscariot is missing. On the left of center, place the boat and fishing pole or net.

Narrator: He 'rose! He 'rose! He 'rose from the dead! Now it is early on Resurrection Sunday. Mary Magdalene and other ladies have already talked with the risen Jesus Christ outside the empty tomb. Jesus told them to go and tell the disciples that He would meet them in Galilee. An angel also told the ladies to make sure Peter knew Jesus expected him to be there, too.

(Pause and allow Peter to walk to the table and sit down next to the picture)

That evening, the disciples were gathered in Galilee. They were meeting behind locked doors, because they were afraid of what the Jewish leaders would do if they found them. They had not yet seen Jesus.

Narrator continued: Then, suddenly, Jesus is standing among them! He showed them His wounds. They became filled with joy. Now they knew that it was really true! Jesus is alive! *(John 20:20)*

(Jesus walks in and shows Peter His hands and points to His side.)
(Peter shows excitement.)

Jesus: Just like my Father sent me to teach you spiritual things, now I am going to send you out to teach other people spiritual things. Receive the Holy Spirit.

(Jesus blows a breath of air towards Peter or play a sound effect.)

Narrator: When Jesus blew that breath of the Spirit on Peter and the other disciples, they became born of the Spirit. You see, before Jesus was resurrected, the disciples had Jesus with them being their Lord and Teacher. But now Jesus was about to return to heaven. Jesus knew the disciples needed to have God inside of them after He was gone, helping to control their human spirit from within. After talking with the disciples some more, Jesus left, and they did not see Him for a few days.

(Jesus leaves off to the right and walks around the back.)

(Peter goes over to the left side of the stage where the fishing pole or net and the box boat are located.)

Peter: I am going fishing!
(Peter gets in the boat, picks up the pole/net and pretends to fish.)

Jesus: *(wearing bright white, gold or purple cloth, walks up to center floor and yells over to Peter)*

Any fish boys?

Peter: No!

Jesus: Try throwing your net on the right side of the boat and you will get plenty of fish!

Peter: *(Puts the net on the right then pretends it is too heavy because of all the fish. He looks at Jesus as if now he recognizes who He is)*

It's the Lord!

(Peter leaves the fishing behind and runs over to meet Jesus in the center of the stage/pulpit area or on the floor.)

Jesus: Peter, do you love me more than being a professional fisherman?

Peter: Yes, Lord, you know I love you!

Jesus: Then I want you to teach my lambs.

(Jesus points to children in the audience. Then asks a second time.)

Jesus: Peter, do you love me?

Peter: Yes, Lord, you know I love you!

Jesus: Then I want you to teach my sheep.

(Jesus points to adults in the audience. Then asks a third time.)

Jesus: Peter, do you love me?

Peter: *(Has a hurt look on his face before he gives his final answer.)*

Lord, you know everything! You know that I love you.

Jesus: Then Peter, I want you to feed my sheep.

(Jesus points to all the people in the audience.)

Before you begin doing this new job of feeding my people my Word, I need you and the other disciples to go to Jerusalem and wait until you are baptized with the Holy Spirit. Then you will have the power you need to enable you to be a great preacher and teacher to all people.

Narrator: After spending 40 days after His resurrection from the dead, walking and talking with Peter and the other disciples, Jesus ascended up into heaven. He returned to His place in Glory beside God the Father.

(Jesus leaves off the scene for the last time.)

Scene 4. Peter After – Filled with the Spirit, Now Unafraid
(Final Scene)

Setting: The Bible setting is an upper room in Jerusalem where 120 disciples are assembled, including women and children. They are all praising God and waiting to be filled with the Holy Ghost. There were also Jewish people from foreign lands in the city of Jerusalem. This drama location could be in the pulpit area or on the floor in the center.

Scenery: Chairs in the center with Peter and disciples praising the Lord. The opening scene should include all in the Play except Narrator, Jesus and the Prop person.

Narrator: With clear direction from Jesus, about 120 disciples, faithful men and women, were waiting in an upper room in Jerusalem to be filled with the Holy Spirit. They did not know exactly what was about to take place. They had spent enough time with Jesus to know that it was going to be wonderful, better than anything they could ever imagine. The disciples were filled with joy, praising the Lord. It is now the 50th day since the Resurrection of Jesus from the dead. They have been in the upper room waiting for the Holy Spirit about 10 days since Jesus left to ascend back into heaven.

Peter and Disciples: (The group sits and sings one or more spiritual songs in praise and worship to the Lord.)

APPENDIX D
DRAMA: PETER BEFORE AND AFTER BEING FILLED

Narrator: All of a sudden, a strong windy sound like a tornado or hurricane could be heard. Then, descending down from above, there appeared cloven, fiery like tongues that came and sat on each disciple's head.

> *(Prop person makes or plays the sound effect of a strong wind and then runs in and touches each person's head with the yellow paper cut outs that in the shape of cloven tongues.)*

> *(After each person gets touched, they raise their arms and move their lips as if they are feeling and speaking something. But do so silently. If possible, let dramatic music play as the actors act out receiving the Holy Ghost.)*

Narrator: To everyone's surprise, the disciples began speaking in many different languages.

> *(If possible, the Prop person plays a tape of different languages that are praising God.)*

Foreigner: *(a new character, a Foreigner enters the scene. This can be the Prop person now dressed in bright colored cloth.)*

> What is this I hear? (points to Peter)
> I hear this person speaking my native language. But I recognize him as being an uneducated person from Galilee? Are these people drunk this early in the morning?

Peter: We are not drunk. We have just been filled with the Holy Ghost just like the Old Testament Prophet Joel prophesied it would happen.
In fact, Jesus of Nazareth, who was crucified, is risen from the dead and has sent this great power to fill all who will believe on Him.

Narrator: After Peter became filled with the Holy Spirit, he was no longer afraid to tell everyone and anyone about Jesus. Peter preached and performed many miracles in Jesus' name. He went to jail and was beaten for the cause of spreading the Gospel of Jesus Christ. Peter became a mighty preacher and Apostle for God.

The End!

This section includes referenced works as noted, but no information was directly quoted, reprinted or copied from any book that was not written by the author in this list, except portions from the Bible and Dictionaries as noted.

Study Prep

[1]Gotquestions.org, *What is Pneumatology?; What is Dunamis?*

[2]Wayne Grudem, *Systematic Theology: An Introduction to Biblical Doctrine* (Grand Rapids, MI: Zondervan; and Leicester, Great Britain: Inter-Varsity Press, 1994 and 2000), p. 21

[3]Jennifer B. Price, *Know His Word Bible Study –1ˢᵗ Quarter, –2ⁿᵈ Quarter, –3ʳᵈ Quarter, –4ᵗʰ Quarter* (Albuquerque, NM: Citi of Books, Inc., 2024), Apologetics: Bible and Christian

Chapter 1

[1]In John 20:21-23, on the evening of Jesus' Resurrection Day, He commissioned the disciples for service. Verse 22-23 says, "And when he *[Jesus]* had said this, he breathed on them, and saith unto them, 'Receive ye the Holy Ghost; whose soever sins ye remit, they are remitted unto them'…" This wording refers to the inauguration of the experience of being born of the Spirit. See Acts 2:38 (Compare with Genesis 2:7). In Acts 1:4-5, forty days later, on Jesus' Ascension Day, Jesus told His disciples to "wait for the promise of the Father… ye shall be baptized with the Holy Ghost not many days hence." This wording refers to the inauguration of the experience of being filled with the Spirit / receiving the gift of the Holy Ghost. See Acts 2:1-4 with Acts 2:38-39.

Chapter 2

[1]*Random House Webster's College Dictionary* (New York: Random House, 1997), p. 84-85

[2]Lester Sumrall, *"The Gifts and Ministries of the Holy Spirit"* (New Kensington, PA: Whitaker House, 1982)

[3]Dake's Annotated Reference Bible (Lawrenceville, GA: Dake Bible Sales, Inc., 1987), New Testament p. 62. The Ten Emblems are used with permission of Dake Publishing.

Chapter 3

[1]Daniel Fuchs, *Israel's Holy Days In Type and Prophecy* (Neptune, New Jersey: Loizeaux Brothers, Inc., 1995), p.9-11

[2]Daniel Fuchs, Israel's Holy Days, Chapters 1, 3, 4, 6, 8 and 11.

[3]*The International Inductive Study Bible, Precept Ministries* (Eugene, Oregon: Harvest House Publishers, 1993, New American Standard Bible), p. 214-215.

[4]Daniel Fuchs, Israel's Holy Days, p. 29

Chapter 4: None

Chapter 5

What does it mean to be born of water (John 3:5)?,Gotquestions.org **Lesson 20. Step 1.** "Born of water" in John 3:5 refers to natural, physical birth by a woman and/or the spiritual birth through cleansing by God's Word and Spirit. Jesus said, "Now ye are clean through the word which I have spoken unto you", which refers to the process of spiritual regeneration by the Holy Spirit, which also points to spiritual cleansing by the blood of Jesus. (John 15:3-5, Ephesians 5:26, Titus 3:5, Hebrews 10:22, 1 John 1:7)

Chapter 6

[1]Howard Carter, *Questions & Answers on Spiritual Gifts* (Tulsa, OK: Harrison House, Inc., 1976)

[2]Sumrall, *The Gifts and Ministries of the Holy Spirit*

[3]Carter, *Questions & Answers on Spiritual Gifts (ref. p. 11-12)* Sumrall, *The Gifts and Ministries of the Holy Spirit (ref. p.54-56)*

[4]Carter, *Questions & Answers on Spiritual Gifts (ref. Chapters 1,2,7)* Sumrall, *The Gifts and Ministries of the Holy Spirit (ref. Chapter 7)*

[5]Genesis Chapters 6 and 37; 2 Kings 5, Exodus 33

[6]Sumrall, *The Gifts and Ministries of the Holy Spirit (ref. p.64,71-73)* Carter, *Questions & Answers on Spiritual Gifts (ref. p.42)*

[7]Sumrall, *The Gifts and Ministries of the Holy Spirit (ref. p.164-166)*

[8]Carter, *Questions & Answers on Spiritual Gifts (ref. Chapters 3-5)* Sumrall, *The Gifts and Ministries of the Holy Spirit (ref. Chapter 8)*

[9]Sumrall, *The Gifts and Ministries of the Holy Spirit (ref. p.89-95)* Carter, *Questions & Answers on Spiritual Gifts (ref. p.60-61)*

[10]Sumrall, *The Gifts and Ministries of the Holy Spirit (ref. p.111)* Carter, *Questions & Answers on Spiritual Gifts (ref. p.100)*

[11]Sumrall, *The Gifts and Ministries of the Holy Spirit (ref.p.166,167)*

[12]Carter, *Questions & Answers on Spiritual Gifts (ref. Chapters 6,8)*
Sumrall, *The Gifts and Ministries of the Holy Spirit (ref. Chapter 9)*

[13]Carter, *Questions & Answers on Spiritual Gifts (ref. p.125)*

[14]Sumrall, *The Gifts and Ministries of the Holy Spirit (ref.p.143)*

[15]Sumrall, *The Gifts and Ministries of the Holy Spirit (ref.p.115-117)*

[16]Sumrall, *The Gifts and Ministries of the Holy Spirit (ref. Chapter 14)*

[17]Sumrall, *The Gifts and Ministries of the Holy Spirit (ref. Chapter 16)*

[18]Sumrall, *The Gifts and Ministries of the Holy Spirit (ref. Chapter 16)*

[19]Sumrall, *The Gifts and Ministries of the Holy Spirit (ref. Chapter 17)*

[20]Sumrall, *The Gifts and Ministries of the Holy Spirit (ref. Chapter 17)*

Appendix C, Lesson 11

[1] Robert Boyd, *Born to Die: Understanding Christ's Life* (Grandville, MI: World Publishing, Inc.), p. 119

Page layouts designed by Jennifer B. Price using artwork as identified below

PICRYL.com Public Domain Images

- The Descent of the Holy Spirit, page 12
- Moses (mozes-ontvangt-de-tafelen), page 54
- The Angel of Death (foster-bible-pictures), page 56
- Glass (minnetta), page 78
- Praying hands (otto-greiner), page 82
- Light bulb, page 198

WikiArt.org Public Domain images

- Fruit (still life, Thomas Hart Benton), page 165

Illustrations by Kathleen L. Kilpatrick*, Copyright 1999

- Spirit-man, page 27
- Descending Holy Spirit Dove, pages 51, 62, 65
- Rain on landscape, page 113

Jennifer B. Price artwork designed by using Shapes in MS Word, or modifications to Public Domain images or illustrations by K.L. Kilpatrick

- Dove, pages 3, 227
- Spiritual Concept of Body of Christ, page 69
- School, pages 75, 126, 127
- Church, pages 126, 128
- Cross with Spirit fire, pages 203, 225

---

*Note:

Special thanks to Kathleen L. Kilpatrick, my co-worker in 1999, who used her drawing talent to create many illustrations used in the first edition of this book that I, Jennifer B. Price, self-published. While the above three illustrations are the only ones included in this second edition, I am eternally grateful for the contribution she made to this ministry work. One of my favorite images is not used in the body of this edition. However, I have included it here to capture the memory of that time. During my ministry formative years, I published my writings under the name of "Lion and the Lamb Ministries." The illustration of the Lion-Lamb by Kathleen is what I desired to become the ministry's trademark.

Lion and the Lamb Ministries
is a teaching ministry by
Jennifer B. Price,
where the deep things of God
are presented so that a child
can understand them.*

Bibles

Holy Bible, King James Version; Peabody, MA: Hendrickson Publishers Marketing, LLC; 2016

Dake's Annotated Reference Bible, Finis Jennings Dake, Authorized King James Version; Lawrenceville, GA: Dake Bible Sales, Inc., 1987

The International Inductive Study Bible, New American Standard, Precept Ministries; Eugene, OR: Harvest House Publishers, 1993

Children's Ministry Resource Bible by Child Evangelism Fellowship, Inc., New Kings James Version; Nashville, TN: Thomas Nelson, Inc., 1987

Bible Study Reference Books

An Expository Dictionary of Biblical Words, W.E. Vine; Merrill F. Unger & William White editors; Nashville, TN: Thomas Nelson, Inc. Publishers, 1985

Know His Word Bible Study – 1st Quarter, 2nd Quarter, 3rd Quarter and 4th Quarter, Jennifer B. Price; Alburquerque, NM: Citi of Books, Inc., 2024

Systematic Theology–An Introduction to Biblical Doctrine, Wayne Grudem; Grand Rapids, MA: Zondervan and Leicester, Great Britain: Inter-Varsity Press, 1994, 2000

Books and Handbooks

A Handbook on Holy Spirit Baptism, Don Basham; New Kensington, PA: Whitaker House, 1969

Born to Die, Robert Boyd; Grandville, MI: World Publishing, Inc., 1997

Israel's Holy Days in Type and Prophecy, Daniel Fuchs; Neptune, New Jersey: Loizeaux Brothers, Inc., 1985

Questions & Answers on Spiritual Gifts, Howard Carter; Tulsa, OK: Harrison House, Inc., 1976

The Gifts & Ministries of the Holy Spirit, Dr. Lester Sumrall; Springdale, PA: Whitaker House, 1993

Tongues, Interpretation & Prophecy, Don Basham; Springdale, PA: Whitaker House, 1971

Videos

Know His Word Bible Study **Video Lessons**, taught by Jennifer B. Price and Pastor Craig I. Carter, can be accessed via www.knowbiblestudies.com or on Williams Temple COGIC Houston, TX Facebook and YouTube pages

Below is a synopsis of Jennifer B. Price's teaching on **Know His Spirit Bible Study** lessons at Williams Temple Church of God in Christ, Houston, Texas, October 2025 to February 2026.

Videos of the 16 teaching sessions are accessible under the "KHS Video Lessons" link on KnowBibleStudies website: www.knowbiblestudies.com

Lesson #	Title/Book Section	KHS Video Lessons Synopsis
01	**Jennifer Price Intro / Study Prep**	Definitions: Trinity, Systematic Theology, Pneumatology, Dumanis, KHS Bible Study Overview
02	**Chapter 1, Lesson 1**	Biblical Hermeneutic, Exegesis, NOT Eisegesis, Bible Versions, Holy Spirit, evil spirits, human spirit
03	**Chapter 1, Lessons 2 and 3**	Born of Spirit, Filled with Spirit, Jesus and the Holy Spirit
04	**Chapter 1, Lesson 4**	Different Baptisms defined in Bible, Role of faith in baptisms
05	**Chapter 1, Lesson 5**	Countdown to Pentecost, Speaking in other tongues
06	**Chapter 2**	Law of Spirit makes us free, Holy Spirit's Power, Omnipresent, Omniscient, Omnipotent; Examples
07	**Chapter 4**	Tabernacle Ex: Glory of God in us, Walk in Spirit to keep God's Glory, Get rid of Sin: Sin roll call
08	**Chapter 5**	Why I Need to Be Filled, How I Can Be Filled, What to do after Filled, Conduct: Decent and in Order

KHS Video Lessons Synopsis continued...

Lesson #	Title/Book Section	Teaching Synopsis
09	**Chapter 6 Intro**	Spiritual Gifts Operations: WHY, WHO, HOW, and WHAT
10	**Chapter 6 Intro Continued**	Nine Spiritual Gifts Defined, 7 General Points to Understand When Studying Gifts of the Spirit
11	**Chapter 6 — Revelation Gifts**	Revelation Gifts Defined; Examples Inspired by 4 Spirit-filled Teachers: William Seymour, Charles Mason Howard Carter, Lester Sumrall
12	**Chapter 6 — Power Gifts**	Power Gifts Defined; Examples Case Study: Passion of Saints Perpetua and Felicity
13	**Chapter 6 — Inspiration Gifts**	Inspiration Gifts Defined; Examples Prophecy displayed in Vocal and Non-Vocal communication forms, Guidelines for Church, for Judging
14	**Chapter 6 — 7 Grace and 5 Ministry Gifts**	7 Gifts of Grace could be viewed as "Spiritual" Personality Types, Five-fold Ministry Gifts; Examples
15	**Chapter 6 — Ministers & Ministries**	False Ministers, Wrong Teachings, True Ministers, True Ministries, Women in Ministry / Leadership, Be Perfected doing Ministry Service
16	**Chapter 7 — Fruit of the Spirit**	Fruit of the Spirit – detail on 9 parts, How to grow the Fruit of the Spirit, Holiness is reason we need Fruit

Jennifer B. Price is the Ministry Head of KnowBibleStudies

Find out more:

knowbiblestudies.com ; youtube.com / @KnowBibleStudies

All of Jennifer's works are designed with youth and adults in mind to inspire all ages to take a fresh look at God's Word.

Find direct links to her works on the website:

- **Know Bible Studies book series**
- **Holy Writ Tales book series**
- **Bible Story Drama Videos**
- **Featured Music**
- **Promo Videos**

Know His Word Bible Study is organized into four "Quarter" books designed to provide an inductive study of the entire Bible in the chronological order events occurred. Therefore, the books are not always studied in the same order as the traditional Bible books layout. Each Quarter book contains most of the daily study lessons for the Bible books as listed below. However, some passages from a Bible book may be found in a different Quarter book. **Know His Word Bible Study—**

1ˢᵗ Quarter:

Genesis, Job, Exodus, Leviticus, Numbers, Deuteronomy, Half of Joshua

2ⁿᵈ Quarter:

End of Joshua, Judges, Ruth, 1 and 2 Samuel, 1 Chronicles, Psalms, 1 Kings, Proverbs, Song of Songs, Ecclesiastes, 2 Chronicles, 2 Kings, Jonah, Amos (small portion of Isaiah & Micah)

3ʳᵈ Quarter:

Hosea, Isaiah, Micah, Jeremiah, Nahum, Habakkuk, Zephaniah, Ezekiel, Lamentations, Obadiah, Daniel, Ezra, Haggai, Zechariah, Esther, Nehemiah, Malachi, Joel

4ᵗʰ Quarter:

Intertestamental History and New Testament

Know His Spirit Bible Study identifies what the Bible says about the Holy Spirit's purpose and work to manifest God's presence on earth, with a focus on His work within Christians.

Know His Blood Bible Study focuses on the power and purpose of the Blood of Jesus.